VARIETIES OF CHRISTIAN-MARXIST DIALOGUE

Edited by
Paul Mojzes

THE ECUMENICAL PRESS
PHILADELPHIA

© *Journal of Ecumenical Studies* 1978

THE ECUMENICAL PRESS
511 Humanities Bldg.
Temple University
Philadelphia, PA 19122

ISBN 0-931214-02-5

JOURNAL OF ECUMENICAL STUDIES
Temple University
Philadelphia, PA 19122

Special Issue, Volume 15, Number 1 (Winter, 1978)

Four issues per year: Winter, Spring, Summer, Fall. Subscription: $10 per year, U.S.A.; $11.25, elsewhere. Student subscriptions: $6, U.S.A.; $6.75, elsewhere. Single copy: $3. Subscriptions begin with first number of each year. Second class postage paid at Philadelphia, Pennsylvania, and at additional mailing offices. Articles appearing in this journal are abstracted and indexed in *Historical Abstracts* and/or *America: History and Life, Index to Religious Periodical Literature, Religious & Theological Abstracts, Elenchus Bibliographicus Biblicus* (Biblical Institute Press, Rome), *Catholic Periodical and Literature Index, Guide to Social Science and Religion in Periodical Literature, Humanities Index, Abstracts of Popular Culture, Theologische Literaturzeitung,* and *Internationale Zeitschriftenschau für Bibelwissenschaft und Grenzgebiete*. Indexing also appears in the fourth issue of each volume. The International Standard Serial Number is 0022-0558.

TABLE OF CONTENTS

INTRODUCTION

Since the inception of the dialogue between Christians and Marxists, a variety of postures or approaches has been assumed by those who favor the dialogue and participate in it. The diversity is so considerable that an average-size volume cannot do justice to all views. We have attempted to collect manuscripts reflecting a considerable segment of the entire spectrum. Not represented here are South American, Soviet, Asian, and African perspectives. With the exception of the South American perspectives, these absences in fact represent the scarcity of writers in this field. Unfortunately this is also true thus far of female and Black input. Thus the volume represents the European and North American mainstream of the Christian-Marxist dialogue.

The writings in this volume often express different, even contradictory, positions. The ideas represented in the various manuscripts do not command equal following in those circles that have been engaged in the dialogue. Some are currently favored by many practitioners and theorists of the dialogue; others, by only a small minority. However, truth is not ascertained by current vogue or popularity. We offer these diverse options not because we agree with them, but because they deserve serious public discussion in regard to their viability and effectiveness.

Paul Mojzes, an American United Methodist historian of religion, provides a survey of the dialogue from its beginning to the present with suggested guidelines for the future. The Austrian Protestant theologian Max Suda presents an analysis of Karl Marx's *Capital,* exploring the critique of religion found therein. Andrija Krešić, a Yugoslav Marxist philosopher, offers a study on the relationship between the Christian concept of the Kingdom of God and the Marxist aspirations for Communism. The place of ideology in theological investigation, a much neglected issue, is treated by the American United Methodist systematic theologian, James Will. Another American contribution is by a Lutheran theologian, Russell Norris, who compares and contrasts the Marxist and Christian views on the relationship of freedom and necessity.

The Study Department of the Lutheran World Federation based in Geneva, Switzerland, sponsored a number of workshops; the Aarhaus Report entitled "Theological Reflection on the Encounter of the Church with Marxism in Various Cultural Contexts" represents a comprehensive and systematic treatment of theological issues arising out of the encounter of the church with Marxism. The basic preparatory paper for the 1977 Paulus-Gesellschaft symposium in Salzburg, the work of Udo Bermbach, a West German Christian political scientist, attempts to summarize the progress achieved in previous Paulus-Gesellschaft meetings and to propose new directions for future dialogue.

Jozsef Lukács, a Hungarian Marxist philosopher, deals with the question of Christian-Marxist relations in Hungary, calling for both cooperation and dialogue and examining the relationship between these two forms of relationships. The same concern is presented by Adolf Niggemeier, a Roman Catholic lawyer and politician from East Germany, who describes what cooperation and dialogue mean in the context of the German Democratic Republic. Jakov R. Romić, a Franciscan friar from Yugoslavia, explores the obstacles and possibilities for the Christian-Marxist dialogue based on analysis of the relationships in his country as well as his participation in the Paulus-Gesellschaft activities. Alceste Santini, an Italian Marxist, offers insight into the Eurocommunist attitude toward Christian-Marxist relations, while Francis Murphy, an American Roman Catholic historian who has long studied the Catholic-Communist relations in France, analyzes the French Communist appeals to Roman Catholics. Ans van der Bent, a native of Holland who is currently with the World Council of Churches in Geneva, analyzes Christian and Marxist responses to secularization and secularism with special reference to China. Gerhard Melzer, a West German Lutheran pastor, attempts to show how it is possible for a person to maintain faith in God and to adopt Marxism as the scientific analysis of the world. A somewhat similar line of reasoning can be observed among certain Latin American and southern European Christians who adopt Marxist analyses.

The Marxist-Christian dialogue is receiving increasing academic scrutiny. Robert Thobaben and Nicholas Piediscalzi, professors of political science and religious studies respectively, from the U.S.A., offer some pedagogical assistance to those who may wish to teach similar courses. Maurice Boutin, a Roman Catholic theologian from Canada, provides an analytic report on the Rosemont symposium on "Peaceful Coexistence and the Education of Youth." George Kline, an American participant in that symposium, offers a further contribution in the ongoing discussion on peaceful coexistence. Piediscalzi and Thobaben finally report analytically on the Salzburg conference of the Paulus-Gesellschaft on the "Future of Europe."

Paul Mojzes, Editor

THE CURRENT STATUS OF THE CHRISTIAN-MARXIST DIALOGUE AND SUGGESTED GUIDELINES FOR CONDUCTING THE DIALOGUE

Paul Mojzes

The purpose of this volume is not merely to report on what is currently taking place in the Christian-Marxist dialogue, but also to promote the dialogue. In view of the history of the dialogue such an approach is entirely appropriate because the dialogue surfaced into public attention primarily by means of the written rather than the spoken word. To this day, be it the weakness or the strength of this dialogue, quantitatively *much* more dialogue has been carried on in print than in public gatherings.

Brief Historical Sketch of Past Dialogues

No comprehensive history of the Christian-Marxist dialogue has been written. Perhaps because of its short duration, little serious historical attention has been given to the various facets of the dialogical encounter.[1]

The Christian-Marxist dialogue emerged in the 1960's.[2] Prior to that period there were surely, in addition to hostile interactions or neglect, more positive interactions such as influences upon each other, attempts at political cooperation, and attempts to synthesize these two views in the lives of individual Marxists or Christians. But the conditions were not conducive to serious dialogue until the decade of the 1960's. De-Stalinization, relaxations of East-West tensions, the papacy of John XXIII, and Vatican II were among the conditions that enabled Christians and Marxists to meet on a dialogical basis. It is difficult to establish precisely where and when the dialogue started first, because the conditions and

---

[1] Instances of exceptions to this generalization are Francis J. Murphy, *"La Main Tendue:* Prelude to Christian-Marxist Dialogue in France, 1936–1939," in *The Catholic Historical Review,* Vol. 40, No. 2 (July, 1974), pp. 255–270; and Paul Mojzes, "Christian-Marxist Dialogue in the Context of a Socialist Society" (Yugoslavia), in *Journal of Ecumenical Studies,* Vol. 9, No. 1 (Winter, 1972), pp. 1–28.

[2] In this respect I take issue with the contention that the dialogue "goes back to the very beginning of the Marxist tradition" made by Harvey Cox, in "The Christian-Marxist Dialogue: What Next," in *Marxism and Christianity,* edited by Herbert Aptheker (New York: Humanities Press, 1968), p. 15.

Paul Mojzes (United Methodist) was educated at Belgrade University Law School and Florida Southern College and received a Ph.D. degree in church history from Boston University. He is associate professor of religious studies at Rosemont College, Rosemont, PA, and managing editor of the *Journal of Ecumenical Studies*. Involved in Christian-Marxist issues since his high school days, he has actively participated in the dialogue since the late 1960's. He is the chairperson for the Task Force on the Christian-Marxist Encounter of Christians Associated for Relationships with Eastern Europe, as well as a participant in many international Christian-Marxist meetings and organizer of some of the recent symposia. He has taught courses on Christian-Marxist relations in Austria and in the U.S.A. since 1969, and has published articles in this field in *J.E.S., Religion in Life, Horizons,* and *Worldview.*

characteristics of the dialogue differed from country to country. Almost simultaneously there were instances of dialogue taking place in Czechoslovakia, Italy, West Germany, and France.

In Czechoslovakia during the period between 1957 and 1962, despite internal opposition, seminars were held by the Marxist professor Milan Machoveč at Charles University in Prague on prominent contemporary Christian thinkers. This included the study of the writings of Professor Josef Hromádka who had taken Marxism seriously and had brought about a serious study of Marxism at the Jan Amos Comenius Theological Faculty in Prague. But actual dialogue took place only in 1964 when Machoveč invited to his seminars a number of Christian theologians passing through Prague, such as Gustave Wetter, S.J., of Rome, Charles West of Princeton, Albert Rasker of Leiden, and H. Braun of Mainz.[3]

In 1964, a book entitled *Il dialogo alla prova* [The Dialogue Put to Test] was published in Florence, Italy. Five Marxist and five Roman Catholic authors contributed to it. These authors reflected the changing situation in Italy since the convocation of the Second Vatican Council in 1962. Likewise the historic pronouncements of Palmiro Toggliati, leader of the Italian Communist Party, shortly before his death in 1964, in which he rejected atheist propaganda and encouraged Catholics to join the Communist Party without abandoning their faith, have also been a culmination of a process of the reexamination of relationships pioneered primarily by the Marxist professor, Lucio Lombardo-Radice, and reciprocated on the Christian side by such people as Mario Gozzini and Giulio Girardi.

The Paulus-Gesellschaft, active primarily in West Germany and Austria, which was organized in the 1950's to promote dialogue between theologians and scientists, turned its attention in the 1960's to the Christian-Marxist dialogue. In the Spring of 1964 at the Munich meeting of the Paulus-Gesellschaft, Ernst Bloch, the German Marxist professor, took part.[4] Later in the fall of that year at Cologne the Polish Marxist professor and member of the Central Committee of the Polish United Worker's Party, Adam Schaff, presented a paper at a symposium entitled "Christianity and Marxism Today."[5] At both symposia only one Marxist appeared among a large number of Christians. But with each succeeding Congress of the Paulus-Gesellschaft (Salzburg, Austria, 1965, with the theme "Christian and Marxist Future";[6] Herren Chiemensee, West Germany, 1966, with the theme "Christian Humanity and Marxist Humanism";[7] Marianske Lazni, Czechoslovakia, 1967, with the theme "Creativity and Freedom"[8]) the

---

[3]Milan Opočensky, "Christlich-marxistischer Dialog in Prag," in *Stimmen aus der Kirche der CSSR* edited by Bé Ruys and Josef Smolik (München: Chr. Kaiser Verlag, 1968), p. 132.

[4]The overall topic of the Munich meeting was "Man: Spirit and Matter." Papers presented by Ernst Bloch, Karl Rahner, and others were published under the title *Der Mensch, Geist und Materie* (München: Paulus-Gesellschaft Selbstverlag, 1965).

[5]*Christentum und Marxismus heute* (München: Paulus-Gesellschaft Selbstverlag, 1966) contains, among others, papers by Johann B. Metz, Adam Schaff, and Alfonso Alvarez-Bolado.

[6]*Christliche und Marxistische Zukunft* (München: Paulus-Gesellschaft Selbstverlag, 1965).

[7]*Christliche Humanität und marxistischer Humanismus* (München: Paulus-Gesellschaft Selbstverlag, 1966).

[8]*Schöpfertum und Freiheit* (München: Paulus-Gesellschaft Selbstverlag, 1968).

number of Marxist participants increased, peaking, naturally, at Marianske Lazni. It was to fall off sharply at the Paulus-Gesellschaft youth congress in Bonn which took place after the Soviet invasion of Czechoslovakia in the fall of 1968.[9] The congresses were discontinued after it was obvious that the Marxist partners in the dialogue, especially the very active Czechoslovakians, as well as Roger Garaudy, were being actively repressed. As an act of solidarity, the Paulus-Gesellschaft suspended its dialogues for a number of years, till 1975, to be precise. The Paulus-Gesellschaft was later made into a scapegoat being accused of mixing into internal affairs of Czechoslovakia and fomenting unrest, and this was given as the official reason for discontinuing the dialogue by the dogmatic Marxists and by those Eastern European Christians who always publicly endorse official positions, whatever they may be.

Over the years the Paulus-Gesellschaft under the leadership of Dr. Erich Kellner, a Roman Catholic priest, has been the organizer of the most numerous dialogues with the largest number of participants. The list of those who took part in their symposia reads like a "Who's Who" in the Christian-Marxist dialogue. They are so far the most publicized meetings with the widest impact on public opinion.

Out of France came the individual who had initially made the greatest impact on the worldwide Christian-Marxist dialogue, Roger Garaudy. His book, *De l'Anatheme an Dialogue* [*From Anathema to Dialogue*] (Paris: Ed. Plon, 1965), which clearly describes the change in Christian-Marxist relations, was obviously prepared earlier and reflects Garaudy's change from a Stalinist to a humanistic Marxist.[10] Garaudy, then a member of the Central Committee of the Communist Party of France[11], was responding to Vatican II, and elaborated on views which he had already expressed in a response to Pope John XXIII's *"Pacem in Terris"* in 1963 in the journal *Cahiers du Communisme.*[12] Roger Garaudy's worldwide involvement in the dialogue[13] made a great contribution to the growth of the dialogue. However, since his expulsion from the French Communist Party, his effectiveness has lessened, though many people still respond to his ideas[14] and he continues to write on the subject of Christian-Marxist interaction.

1964 can be regarded, then, as the date of the actual beginning of the Christian-Marxist dialogue. In its first, spontaneous, even exhilarating form it

---

[9]*Evolution oder Revolution der Gesellschaft* (München: Paulus-Gesellschaft Selbstverlag, 1969).

[10]Manfred Spieker, *Neomarxismus und Christentum: Zur Problematik des Dialogs* (München, Paderborn, Wien: Verlag Fredinand Schöningh, 1974), pp. 63 ff.

[11]In 1970, Garaudy was not only relieved of his high post but expelled from the Communist Party of France because of "revisionism."

[12]Spieker, *Neomarxismus*, p. 75.

[13]In addition to his participation in the Paulus-Gesellschaft symposia, he carried on a dialogue with many theologians. See, for instance, Roger Garaudy and Quentin Lauer, S. J., *A Christian-Communist Dialogue* (Garden City, NY: Doubleday and Company, 1968); Roger Garaudy, "Christian-Marxist Dialogue," and Johann B. Metz, "The Controversy About the Future of Man: An Answer to Roger Garaudy" in *Journal of Ecumenical Studies,* Vol. 4, No. 2 (Spring, 1967).

[14]E.g., Russell Norris, "Transcendence and the Future: Dialogue with Roger Garaudy," in *Journal of Ecumenical Studies,* Vol. 10, No. 3 (Summer, 1973), pp. 498–514; and Russell B. Norris, *God, Marx and the Future: Dialogue with Roger Garaudy* (Philadelphia: Fortress Press, 1974).

did not last very long. Abruptly the dialogue ended in Czechoslovakia by late 1968, and shortly thereafter in Austria, Germany, and France. Many of those who participated in these dialogues concluded that the dialogue was dead.[15] Some maintain that position to this day. Soviet Marxist scholars delivered sharp attacks on this form of the dialogue, charging that it leads to a convergence which falsifies and weakens the Marxist position.[16] Ideological dialogue was seen as a threat by dogmatic Marxists and to a lesser degree by establishment Christians.[17] Others argued that, while dialogue was dead, Christians and Marxists could cooperate on concrete projects.

This indeed became the case in Latin America. The Latin American motto became liberation, and for the sake of liberation many Christians were willing to cooperate with Marxists in revolutionary endeavors. Marxists, too, sought such cooperation.[18] First a large number of essays and books were published by Latin American theologians proposing a "liberation theology" which was implicitly or explicitly inspired by some Marxist insights. Later a whole battery of books specifically on the dialogue was written by such Christian writers as José Miguez-Bonino and José Miranda. Such theological treatises indicate that some Latin American writers do not reject ideological or theological reflection on issues of Christian-Marxist relations. However, public dialogues are rarely, if ever, taking place. This is not surprising in light of the oppression which followed the fall of Allende's regeme in Chile or the political situation in Argentina, Brazil, Uruguay, and most other Latin American countries.

This Latin American self-conscious reflection on Christian-Marxist relations started just about the time when the formal European dialogues came to a close. But in Europe matters were not uniform by a long shot. In Yugoslavia, Poland, Italy, Spain, and England, fascinating interactions were taking place. The Yugoslav Marxists and Christians who had attended the Paulus-Gesellschaft meetings decided to continue their dialogues at home, and from 1968 to 1972 a very fruitful and active period of dialogue ensued. Marxist philosophers and sociologists such as Bošnjak, Ćimić, Roter, Kerševan, Krešić, and Vrcan were publicly, privately, and in print involved in dialogues with Christians such as Archbishop Franić, Bajsić, Šagi-Bunić, Šimundža, Vereš, and Romić. Only an internal purge and tightening of ideological lines by the League of Communists of Yugoslavia brought this dialogue in public virtually to a halt, but it continues to the present in private and to some degree in print.

[15]E.g., Günther Nenning, "Warum der Dialog starb" in *Neues Forum* (Vienna), March, 1972.

[16]E.g., Lev N. Mitrokhin, "About the 'Dialogue' of Marxists and Christians," in *Voprosy filozofii* (Moscow), July, 1971.

[17]Most notorious is the removal of Giulio Girardi from the Salesian University in Rome. Eventually he moved to Paris and continued to write on the topic but was expelled from the Salesian order in September, 1977, apparently for his continued involvement with Marxists. His most important book is *Christianity and Marxism* (New York: The Macmillan Co., 1968).

[18]Nicholas Piediscalzi and Robert G. Thobaben, eds., *From Hope to Liberation: Towards a New Christian-Marxist Dialogue* (Philadelphia: Fortress Press, 1974); John Eagleson, ed., *Christians and Socialism* (Maryknoll, NY: Orbis Books, 1975).

In Poland the dialogue assumed a form very different from other countries. There were no spectacular public meetings and only very little in print, but a good deal of lively interaction in the Clubs of the Catholic Intelligenzia.[19] After the short period when Adam Schaff and Lezsek Kołakowski attempted to focus on philosophical issues, the Marxist thinkers of Poland tend to lay stress on practical issues. Taking into consideration the strength of the Roman Catholic Church in Poland, it is not surprising that Marxists seek a dialogue on practical issues and are willing to include in the package some ideological dialogue.[20]

The Italian situation appears to be the opposite of Poland's. While Poland has a Marxist government which must reckon with the power of the Roman Catholic Church, the reign in Italy is in the hands of Roman Catholics who must reckon with a very powerful Communist Party. Under such circumstance the Italian Catholics and Marxists are in constant dialogue through "Christians for Socialism," through the Communist attempt to work out the "great compromise" with the Christian Democrats, through the Communist attempt to woo a Roman Catholic electorate, or through the Catholic intellectual's perception that the Italian Communists are a new breed of Communists with whom one may work jointly. All these dynamics and more are going on simultaneously.

In Spain the original initiative seems to have been by such theologians as José Maria Gonzales-Ruiz,[21] an initiative not surprising under conditions of illegality for the Spanish Communists during Franco's regime. Spanish Communists and Catholics gradually changed their mutual perceptions and sought ways to cooperate against oppression.[22] With the emergence of "Eurocommunism" in which the Spanish and French Communists seem to follow the example of the Italian Communists, one may expect further impulses for the dialogue.

In England, where there is a longer tradition in Christian socialism and common action between Christians and the labor movement, the dialogue which emerged in 1966 first in the series of published dialogues in *Marxism Today* soon spread to many smaller public dialogues in churches, universities, Communist Party branches, and so forth. The novelty of this dialogue was that English Catholics joined the discussion for the first time. The major brunt of the discussion was carried by Protestant churches primarily through the British Council of Churches and the Society of Friends. Many of the dialogues were published in newspapers, journals, and in book form.[23]

---

[19]Ordered to cease activity by governmental order in 1977.

[20]Tadeusz M. Jaroszewski, "Confrontation, Dialogue, and Cooperation," in *Church within Socialism,* edited by Erich Weingartner and Giovanni Barberini (Rome: IDOC International, 1976), pp. 186–192.

[21]Jose Maria Gonzales-Ruiz, *The New Creation: Marxist and Christian?,* tr. Matthew J. O'Connell (Maryknoll, NY: Orbis Books, 1976).

[22]Santiago Alvares, "Towards an Alliance of Communists and Catholics" in Paul Oestreicher, ed., *The Christian-Marxist Dialogue* (London: The Macmillan Company, 1969), pp. 68–93.

[23]James Klugmann, "The Pattern of Encounter in Britain," in Oestreicher, *The Christian-Marxist Dialogue,* pp. 170–188.

The Present Status of the Dialogue

Showing much more vigor than opponents and some supporters of the dialogue expected, a new phase of the dialogue emerged in the 1970's. It is characterized by much less publicity and seems to be more widely diffused. For its base it has a considerable literature that has emerged from the protagonists in the first phase and from a new group of authors reacting to those writings. It consists of a series of peace symposia, reactivation of the Paulus-Gesellschaft activities, and a new North American involvement.

The writings of both Marxists and Christians produced in the 1960's were published as books only toward the end of the decade and continued to be translated and disseminated in the 1970's. Themes regarding the nature of human beings, transcendence, Christian attitudes toward evolution, Marxist attitudes toward religion and the Bible, as well as those dealing with the question of the relationship between Christians and Marxists were reaching an increasingly wider audience. Some were asking questions as to whether Christians could be socialists; others were wondering if it might not be mandatory that Christians be socialists. Courses dealing with the dialogue appeared at a number of universities and colleges. International travel and conferences kept the interest alive. The policy of détente and the Helsinki Agreement provided the atmosphere for continued Marxist-Christian interaction.

The Institut für Friedensforschung of Vienna University (initiated by the Roman Catholic Theological Faculty) under the leadership of Prof. Rudolf Weiler, and the International Peace Institute of Vienna under the leadership of Dr. Vladimir Bruskov from Moscow, jointly organized a symposium on "The Problems of International Peace and of Peaceful Co-Existence," held in Vienna in November, 1971.[24] This was followed by symposia in Moscow, 1973; Wallersee (near Salzburg), 1974; Tutsing (near Munich), 1975; and Rosemont (near Philadelphia), 1977. The first four symposia consisted of participants from East and West Europe, while at the last there was, in addition, a significant North American group. These symposia were carefully prepared, with participation by invitation; each group had both Christian and Marxist participants, though the Eastern groups were predominantly Marxist, and the Western were predominantly Christian. Usually only two major papers with two respondents were read; hence, the emphasis was on discussion.[25] A good deal of time was given for informal interpersonal contacts. For this reason the number of participants in each of the symposia was between thirty and sixty. For this dialogue the most significant is the Soviet participation. Outside of this context no Soviet Marxists and no Russian Orthodox theologians have taken part in dialogue. Very highly

---

[24]Rudolf Weiler, "Der Ausbau des Institutes für Friedensforschung in den Jahren 1972 und 1973," in *Wienner blätter*, No. 1 (January, 1974), p. 6.

[25]The papers and discussion of the first three symposia are published by Rudolf Weiler and Walter Hollitscher, eds., *Christen und Marxisten in Friedengeschpräch* (Vienna, Freiburg, and Basel: Herder, 1976). Papers from all symposia have been published in English and German in *Peace and the Sciences* (Vienna: International Institute for Peace), March, 1972; December, 1973; March and June, 1977.

placed and competent representatives came to these symposia. Since 1975, American contacts have been made with the two Vienna institutes through Paul Mojzes and the symposia have been supported by the Institute of International Understanding, Christians Associated for Relationships with Eastern Europe (C.A.R.E.E.), and the *Journal of Ecumenical Studies*. The next symposium is scheduled for Spring, 1978, in Yerevan, U.S.S.R. Stockholm may be the locus of a 1979 meeting.

By 1974 the Paulus-Gesellschaft decided to resume sponsorship of Christian-Marxist meetings. The major partner for Christians in this dialogue would be the Italian Communists, though others were not excluded. In October, 1975, a symposium was held in Florence with a primarily Western European participation (Yugoslav participants were the only ones coming from a socialist country). At the symposium it was agreed that the Paulus-Gesellschaft and the Italian Communist Party would sponsor a major European Congress on the theme, "The Future of Europe," to be held in Strassbourg, France. The meeting took place instead in Salzburg, Austria, in September, 1977, on a somewhat less ambitious scale. The Italian Communists, however, did not attend the meeting. Nor did the French. The only Marxists present were from Spain and Hungary.

On the national level several dialogues were taking place in the 1970's. In Hungary the normalization of church-state relations and the increasingly liberal policy of the Kadar regime has brought about a dialogue, mostly in journals between Marxists (led by Professor Josef Lukács) and prominent Catholic and Protestant theologians. The Hungarian Reformed theologian Károly Tóth, the General Secretary of the Christian Peace Conference, constantly stresses that conditions for the Christian-Marxist dialogue are improving. A major impetus for the dialogue came from the East Berlin Conference of European Communist parties (July, 1976), where dialogue and cooperation with Christians has been included in the final document. Particularly significant is the usage of the word "dialogue," because it has been a problematic one, particularly for the Soviets. It has finally been accepted as official terminology.

With the emergence of "Eurocommunism," the Communist parties of Italy, Spain, and France have made repeated political appeals to Christians and are trying to give continued assurances that if they come to power they will not persecute the churches and in general will preserve the democratic heritage including the multi-party parliamentary system. Berlinguer, Marchais, and Carrillo have all made their "policy of outstretched hands" speeches. Some Christians regard them with suspicion; others are convinced of their sincerity.

In the United States the interest in the dialogue was marginal until very recently. Individuals involved themselves in the European dialogues or Latin American cooperation. Those involved in Latin America were frequently radicalized by their experiences and were very sympathetic to Archbishop Helder Camara's call for dialogue.[26] "Liberation theology" has made a considerable

---

[26]Delivered at the University of Chicago, November 6, 1974. A special issue on the dialogue in response to this speech was published by *New Catholic World*, Vol. 220, No. 1317 (May/June, 1977).

impact on American theologians, and made many of them receptive to dialogue. Those involved in the European dialogue became convinced that the European experiences are unsuitable for the American circumstances. American Christians are aware that Marxism is relatively marginal in the U.S.A. and Canada and that it is badly splintered. Thus the tendency was for American Christians to look for foreign Marxist dialogical partners,[27] or else they entered into smaller-scale public dialogues with local Marxists.[28] Writings and papers delivered at professional academic societies were another American contribution to the worldwide dialogue.[29] Conferences on the relationship of Christianity and socialism were held in 1977 in San Francisco, Washington, and Chicago.

The Task Force on the Christian-Marxist Encounter of C.A.R.E.E. increased its activities and found many people in academic and ecclesiastical circles interested in the dialogue. Judging this to be an "auspicious" time, C.A.R.E.E. is convening the North American Christian-Marxist Conference on the theme "U.S. Socio-Economic Order in the Next Decade: Christian and Marxist Perspectives," to be held in May, 1978, at Rosemont College. It is hoped that this will turn out to be the first large-scale Christian-Marxist dialogue.

Ground Rules for the Dialogue

Historical conditions vary so much that it is impossible to prescribe uniform guidelines or ground rules for successful dialogue. They could turn out to be a "Procrustean bed" rather than an aid to the dialogue. Nevertheless, a number of suggestions can be made which, if implemented, might be beneficial in making a dialogue more constructive. It would appear that these ground rules could be used not merely in the Christian-Marxist dialogue but in other dialogues as well, although they were formulated specifically with the Christian-Marxist dialogue in mind.

1. Both partners must have a need for dialogue.
2. Have a preliminary knowledge of your partner and the position with which you are going to dialogue.
3. Have a clear understanding of your own position.
4. Be well informed about the topic being discussed and present it clearly.
5. Set concrete areas of discussion ahead of time.
6. It is more promising to discuss specific issues than general, abstract issues.
7. Do not stereotype. Be open to the presentation of your partner's viewpoint.
8. Interpret your partner's view in its best light. Look at the whole picture and do not try to belittle that view.

---

[27]E.g., symposia in Florence, Salzburg, and Rosemont; the Korčula and Dubrovnik schools; etc.

[28]E.g., dialogue at World Fellowship Camp, Conway, NH, in 1965 and 1977, as well as on various campuses (e.g., Wright State University, Rosemont College, Temple University). The most important Marxist partner in these dialogues so far has been Herbert Aptheker.

[29]E.g., Thomas Ogletree, ed., *Openings for Marxist-Christian Dialogue* (Nashville, New York: Abingdon Press, 1968); Herbert Aptheker, *The Urgency of Marxist-Christian Dialogue* (New York: Harper and Row, 1970).

9. Look at the weaknesses and strengths of both views.
10. Emphasize things you have in common.
11. Listen to what your partner is saying. Strive for a clearer understanding of his or her position. Be willing continually to revise your understanding of the other's views.
12. There should be no hidden agendas. There should be no tactical or selfish motive initiating the dialogue.
13. Be open to constructive criticism, and avoid destructive criticism. Be aware of your partner's sensitivities.
14. Each member of the dialogue should be self-critical and honest. This should not mean giving up dignity and self-respect.
15. Do not assume that the conclusions reached are final. There will always be a need for continual dialogue regarding these views.
16. Each partner must accept responsibility for the good and bad his or her group has done or is still doing.
17. Both the ideals and the realities of each group should be taken into account.
18. Face issues which cause conflict, but emphasize those things upon which partners agree. Antagonistic relationships may then give way to cooperation.
19. Challenge one another to be faithful to your own search for truth.
20. Soul-searching and mutual enrichment should be part of the dialogue. Neither's truth is absolute. Each partner needs the other in order to get a more complete picture of truth. Monopoly in thought leads to sluggishness in thinking and to the perversion of truth.
21. Dialogue is impossible if either partner claims to have already solved the problem for all time to come.
22. Dialogue should present a new appreciation for the value of both positions.
23. Dialogue occurs between persons or groups of persons, not between disembodied ideas.
24. You must not try to convert your partner, or the dialogue may turn again into a monologue. Differences must be maintained, although they should change from irreconcilable ones to a diversity of approaches for the common good.
25. Dialogue should enable easier cooperation.
26. Work toward accomplishing something for the better. Work at improving the situation.
27. Observe the dialectical nature of the dialogue. Both views should be included in final conclusions, though not necessarily in equal measure. Both partners ought to move to new positions (not necessarily convergent ones) which would not have been possible without the dialogue.
28. Be aware that there are other people involved. The dialogue should be for the benefit of the whole community.

This list is not comprehensive, nor is it offered as a sequential order of guidelines, but is rather meant to serve as a check list of items which should be included in our dialogical "baggage" for the long, common journey which we are to undertake.

Future Prospects for Dialogue

The Christian-Marxist dialogue is unusually susceptible to political pressures. Any basic change in political constellations can affect the dialogue detrimentally or stimulatingly. The current crisis in deténte and the fortunes of "Eurocommunism" would appear to have the most immediate impact on the dialogue.

No dramatic increase in the dialogue is on the horizon. This is probably good. A slow, steady improvement in relations promises more realistically long-range success. One may expect a number of challenges to the dialogue from both the Communist and the Christian side, not only from those who oppose the very idea of dialogue, but also from those who warn against a too-quick synthesis which may lead to surrender of identity.[30]

The symposia which are co-sponsored by the Institut für Friedensforschung, International Institute for Peace, Institute for International Understanding, and C.A.R.E.E. are likely to continue with a dual emphasis on cooperation for peace and discussion of ideological issues. The Paulus-Gesellschaft will continue to seek partners for ideological dialogue. Those socialist countries where political relaxation takes place are likely to permit or even encourage dialogue. Poland, Hungary, and Yugoslavia appear at the moment the only likely candidates. Italy, France, and Spain are probably going to produce the largest number of national Christian-Marxist interactions. As long as political and economic oppression is so prevalent in Latin America, Christians and Marxists will continue to cooperate. Marxists are going to welcome Christian support and will promise to be tolerant of religion; many Christians are likely to embrace Marxist social analysis or methodology. A fundamental reevaluation of the Marxist analysis of religion or acceptance of some Christian principles is not to be expected soon. Nor is one to expect large-scale public dialogues.

In the U.S.A. and Canada, a considerable increase of interest in the Christian-Marxist dialogue on the part of Christians is already evident and is to be expected in the near future. This is likely to express itself in increased publishing activity and national and local conferences. One of the basic issues to be discussed among Christians is to what degree a Christian can embrace Marxist views. The minority will opt for a synthesis; most will look for a dialogue without convergence. The initiative is clearly on the Christian side. U. S. Marxists are not only divided and marginal but too antagonistic to each other to be a significant social phenomenon. It remains yet to be seen to what degree they are willing and capable to respond to this Christian initiative. Some may see it as a

---

[30]E.g., Dale Vree, *On Synthesizing Marxism and Christianity* (New York, London, Sydney, Toronto: John Wiley & Sons, 1976).

change for "legitimization," a chance to surface in public not merely as an opposition ready to debate and combat prevailing views, but also to be treated as partners.

In West Germany there is a good deal of Marxist theoretical thinking and left-wing political activity, but the Communist Party is not a significant political force. The serious concern in Germany is the restrictive legislation against Communists and the question as to whether Christians, especially pastors, may join the Communist Party. Some West German thinkers are raising the issue whether under circumstances of advanced capitalism it may be a Christian imperative to be a socialist.[31] In East Germany much is written about cooperation between Christians and Communists, but no ideological dialogue is carried on.

Three other countries which so far have not figured prominently in the dialogue may assume some importance in the future—Cuba, India, and China. With improved relations between the U.S.A. and Cuba, an increasing number of church leaders from the U.S.A. and Canada are visiting that country and communicating their experiences. Some of these communications have already provoked controversy in the churches. It is likely that in the next decade American Christians will interact more intensely and more positively with Cuban Marxism. In India a number of Christian scholars have already undertaken an evaluation of Marxism and engaged in at least a written dialogue.[32] The Christian Institute for the Study of Church and Society in Bangalore seems to be setting the pace in this encounter. In China there is no likely Christian-Marxist dialogue, but the Chinese Communist experience has recently been given a good deal of Christian scrutiny. Many western Christian leaders traveled to China and have given not altogether negative responses. The most serious study on China so far is probably that of the Study Department of the World Lutheran Federation in cooperation with *Pro Mundi Vita,* a Roman Catholic organization.[33] The National Council of Churches of Christ in the U.S.A., through its department for the study of China, and similar groups have also become more active in attempting to determine the best Christian response to China. No active Chinese Marxist response is to be expected in the near future.

The World Council of Churches sponsored a Christian-Marxist Consultation several years ago, and the Lutheran World Federation more recently sponsored a number of seminars in Switzerland, Belgium, Sweden, and Denmark. Such study seminars will probably continue, and national churches will probably conduct them. It would be desirable if some Marxists were to be invited to such seminars. IDOC International, an ecumenical documentation center in Rome,

---

[31]Raised by such thinkers as Helmut Gollwitzer, "Müssen Christen Sozialisten sein?" *Junge Kirche,* Vol. 37, No. 10 (1976), pp. 497–505.

[32]P. M. John, *Marx on Alienation* (South Asia Books, 1976).

[33]Lutheran World Federation Study Dept./*Pro Mundi Vita, Christianity and the New China* (So. Pasadena, CA: Ecclesia Publication, 1976). Also significant is their publication, *The Encounter of the Church with Movements of Social Change in Various Cultural Contexts* (Geneva: Lutheran World Federation, 1977).

has already been useful in collecting and publishing data regarding Christian-Marxist encounters. Their continued activity could be a great service for an informed worldwide dialogue.

One of the major questions for the future is whether Marxists will become more eager to involve themselves in the dialogue than they are at the present. In the past several years it seems that more Christians have sought to engage themselves in dialogue with Marxists than vice versa. In many instances these Christian initiatives were meagerly accepted. In most public encounters the number of Christian participants and observers vastly outnumbered the Marxists. While for Marxists political considerations naturally play a greater role and party discipline seems to be much more tight than ecclesiastical centralism is in the more authoritarian churches, there is still going to be a negative impact on the overall dialogue if the Marxist response continues to be so guarded. Fairly soon people in leadership positions in Communist parties will need to take a long, hard look as to whether their caution and suspicion toward dialogue with Christians is not going to hurt rather than assist their own interest. And if they are concerned about the interest of the world, their hesitation should practically dissolve at once.

We Christians are waiting and wondering. But while we are waiting we must do a lot of education and dialogue within the churches in order to rid ourselves of primitive anti-Communism and of incriminating alliances with oppressive forces. A serious discussion in the churches needs to be carried out as to what degree a dialogue with Marxists represents an incriminating engagement with a repressive movement. It should be clear to Marxists and non-Marxists alike that the primary interest of Christians is not the dialogue with Marxists but the enhancing of human dignity, wholeness, freedom, creativity, and happiness. Insofar as the dialogue contributes to this, it is desirable for Christians. If it does not, it may need to be modified or even rejected. Ultimately, the future of the dialogue depends on the degree of future humanization of both Christianity and Marxism.

THE CRITIQUE OF RELIGION IN KARL MARX'S *CAPITAL*

Max Josef Suda

Preliminary Note

The latest discussion on Karl Marx's critique of religion[1] essentially refers to the critical remarks on religion of the young Marx—and it does so legitimately: for it was the young Marx who had a particular interest in the critique of religion and, in those years of his life, laid the foundation for the attitude of the entire Marxist movement toward religion. The mature Marx was more concerned with the critique of politics and economy. The critique of religion strongly recedes, for instance, in Marx's principal work, *Capital,* but that receding critique of religion has taken such a peculiar turn compared to the earlier times that it is worthwhile to analyze it in detail.

1. The Ironic Treatment of Religion

A Christian or even a theologian who reads *Capital* cannot avoid feeling awkward. First of all one is faced with sarcastic remarks regarding the Christian religion, such as ''The fact that it is value, is made manifest by its [of the linen,

---

[1]The literature includes: Frederick J. Adelman, *From Dialogue to Epilogue, Marxism and Catholicism Tomorrow* (The Hague, 1968); Walter Bienert, *Der überholte Marx, Seine Religionskritik und Weltanschauung kritisch untersucht* (Stuttgart, 1974); Klaus Erich Bockmühl, *Leiblichkeit und Gesellschaft. Studien zur Religionskritik und Anthropologie im Frühwerk von Ludwig Feuerbach und Karl Marx* (Göttingen, 1961); Iring Fetscher, ''Wandlungen der marxistischen Religionskritik,'' *Concilium* 2 (1966): 455 ff.; Helmut Fleischer, *Marxismus und Geschichte* (Frankfurt/M., 1970); Erich Fromm, *Marx's Concept of Man* (New York, 1961); Roger Garaudy, J. B. Metz, and Karl Rahner, *Der Dialog oder: Ändert sich das Verhältnis zwischen Katholizismus und Marxismus?* (Reinbek bei Hamburg, 1966); Roger Garaudy, *Perspectives de l'homme. Existentialism, pensée catholique marxism* (Paris, 1959); Helmut Gollwitzer, *Die marxistische Religionskritik und der christliche Glaube* in Marxismusstudien, 4th ed. (Tübingen, 1962), pp. 1 ff.; Johannes Kadenbach, *Das Religionsverständnis von Karl Marx* (München/Paderborn/Wien, 1970); Walter Kern, *Atheismus—Marxismus—Christentum* (Innsbruck/Wien/München, 1976); Traugott Koch, ''Revolutionsprogram und Religionskritik bei Karl Marx,'' *Zeitschrift für Theologie und Kirche* 68 (1971): 53 ff.; Jan Milic Lochman, ''Dimensionen Marxscher Religionskritik,'' *Internationale Dialog-Zeitschrift* 6 (1973): 351 ff.; Heinrich Popitz, *Der entfremdete Mensch. Zeitkritik und Geschichtsphilosophie des jungen Marx* (Frankfurt/M., 1967); Werner Post, *Kritik der Religion bei Karl Marx* (München, 1969); Marcel Reding, *Der politische Atheismus* (Graz/Wien/Köln, 1957); Robert Steigerwald, *Marxismus—Religion—Geganwart* (Berlin, 1973); Robert C. Tucker, *Philosophy and Myth in Karl Marx* (Cambridge, 1961); Charles Wackenheim, *La faillite de la religion d' après Karl Marx* (Paris, 1963); Gustav A. Wetter, *Der dialektische Materialismus* (Wein, 1952).

Max Josef Suda (Lutheran Church-Augsburg Confession) is Universität assistent at the Evangelisch-theologische Fakultät, University of Vienna, Austria. He received his education at the University of Vienna (Ph.D.) and University of Geneva, as well as a diploma from the Akademie für sozialarbeit für Berufstätige. Recent articles include ''Das Gottesbild aus dem Unbewusten'' and ''Theoretische und praktische Überlegungen zur Grundlegung der christlichen Anthropologie in Diskussion mit Karl Marx.''

M. J. S.] equality with the coat, just as the sheep's nature of a Christian is shown in his resemblance to the Lamb of God.''[2] Or Marx ironically paraphrases a psalm: ''As the hart pants after fresh water, so pants his [the bourgeois', M. J. S.] soul after money, the only wealth.''[3] A third example is:

> But even in the colonies properly so called, the Christian character of primitive accumulation did not belie itself. Those sober virtuosi of Protestantism, the Puritans of New England, in 1703, by decrees of their assembly set a premium of £40 on every Indian scalp and every captured red-skin: in 1720 a premium of £100 on every scalp; in 1744, after Massachusetts-Bay had proclaimed a certain tribe as rebels, the following prices: for a male scalp of 12 years and upwards £100 (new currency), for a male prisoner £105, for women and children prisoners £50, for scalps of women and children £50.[4]

One of the main reasons for this feeling of embarrassment or even anger is the fact that in *Capital* Marx does not criticize religion genuinely, nor does he argue against religion seriously. Instead, he only strikes at the Christian religion with side-cuts. This is to be seen in connection with the fact that for Marx, since 1843–44, there is no need for a critique of religion. Enlightenment philosophers up to Feuerbach had been of the opinion that religion was a stupefying and suppressing power from which human beings have to liberate themselves. For Marx, however, the source of suppression lies in the political conditions (1843–44, *Critique of the Hegelian Philosophy of Right. Introduction*) and, from 1844 onward (*Economic and Philosophic Manuscripts*), in the economic conditions. After that time religion for Marx no longer had the meaning of an independent sphere of life. It is but cold comfort for the oppressed and an epiphenomenon veiling the view of the real conditions.[5]

Marx no longer needs to criticize religion. Sarcastic remarks is all he has for it. But what is the point of these remarks? A critique of religion and religion itself could be overcome to such an extent that there is no longer any demand for mentioning them in *A Critique of Political Economy* (subtitle of *Capital*). But, obviously, Marx wants to give certain hints for the reader (and for himself?) by referring to religion. What kind of hints?

Let us look at our first quotation: in the context of this quotation Marx is

---

[2]Editions of *Capital:* Karl Marx, *Das Kapital*, Vol. 1–3 (Berlin, 1969–70) (= *Marx-Engels-Werke*, Vol. 23–25); Karl Marx, *Das Kapital*, Vol. 1–3, ed. Hans-Joachim Lieber and Benedikt Kautsky (Stuttgart, 1962/63/64) (= *Karl-Marx-Ausgabe*, ed. Hans-Joachim Lieber, Vol. 4–6. [The quotations in this translation of Suda's article follow the English edition: Karl Marx, *Capital*, tr. Samuel Moore and Edward Aveling, ed. Frederick Engels, Vol. 1–3 (Moscow, 1954/56/59, reprinted 1974).] The quotation is from 1:58.

[3]Ibid., 1:138.

[4]Ibid., 1:705.

[5]In *Die deutsche Ideologie* we read: ''Auch die Nebelbildungen im Gehirn des Menschen sind notwendige Sublimate ihres materiellen, empirisch konstatierbaren und an materielle Voraussetzungen geknüpften Lebensprozesses. Die Moral, Religion, Metaphysik und sonstige Ideologie und die ihnen entsprechenden Bewusstseinsformen hehalten hiermit nicht länger den Schein der Selbständigkeit'' (*Marx-Engels-Werke*, Vol. 3 [Berlin, 1969], pp. 26–27).

examining the value of the linen and the coat. The coat and the linen have a different physical form; they are also things with a different use-value, but they can be exchanged one for the other in the market. That is, a coat and a certain quantity of linen can be exchanged for each other; they have the same exchange-value or the same money-value. At first sight it is a mystery as to how a coat and a certain quantity of linen should be "equal." Here Marx makes use of a comparison. How is it possible that Christians can be like Christ, can be "equal" to Christ? Marx doesn't answer this question, but he solves the problem of the equality of the coat and the linen. In a society producing commodities every product has, in addition to its "natural or physical form," a "value form" which is measured in a definite quantity of another commodity or in money, and when two commodities have the same "money measure," that is the same price, even though they are not equal in any other respect, they are considered to be equal. Marx thus draws a comparison between a fact of belief which for the believer contains a mystery and a fact of a society producing commodities which for a member of this society also includes a mystery.

The following quotation is a continuation of the above-mentioned but also serves as a new example:

> In simple circulation, C-M-C, the value of commodities attained at the most a form independent of their use-values, i.e. the form of money; but that same value now in the circulation M-C-M, or the circulation of capital, suddenly presents itself as an independent substance, endowed with a motion of its own, passing through a life-process of its own, in which money and commodities are mere forms which it assumes and casts off in turn. Nay, more: instead of simply representing the relations of commodities, it enters now, so to say, into private relations with itself. It differentiates itself as original value from itself as surplus-value; as the father differentiates himself from himself qua the son, yet both are one and of one age: for only by the surplus-value of £10 does the £100 originally advanced become capital, and so soon as this takes place, so soon as the son, and by the son, the father, is begotten, so soon does their difference vanish, and they again become one, £110. [In the original Marx writes God Father" and "God Son," but this is changed into "father" and "son" in the English translation!][6]

In this context Marx uses the theological pattern of thinking about the relations of God as "father" and Christ to illustrate the relations of the original capital-value and surplus-value and thus "explains" the economic process in capitalism. One is at a loss to point out or understand the irony of the comparison. A Christian, of course, feels insulted by those lines in which matters of faith are compared with something so trivial as the economic process; but when we consider that economy is for modern people the basis of their existence, is the comparison then still offensive? On the other hand, one notices, of course, that Marx is not going to acknowledge the mysterious identity of original capital-value and surplus-value

[6]*Capital*, 1:152–153.

as the identity of God as "father" and Christ is acknowledged in faith. For the entire context of *Capital* Marx enlightens us on the genesis of surplus-value. The parallel from Christian theology is thus once more used rather for the sake of irony.

Another impressive example is that passage of Vol. 3 of *Capital* wherein Marx refers to the three relations (capital—interest, land—ground-rent, and labor—wages) as the "economic trinity."[7] But here, too, both kinds of trinity are ridiculed:

> On closer examination of this economic trinity, we find the following: First the alleged sources of the annually available wealth belong to widely dissimilar spheres and are not at all analogous with one another. They have about the same relation to each other as lawyers' fees, red beets and music.[8]

Marx ironically parallels the Christian religion with the modern capitalist economy. In both systems processes are found which interpret each other. I do not, however, want to give the impression that the entire analysis in *Capital* made use of this parallelism. No, there are only sporadic instances, not many, but still sporadic within the enormous architecture of *Capital,* which, however, touch upon central issues of both religion and capitalism.

One thing can be seen clearly by these quotations: the paralleling of central topics of capitalism with central topics of the Christian religion serves the purpose of critique. Marx uses irony and mockery in the way shown above to bring humor to his otherwise dry examinations and, on the other hand, because it is the best way to unmask certain views. But what is the aim of his criticism? Obviously not only theologumena and ideas of faith, but also the economic conditions paralleled and the theories pertinent to these conditions. Marx seems to say that these economic ideas are as naive or anachronistic as those Christian ideas! Those who do not notice that the economic conditions of capitalism are obsolete but, instead, admire them as quasi-eternally valid relations have to be made aware of the antiquated religious ideas of Christianity. The theories which support capitalism are just as antiquated as Christian dogmas!

Marx, however, does not content himself with paralleling capitalism with an antiquated or obsolete Christian religion; when we read *Capital* another totally different religious world dawns upon us.

2. Fetishism

In important passages of *Capital,* Marx no longer with a hidden sarcastic tone but almost in earnest uses a term from the science of religion which, this time, does not refer to the world of Christian dogmas—the term "fetish." He talks of

---

[7]Ibid., 3:814, 830.
[8]Ibid., 3:814.

the fetish commodity,[9] the fetish money,[10] the fetish gold,[11] and the fetish capital.[12]

It is very well possible that Marx came across the term "fetish" through Hegel's philosophy of religion. In Hegel, in any case, the contemporary knowledge of the history of religion is reflected. For Hegel fetishism is part of the most primitive forms of "natural religion"; he describes fetishes as carved things, wood, animals, rivers, trees, etc.; that is, natural objects turned into idols.[13]

The word "fetish," from the Portuguese "*fetiço*" (Lat., *factitius*), generally refers to cult objects either modelled by humans or not. Van der Leeuw, a phenomenologist of religion, defines fetishism as follows: "We speak of fetishism when people regularly count on the power inherent in things and then act according to this belief."[14] Is Marx of the opinion that the people in industralized regions "believe" in such things as commodities, gold, money, capital? Why, for goodness' sake, should these things carry a religious meaning?

Marx says that a commodity as an article of utility is in no way a mysterious thing. The article of utility is the result of labor and satisfies human wants. But a commodity does not have use-value only; in addition to that it has an exchange-value. For a person—e.g., a dealer—who wants to exchange an object for another object (or money), use-value is utterly unimportant. It is the buyer who then takes an interest in it. To the dealer the object exists as exchange-value only. Use-value and exchange-value are united in the object, but they are not identical, for when we consider the exchange of one commodity for another (or money), both objects have different use-values but are equal in the exchange process (purchase or sale). The equality of commodities is their exchange- or money-value—in short, their value as commodity. In our society the most different things can be called commodities.

In the first chapter of *Capital*, Marx studies how unequal things can be equal as commodities. The result is the insight that complicated social mechanisms are at the basis of this equality: not everybody can produce all articles of utility for himself or herself, and with the increasing development of human wants the need for division of labor increases, too. People produce for each other, and in this reciprocity they depend upon each other. Thus a key of distribution is found which guarantees the existence of equality in the amount one person produces for another and the other way around. This key of distribution is "the measure of the

[9]Ibid., 1:76–87, 96. On page 96, the translation omits the term "fetish" by translating *"Geldfetisch"* into "money" and *"Warenfetisch"* into "commodities."

[10]Ibid., 1:86, 96. Cf. note 9 above!

[11]Ibid., 1:133.

[12]Ibid., 1:86 (the German *"Fetischismus"* of capitalist economy is reproduced by "superstition"); 3:391–399, 829.

[13]G. W. F. Hegel, *Jubiläumsausgabe*, ed. Hermann Glockner, Vol. 15 (Stuttgart/Bad Cannstatt, 1965), pp. 316–317.

[14]G. van der Leeuw, *Phänomenologie der Religion*, 3rd ed. (Tübingen, 1970), pp. 19–20. [The quotation is translated from the German edition.]

expenditure of labour-power by the duration of that expenditure.''[15] This does not mean that a product increases in value with the worker's slowness in producing the object, but depends upon the average labor-time socially necessary. In addition, a social institution must be established—the market—in which the products equated with each other can change their owners.

Thus we can see that there are certain social relations hidden behind commodities. Indeed, commodities as exchange-values *are* these relations. As long as human beings do not understand these social relations but consider them to be things (commodities), they are prone to fetishism:

> There is a definite social relation between men, that assumes, in their eyes, the fantastic form of a relation between things. In order, therefore, to find an analogy, we must have recourse to the mist-enveloped regions of the religious world. In that world the productions of the human brain appear as independent beings endowed with life, and entering into relation both with one another and the human race. So it is in the world of commodities with the products of men's hands. This I call the Fetishism which attaches itself to the products of labour, so soon as they are produced as commodities, and which is therefore inseparable from the production of commodities.[16]

The fetishism of gold and money is the further development of the fetishism of commodities. Gold is itself a commodity whose production requires a "measure of the expenditure of labor-power by the duration of that expenditure." Then gold is, in certain societies, turned into a commodity for which all other commodities can be exchanged; gold becomes a universal means of payment. The development of silver money, paper money, and credit money veils the commodity character of money and results in the fact that the fetishism of money is less easily perceived than that of commodities.

Fetishism reaches a climax in the fetishism of capital. Capital is not only the objective representation of human relations in a thing, as is the case with commodities, nor is it only the additional abstraction from these commodities, as is the case with money. Capital is in addition the self-expanding value *(der sich selbst verwertende Wert)*, that amount of commodities or money which, in a "mysterious" way, increases after some time. Marx uses most of his energies to solve the riddle of this mysterious increase. For that purpose he develops his surplus-value theory which takes up the major part of his great opus, *Capital*. Here the results can only be summarized.

Surplus-value is, according to Marx's analysis, not the result of clever bargaining or usury but of the legal-economic organization of industrial production. In modern industrialized society commodities are, of course, no longer exchanged. They are paid with money. But we also get money without selling commodities (objective exchange-value). We get money for our labor. The

---

[15]*Capital*, 1:77.
[16]Ibid.

workers who produce commodities never own these commodities so that they could sell them. They can on no account own them, since they own neither the raw material nor the means of labor (the two together form—according to Marx—the means of production) to be able to produce the commodity, as, for instance, a farmer gets the fruit from his or her field. In modern industrial society a separation has developed between the owners of the means of production and commodities on the one hand, and the workers on the other. The workers own only their labor. Since they no longer have the means of production, they have to sell their labor to the owners of industrial firms. Labor has thus become a commodity.

The following produces surplus-value: The workers own their labor which they can sell. Not only *can* they sell it; they *must* sell it, or perish. Labor is, therefore not like any other commodity. It is the worker's very existence. The owner of the means of production (capitalist) is thus in the position of dictating conditions. This is the one prerequisite for exploitation. The other is the tendency of modern economy to expand, to produce quantitatively and qualitatively more—in a word, the progressive character of modern industrial society itself. More and better goods must be produced. This is possible only with the help of more raw material and better technologies. Raw material and better technologies in the form of better machines have to be bought before they can be employed for production. A greater production potential (more means of production) has to be accumulated, but it is accumulated in the hands of the owner of industrial companies. What is at the basis of this?

In a detailed study Marx proves that this "surplus" is the result of surplus-labor done by the workers without being paid for it. They are paid for the work, but not for all the work they do. The owner of the means of production buys their labor and uses it for a given span of time. The workers work part of this time for the equivalent which they are paid later. They use this money to buy their means of subsistence and—to a rather modest extent—other goods. But for the other part of their work they do not work for themselves, not for payment, but for the owner of the means of production or the anonymous firm—and that without payment. This is not at all included in the labor-contract. This contract actually includes only one thing, namely, that the owner can employ the worker for a given period of time. The way which this time is used so that the worker produces a surplus-value for the expansion and increase of production is up to the owner. Expansion and increase are the most important aspects of capitalist production. Without them capitalist production is not possible.[17] When we speak today of the necessity of "zero growth" of the economy in connection with the

---

[17]Interesting ideas with respect to a theological discussion of Marxian economic theory can be found in: Friedrich Delekat, *Vom Wesen des Geldes. Theologische Analyse eines Grundbegriffes in Karl Marx: Das Kapital,* in Marxismusstudien (Tübingen, 1954), pp. 54 ff. But I do not think Delekat's judgment is right that the Marxian theory of surplus-value was unintelligible or mythological (*"mythologisch,"* ibid., p. 69). For the topic of religion and economy, see also: Louis Althusser, et al., *Lire le Capital,* Vol. 1–4 (Paris, 1968 ff.); Helmut Gollwitzer, *Die kapitalistische Revolution*

ecological crisis and a scarcity of energy, since the natural foundations of life and resources cannot be exploited *ad infinitum,* it might be that we have reached an insight regarding the impending end of capitalism—an insight gained in a manner different from that of Marx.

An economy which no longer expands, no longer increases production, no longer opens up new markets, no longer stimulates new wants to find consumers for its commodities need no longer be a capitalist one. For Marx points out explicitly that the characteristic feature of capitalism is the accumulation of surplus-value. Marx, of course, points out the injustices done to the workers by giving them less than the value of their work. But what Marx really criticizes is the perverted and inhuman character which industrial society as a whole has acquired by producing according to a capitalist structure. This is what we now have to study at greater length.

We have already seen that commodities are in reality not things but social relations. Money is only a commodity which is no longer recognizable as a commodity. Capital equally is a social relation, but an even more complicated one.[18] It does not suffice to see capital as a big amount of commodities or a large sum of money. It is a *growing* amount of commodities and a *growing* sum of money. As we have seen, it grows with the help of surplus work of industrial workers. The increase is unpaid labor-time and work transformed into money or commodities. Workers do not voluntarily offer their surplus labor to capital. For accumulation purposes capital must have the power to force the worker to do surplus labor. Capital is thus not only a social relation, but also a social power![19] In capitalist societies this social power relation can again be regarded as a thing.

The fact—or, rather, that which only appears to be a fact—that capital is nothing but a "mass" of commodities and money is connected with another seemingly mysterious fact, i.e., that capital bears interest. The belief that capital increases itself, that it "grows" like a living thing or has "young ones," is, for Marx, the climax of modern fetishism:

> Capital appears as a mysterious and self-creating source of interest—the source of its own increase. The *thing* (money, commodity, value) is now capital even as a mere thing, and capital appears as a mere thing. The result of the entire process of reproduction appears as a property inherent in the thing itself. It depends on the owner of the money, i.e., of the commodity in its continually exchangeable form, whether he wants to spend it as money or loan it out as capital. In interest-bearing capital, therefore, this automatic fetish, self-expanding value, money generating money, are brought out in their pure state and in this form it no longer bears the birth-marks of its

(München, 1974); Friedrich-Wilhelm Marquardt, "Muss ein Christ Sozialist sein?" *Evangelische Theologie* 37 (1977): 148 ff.; R. H. Tawney, *Religion and the Rise of Capitalism* (1926); István Mészáros, *Marx's Theory of Alienation,* 3rd ed. (London, 1972); Jindrich Zelený, *Die Wissenschaftslogik und Das Kapital* (Frankfurt/Wien, 1968).
   [18]Capital is a social relation: *Capital,* 1:477, 717; 3:195, 264, 399, and passim.
   [19]Ibid., 3:195, 264.

origin. The social relation is consummated in the relation of a thing, of money, to itself.[20]

It can hardly be shown here how Marx deduces the interest which is paid by the bank as part of the industrial surplus-value or profits, just as trade profits, too, are due to this industrial surplus value.[21] Marx says explicitly that in this instance he can go back to the result of classical economy.[22]

Marx' words on fetishism differ greatly from his remarks on the Christian doctrine. When we read *Capital,* it becomes quite obvious that Marx has no interest in criticizing fetishism as religion. With regard to Christianity Marx has a number of critical intentions, critical with respect to religion. He parallels the Christian religion with certain awkward characteristics of the capitalist mode of economy. He speaks with irony about central Christian dogmas. But there he also changes the direction of his criticism, turning it toward capitalism by holding to it the mirror of a naive, wrongly mysterious, and anachronistic Christian religion, in which capitalism is to see its weak points. Fetishism, in the sense just mentioned, serves only as a means of a critique of capitalism.

It is quite clear from the beginning that Marx need not imply on the part of his readers any fetish cult which he would have to criticize, at least not a fetishism in the original sense of a scientific-religious definition. It is, however, a new fetishism! Marx no longer uses parallels and comparisons as in the case of the Christian religion (the form of capitalism needing criticism on the one hand; on the other, the form of faith as much in need of criticism). To him capitalism *is* fetishism. He speaks of a fetishism of commodities, capital fetishism, etc. We are here faced with a form of a critique of religion different from that of Christian religion!

3. The Religion of Capital

Marx uses the term fetishism to identify capitalism. Capitalism is fetishism. This is in no way intended to give the impression that Marx's critique of economy is less important and that his critique of fetishism is the crux of *Capital.* Rather, Marx analyzes the process of production and accumulation of capital in every detail. He summarizes laws which had been discovered by earlier theorists of economy, and formulates theories of laws which had not been known before—especially his theory of surplus-value. But Marx also shows us the great power òf irrationality of capitalism. The most important manifestation of irrationality is the market mechanism leading to over-production, to stagnation in selling the commodities, and thus to crises in the economic system. Another manifestation of irrationality is the disproportion between the means of production and their organization (conditions of production) in the way that the produc-

---

[20]Ibid., 3:393.
[21]This is deduced in Vol. 3 of *Capital,* parts IV and V, pp. 267 ff. and 338 ff.
[22]Ibid., 3:830.

tive forces are developed further than their forms of organization, so that these forms of organization become bonds of the economic and social development. But the greatest irrationality lies in capital itself, which shows an insatiable tendency of accumulation, to expand, to overpower all spheres of economy and politics.

Marx seems to think that the most adequate way to describe this irrationality of capital is to use quasi–mythological phrases: capital incorporates "with itself the two primary creators of wealth, labour-power and the land";[23] capital is, so to speak, a living thing with an "all-engrossing appetite."[24] Marx knows, of course, that it is not a mythological figure which is at work here, but human beings. Neither is it the capitalist's personal love of consumption which is the source of this irrationalism. "For capitalism is abolished root and branch by the bare assumption that it is personal consumption and not enrichment that works as the compelling motive."[25] The capitalist is "actually but personified capital endowed with a consciousness of its own and a will."[26]

Capital is really a social relation, a power relation, or, to put it even more precisely, a class relation inasmuch as in the capitalist mode of production, the owner of the means of production, and the "owners" of labor are separated from each other.[27]

Capitalist society, which will not realize the true relations and conditions existing in it is, according to Marx, subject to fetishism. The true conditions are twisted and renamed, and society surrenders itself to its own irrationality. The relations among human beings are declared to be a thing, and society is alienated from itself:

> Capital comes more and more to the fore as a social power, whose agent is the capitalist. This social power no longer stands in any possible relation to that which the labour of a single individual can create. It becomes an alien-ated, independent, social power, which stands opposed to society as an object, and as an object that is the capitalist's source of power.[28]

The alienation of society is, so to speak, an archaic state of consciousness: fetish cult. The blame of fetishism derives its critical pathos from the temporal and cultural distance between a primitive religion of nature and an enlightened bourgeois society. Bourgeois society thinks it has climbed a high ladder, but in reality, it has fallen very deep! It fancies to arrange its relations rationally. Perhaps it believes it has purified its religion with the help of philosophy and enlightenment. But in reality it is dominated by a superstition which penetrates its whole life and is based upon the form of organization of its economy. The

---

[23]Ibid., 1:566.
[24]Ibid., 3:397.
[25]Ibid., 2:123.
[26]Ibid., 3:289–290.
[27]E.g., ibid., 2:31 and passim.
[28]Ibid. 3:264.

economy in its capitalist form has admittedly become the engine of every progressive development. Incidentally, Marx speaks of capitalism as the "religion of everyday life."[29] Capitalism is capital-religion!

Maybe we can now understand better why Marx treats the Christian religion in *Capital* with such great irony. The Christian religion no longer has the meaning which it would attribute to itself. Bourgeois society has long ago replaced the Christian faith by a religion far more powerful, the religion of capital, i.e., subjection to the power of capital.

In the reproach of fetishism another aspect can be seen besides the one that in capitalism a regression to an obsolete form of religion has taken place. Let us start from Hegel's philosophy of religion where the word "fetish" is used in the same meaning as "idol" and *"Götzenbild."*[30] When we now put "idol" for "fetish" we see clearly that Marx does not fight against some neutral phenomenon, which could be described in cool scientific-religious terms, but against a phenomenon which in the history of the Christian religion and even more so in the history of Israel was of outstanding emotional importance. Aren't we reminded here of the prophetic critique of statues of gods and idols, of the critique of "sacred" trees and places, of the critique of the Yahweh cult insofar as it had a hostile effect on ethic and humane behavior? Are we not reminded of Jesus' prophetic words and actions against ritualism and the cult of laws and of Paul's critique of the Jewish law? Are we not reminded of the reformers? This production and worship of stone images, this hypostatization into gods of human sexual functions, this submission to a rigid law, this belief in human works—is not that the same as Marx's *"Verdinglichung"* (reification) and *"Entfremdung"* (alienation)?

There is no doubt that Marx's arguments in this case are similar to the arguments of the Old and New Testament against idolatry. The critique of fetishism is not a critique of religion with respect to Christianity or Judaism, but rather a critique, together with Christianity and Judaism, of idolatry. But Marx on the one side and Judaism and Christianity on the other fight against different idolatries. Marx is attacking the modern idolatry of economic *"Verdinglichung"* (reification, hypostatization). What are Judaism and Christianity attacking? In former times they assailed idolatries which were then virulent, but do they still have the prophetic vigor and critical power for a critique of fetishism? Or, and this is obviously Marx's opinion (that is why here they go again different ways), have Judaism and Christianity themselves become such idolatrous factors, or at

---

[29]Ibid., 3:830. The full sentence with the context is: "It is the great merit of classical economy to have destroyed this false appearance and illusion, this mutual independence and ossification of the various social elements of wealth, this personification of things and conversion of production relations into entities, this religion of everyday life. It did so by reducing interest to a portion of profit, and rent to the surplus above average profit, so that both of them converge in surplus–value; and by representing the process of circulation as a mere metamorphosis of forms, and finally reducing value and surplus-value of commodities to labour in the direct production process."

[30]Cf. note 12 above. Schleiermacher also identifies idolatry and fetishism in his principal work, *Der christliche Glaube,* 8/1.

least diminishing factors, which do not see that the new, all-embracing fetish-religion of economic reification and petrification of human relations has long seized the reigns of power?

There is one exception which proves that Marx—if only to a small extent—has had the support of theology in his critique of economy. Hardly any theologians are quoted in *Capital*. But the theologian quoted conspiciously frequently with respect to these conditions is Martin Luther. Unless I have missed a quotation, Marx quotes Luther's critique of the interest usury in seven different passages of *Capital*.[31] The especially interesting quotation is the one in which Luther calls the usurer the greatest "enemy of man" who wants to be "God over all men."[32] Luther, too, in regard to inhuman economic conditions uses the pattern of argumentation "denunciation of a false religion," but to Luther the false god is a person (usurer), whereas to Marx it is a thing (capital) which is unmasked as an idol.

But this contact between Luther and Marx is, on the whole, only an episode. There is no explicit mention that Marx regards himself as standing in the tradition of the Jewish or Christian critique of idolatry. Marx is not at all interested in true religion whose support he wants in the battle against idolatry. To him religion is totally *passé*. Contemporary religion is to Marx, at the best, ideology, a deceptive veil hiding the real state of affairs and preventing the critique or change thereof.

4. Consequences

Reading *Capital* makes clear how closely religion and economy are connected, not only in the sense that religion is dependent on economy as its condition—a common one-sidedness—but also to the extent that the economic process is organized with the help of a religious (or pseudo-religious) world of ideas. Marx describes this world of ideas as "capital-religion," as a complex of illusions standing in the way of a humane practice. Yes, "capital-religion" makes humane practice itself impossible, since human beings put themselves into dependency to a power—the self-expanding capital. But, as soon as human beings put themselves into dependency to a power, they can be at best executive organs but cannot act autonomously. And human practice is nothing if not autonomous acting. This is the kind of practice for which Marx wanted to liberate human beings. In doing so Marx aimed at an emancipation under the conditions of modern economy, an emancipation which must be a social conduct understanding those conditions. Marx saw no need for himself to contradict or repeat fundamental ethical theories of freedom, such as those of Kant or Fichte. Marx

---

[31]Luther's treatise *Von Kaufshandlung und Wucher* of 1524 is quoted from *Capital,* 3:331, note 48; the treatise *An die Pfarrherren, wider den Wucher zu predigen* of 1540 is quoted from *Das Kapital,* vol. 1 (Berlin, 1969), p. 149, note 96 (omitted in the English translation!); *Capital,* 1:187, note 1; 1:555–556, note 1; 3:346, note 56; 3:394, 611.

[32]Ibid., 1:556, note.

was, however, a great destroyer of illusions by proclaiming freedom as the only humane and decent possibility of existence and exposing as a myth the dangerous but perhaps comfortable hope for a subject "capital" which could steer the economic process to a good end.

Christianity is as deeply concerned for humane practice as Marx. Only the faith which has become practical is true faith. Such faith, however, will do everything to show in word and in action that the capital-religion unmasked by Marx is a pseudo-religion. This is for me the pivot of a theological discussion of Karl Marx's *Capital*. To Marx any form of religion is an alienation of humans, i.e., a system leading humans to accept themselves as dependent and as "things," and preventing a practice in the humane sense of the word, that is, as self-determination and autonomy.

From whence does Marx derive this negative concept of religion under which he also subsumes the Christian faith? In his social analysis Marx assumes that the Christian religion contributes to the repressive organization of society and particularly to economic exploitation. But we cannot spare Marx the reproach that he assumes an undialectical connection between Christianity and economy. Just as the Christian religion on the one side supported the development of a modern industrial society, on the other side, it did not trust that society and attacked it heavily. In doing so the Christian religion, no doubt, not only attacked the inhuman aspects of this industrial society, but also the progressive ones. We must admit that. But this shows the strained relations of the Christian faith and industrial society. Since the famous turn under the emperor Constantine in the fourth century, Christianity has changed from an exclusively eschatologically-orientated community to a political factor. In politics as in any other "worldly" business, hands get dirty. But this must be no excuse. On the contrary, the mistakes of politics with Christian motives must be laid open without mercy. This, however, cannot lead to a neglect of the critical, conciliatory, and justice-supporting power of Christianity. No doubt, the conciliatory power of Christianity was seen very clearly by Marx, but he had no esteem for it. Conciliation in a social context is for Marx simply the hushing-up of antagonisms, i.e., appeasement. Conciliatory conduct, however, must never result in appeasement. A Christian has to face antagonisms and carry out conflicts. Furthermore, in the sense of Christian ethics, a Christian must line up on the side of the oppressed in class struggles. But conflicts and struggles aim at pacification, that is, at the reconciliation of humans. Therefore, a Christian has to examine in every single case of class struggle if it could not lead to new oppression and new injustice. Christians must especially see that with fighting against injustice in capitalism they merely fight a specific form of injustice. They do so legitimately, but they must also realize that by doing so they cannot prevent injustice as such or prevent new forms of injustice.

At this point we have to differentiate between capitalism as a real social system and capitalism as an ideology. In the first instance, capitalism is a necessary and important phase of human history without which there would be no industrialization and no technological progress. Marx has acknowledged this himself.[33] In the sense of ideology, however, capitalism is a power system used by the bourgeoise class, which owns the means of production, as a means for oppressing the working class. But beyond this common formula *Capital* offers other insights as well. It is a bad capitalist who enjoys his or her profits and does not invest them. Sooner or later he or she will no longer belong to the class of capitalists. Capitalism consists in the ever-expanded accumulation and reinvestment of surplus-value. From that point of view it is both the working class and the class of capitalists who are alienated. Capitalism as ideology is, as we have seen, a power system in which those who seemingly rule are as much ruled as those who are obviously ruled. They are all under the rule of an inhuman principle—the principle of self-expanding capital. The principle to which they submit, for which they sacrifice,[34] has been created by the people themselves. That is why it is an idol, a fetish. Capitalism as ideology implies the submission to a principle which is no principle at all, since humans create capital in their social labor, and thus it is human society which is the principle of capital and not vice versa.

A Christian should not feel in this issue the urge to criticize the motives of the Marxist critique of capitalism as "nothing but humanistic." A Christian is, out of faith, an unshakeable humanist, since he or she is motivated to humanism by God, who as logos has become human, and who as Holy Spirit continues to become human in the society of human beings.

With respect to atheism in Marx and in Marxism a Christian will, of course, have to bring forward many critical remarks. Within the context of this paper I only want to point out that the quotations from Marx referring to Christology and Trinitarianism show clearly that Marx regards these doctrines only as parallels or models of capitalist fetishism (the exact relation remains open). This leads us to suppose that he did not have enough knowledge of these tenets. Otherwise he could not have missed their fetish-critical and humanist features. The critique of the Christian religion is, with Marx, far less important than the critique of the religion of capital.

The question has, however, to be raised whether the Marxists do not place too great an emphasis on atheism instead of on anti-fetishism. How much of the Marxian critique of capitalism has been put into concrete socialist practice? Is it enough to socialize or nationalize the means of production? Has it not been and is it not still the case that those societies and nations in which the means of production have been socialized nevertheless submit to the principle of the greatest possible accumulation of capital, that is, the capital fetish?

For the purpose of an effective conclusion, let me formulate my thesis in a Marxian vein: Human society exists not for capital, but capital for human society.

Translated from German by Ulla Ernst

---

[33]Ibid., 3:259: "Development of the productive forces of social labour is the historical task and justification of capital." Cf. 3:441, 819.

[34]Ibid., 1:133; 3:516.

THE KINGDOM OF GOD AND COMMUNISM*

Andrija Krešić

Pro-Existence and Property

There are some characteristic New Testament notions about material riches and poverty which are in accord with the principle of Christian love or pro-existence.[1]

It is logical that the rich were non-desirables among those Christians who regarded that service of God and service to wealth are mutually exclusive, because "no one can serve two masters" (Mt. 6:24). Or to put it differently, one whose life principle is invested in things will not follow the principle of living for people. Devotion of person to person is salvific; hence the rich had no chance for salvation ("It is easier for a camel to go through the eye of a needle than for a rich man to enter the kingdom of God"—Mt. 19:24).[2] They will be left to "weep and howl" on account of the troubles which will beset them because they condemned and killed the just one who could not resist them (James 5:1–6). When things are imposed as mediators and regulators of relations among people, then there is no place for Christ as the principle of love for the neighbor. Even desire for wealth leads to ruin, "for the love of money is the root of all evils" (1 Tim. 6:8–10). The early Christian morality did not allow speculative accumulation of wealth. Hence Jesus bitterly drove out the merchants and moneychangers from the Temple because he considered their business to be robbery and looting (Mt. 21:12–13).

While the possession of riches was judged to be sinful and perilous, poverty was proclaimed to be virtuous and saving. " 'If you would be perfect, go, sell what you possess and give to the poor, and you will have a treasure in heaven; and come follow me' " (Mt. 19:21). This means not only that poverty is just for the perfect, but also that poverty is perfect and that Christ's followers should not have private wealth. After all, his first followers were poor fisherfolk.

Poverty, however, was not praised in its sense of destitution or complete lack

---

*By permission of the author, this is a translation of a chapter from *Kraljevstvo božje i komunizam* (Belgrade: Institut za medjunarodni radnički pokret, 1975), pp. 132–146.

[1]Andrija Krešić uses the term for an attitude which tends to be supportive of the continued existence and activity of those who do not agree with one's own position. The partners would be in a dialogical relationship. [Translator's remark.]

[2]All biblical quotations are from the Revised Standard Version.

Andrija Krešić (Marxist) studied philosophy in Moscow, Leningrad, and Belgrade, where he received his doctoral diploma in 1951. He taught philosophy at the Universities of Sarajevo and Belgrade. In 1939 he joined the Communist Youth of Yugoslavia and, in 1941, the Communist Party of Yugoslavia, and joined the Partisans in the war of national liberation. Involved in the political life of the country, he became a member of the Yugoslav Federal Congress and a highly placed official of the Communist Party and the Socialist Alliance of the Working People of Yugoslavia. He is a past president of the Yugoslav Association for Philosophy and director of both the Institute for the International Workers' Movement and the Center for the Publishing of Marxist Classics. Among his publications are six books, translations of books from Russian and French, and many articles.

of goods, nor was wealth damned as wealth in and of itself. The real goal of Christian condemnation was private property. In their desire for the common good they strove for the common material good. "And all who believed were together and had all things in common; and they sold their possessions and goods and distributed them to all, as any had need" (Acts 2:44–45). The distribution of common wealth according to individual need is a well-known communist principle, quite different from ascetic self-denial and individual destitution. "There was not a needy person among them, for as many as were possessors of lands or houses sold them, and brought the proceeds of what was sold and laid it at the apostles' feet; and distribution was made to each as any had need" (Acts 4:34–35). Thus conceived, the virtue of poverty did not mean the suppression of natural human needs but only the suppression of private property. From the above it follows that early Christian proclamation of poverty was not the proclamation of asceticism but of a special kind of communism as a social form of the use of goods. Morality was in the service of this communism requiring the owner of private property to give that possession to the Christian commune.

In early Christian communes, similarly as in the prehistoric communist extended family communities, there was no egoism of private property to disturb the spontaneous pro-existence of "brothers in Christ" and to push it out of real life into the sphere of moral laws. These communities can be regarded as the incarnations of the communal ideal, of realized moral principles or humanized divinity. "Now the company of those who believed were of one heart and soul, and no one said that any of the things which he possessed was his own, but they had everything in common" (Acts 4:32). This "company" was united and behaved as a self-conscious subject ("one heart and soul") when each individual actualized it as his or her own need, i.e., when it was in his or her heart and soul. Just as the identity and harmony of the individual and common good were established through the usage of goods, so had common togetherness come to rule the heart and mind of the individual, spontaneously expressing the principle of social harmony: "one for all, all for one." At that time the dualism of principle and empire, spirit and body, heaven and earth, sanctity and sin, God and the world could relate primarily to the duality and conflict between the Christian and non-Christian world. The Old Testament moral dilemma between life in a worldly paradise and suffering in the surrounding desert was now expressed as opposition between Christianity and paganism, between the early Christian commune and its non-Christian surroundings.

While the gospel notions of wealth and poverty express the experience of early Christian communism, the Christian consciousness did not vacillate in holding that wealth belongs to the community of the poor and that the owner is but a steward. The owner, however, is not a steward but a usurper if he or she gives a gift of something that is his or hers, because in principle everything is given for use to all. Pointing to such an understanding of the Church Fathers, Pierre Bigo writes that they remind him of Karl Marx.[3] The principle of common

---

[3]Pierre Bigo, *La doctrine sociale de l'Eglise* (Paris: PUF, 1954), p. 33.

usage of wealth remained a part of Christian consciousness along with the fact of private property. Bigo points out that Thomas Aquinas refused to define ownership as the designation of a thing for the use of its owner. For him ownership is not such a designation, but a responsibility.[4] Still, Christian consciousness did not succeed in resisting the pressure of facts which comprise the world of private property.

The early Christian communism of usage or consumption of wealth could not develop in the framework of the organization of *production* based on private property. Therefore it remained only in an undeveloped form through esoteric monastic orders which followed the vow of poverty. Christianity, on the other hand, survived by finding a *modus vivendi* with the world. It shared the fate of the world which was divided, and it even divided itself along the lines of rich and poor Christians. The owner always prefers the freedom of usage of property rather than the obligation to place it at the disposal of the community. The purpose of private property is indeed to use property privately. Therefore, in addition to communal or monastic Christianity, private-propertied and wealthy Christianity made an appearance and prevailed. Its spirit can already be recognized in the New Testament scriptures, as in Paul's letter to the Corinthians, wherein the obligation of the surrender of ownership for common use was replaced by charity and similar attitudes (2 Cor. 8–9).

As early Christian communism disappeared in the divided society of private property, so Christianity gradually affirmed the interpretation that Christ never did condemn private property but only wealth which the owner uses over and above his or her own needs. "It is not ownership in itself which Christ condemns as sin. Sin is wealth, or accumulation and consumption of things above one's needs."[5] It is not clear why one needs to hoard and use something "above one's needs." What is unnecessary and superfluous ceases to be owned; it is turned over to anyone, without virtue or charity toward the poor.

The morality of sharing the surplus "above the need" is based on the notion that until there is no surplus for some people others cannot even satisfy basic needs. Be that as it may, Christ's condition to the rich young man—to distribute his entire property to the poor so he could follow the way of salvation—was interpreted in a non-communist, private-propertied Christian spirit.

> The real community of goods is optional. Effective poverty, as perfect purity, is an advice directed only to those whose role is to witness the nearing of the kingdom of heaven and to anticipate its realization by placing themselves, so to say, on the edge of history as Christ did, not to avoid history, but, to the contrary, to be moved because in it already lives something of the kingdom of heaven to which it aims.[6]

Thus it follows that a complete (communistic) denial of private property is not obligatory and relates only to exceptional Christians (for instance, the holy

---

[4]Ibid., p. 40.
[5]Ibid., p. 20.
[6]Ibid., p. 23.

ascetics or the Christ of the gospels) which exemplify an ideal. Thereby is affirmed the possibility and the reality of the division of Christianity into a closed minority of ordained "witnesses of the kingdom of heaven," and the rest of the mass of believers who are situated very differently in the worldly kingdom. In the form of those rare exemplary Christians who are in isolated communal orders, the "kingdom of heaven" participates a bit in history, but it can become a kingdom for the people only "at the end" or "on the other side" of history. Therefore the final salvation of the human species takes place under extra-historical ideal conditions, "in heaven," but in real life there remains only the unquenching thirst for an all-encompassing "brotherhood in Christ" which is proportional to the privation of the poor in worldly goods.

While the multitude in early Christian communities truly lived with "one heart and soul," there was no discrepancy between Christian life and morality, words and deeds, ideal and real, soul and body, mind and experience. It was not necessary to command love between people in those communities. The command of love was more directed to the non-Christian world of social division and antagonisms. But when effective love evaporated from the world with the disappearance of the early Christian communities, it turned into a mere philanthropic ideal, into moralistic preaching, into a promised salvation which will not take place in history. The symbolism of Christ's ascent into heaven expresses the need for transcending the sinful world, but it also says that God-love (*Deus caritas*) or the spirit of love is departing from the earth, that it is no longer in an historical human body, but that it is somewhere outside the world and that it will return from that transcendent residence only at the end of time. Thus the worldly revolutionary movement of Christians has been reduced to religion: God the Son returned to God the Creator, the New Testament God became equalized with the Old Testament God, redemption from the contradictions of life was transferred to the realm of death, salvation of the world became salvation from the world. With its transformation into religion, by which the ecclesiastical hierarchy sanctifies the worldly hierarchy, Christianity has renewed in itself the duality of God and the world, soul and body, sanctity and sin, ideal and reality, mind and experience, ascetic repudiation of all that is related to the senses, and life according to human needs. All this because the Christian owners do not approve of anything like the early Christian community of goods.

In the many historical efforts to save humanity from burdensome divisiveness, Christian efforts toward salvation have made their appearance. The most radical ones made a prognosis of Christian salvation of the world by means of a return to evangelical roots, i.e., togetherness of love in the form of early Christian communism. The most radical contemporary protagonists of the evangelical transformation of Christianity and the Christian transformation of the world have at their disposal all previous experiences of this kind, both Christian and non-Christian, positive and negative. There is, first of all, the early Christian negative experience that the community of love cannot develop or survive as the communism of consumption at the complete mercy of the owners. In other words, communism has a chance if it is based on itself, if communist consumption depends on communist production.

The Christian changing of the world (Salvation of the world is indeed its concern.) does not have to mean departing from the "kingdom of heaven" in every sense. To the contrary, the concern is to uplift this worldly life to the heights of the "kingdom of heaven," the human to the pedestal of divinity, reality to the level of the ideal, experience to the level of the mind—and this now and everywhere, as a non-delayable worldly-historical event. The principle of love was proclaimed for all people, for the whole world, and not only for the select "witnesses" of God's kingdom.

Communism in Marx's sense, which also establishes the community of goods (including particularly means of social production), is not a mere rejection of earlier communistic ideals (including those of the gospels), but the transformation of the ideal into reality, connecting the theory and action of the communist movement.

Today there is a new possibility of tactical and strategic, practical and doctrinal encounter and growing together of Christianity and Communism, which, of course, does not mean that all this will actually take place. This possibility is not being used and is not wanted by those trends of Christian renewal which restrict themselves to adjusting Christian traditions to the contemporary bourgeois world. A similar lack of action in this direction is evident by that kind of Communism which lost itself in its preoccupation with its own rule over people and which identified itself too closely with this world, using too much its institutions and methods, to be able fundamentally to change the world. Though permanent partnership and merger of Christianity with Communism are not "things of this world," i.e., are not typical phenomena of our contemporary world, still there is a real possibility of such an occurrence.

Alliance and synthesizing of Christianity and Communism, as an event "on the other side" of the contemporary world, are being affirmed today within Christianity by the protagonists of radical renewal, by which Christianity is liberating itself from the superhuman (mystical) connection and is participating in the revolutionary mission of liberating all who are oppressed and abolishing all powers over people. Among Communists there is a similar group of revolutionaries inspired by that original humanism for whom authentic human behavior in the world is not adaptation to the given order with perhaps some improvement in it, but its abolition and creation of a new world based on humane measures. With their activity "the other world" comes instead of "this world"; the future—as a completely different era—transcends the present; the human kingdom of liberty replaces the superhuman and inhuman rule of necessity. We are talking of people who are expressing best the generic nature of humanity—to transcend one's own humanity. To them, all are near and dear who—in whatever manner—carry the same human "power of transcendence." Because of this work of transcending "this world," it is quite logical for the Marxist Ernest Bloch to point out in his non-conformist philosophy of hope and "dialectical-concrete utopia" the possibility of reading the Bible "with the eyes of the Communist Manifesto,"[7] and the possibility that Christianity should again form an alliance with the revolution (after the alliance of the period of peasant wars).[8]

Money and Transcendence

The unusual divine existence (individual-general, natural-supernatural, immanent-transcendent) can be understood by an analogy with money. Namely, merchandise when exchanged has an exchange value which is its socio-economic and quantitative existence, in distinction to its natural, qualitative value. Before its exchange, the merchandise changes in one's mind into a quantitative amount or sign in order that it be measurable and exchangeable with other merchandise. This imaginary transformation of quality into quantity or transformation of merchandise into exchange value becomes, in the act of actual exchange, a real duplication of existence. The exchange value of merchandise acquires a material existence apart from the material existence of the merchandise. This we call money.

We read in Marx that the exchange value of merchandise is its immanent monetary characteristic. This monetary characteristic separates from the merchandise in the form of money which exists outside the merchandise. Money is general merchandise, but it exists as separate merchandise side by side with other merchandise. The spirit became incarnate, the "word" became "flesh." Money is the objectivized exchange value, the "incarnation" of the imaginarily existing merchandise—quantity "returned" into quality (silver or gold).

Money is the measure of the relation of merchandise in exchange, the measure of value of all products which exists outside all products. Money is, then, a means or mediator of exchange. With its double nature it is an intermediary between the natural (sensible) and the unnatural (socio-economic) existence of merchandise. Thus, too, the God-Human mediates between God and humanity, between the social and natural existence of humankind.

Money is the means (mediator) transformed into an end which one desires more than the greatest pleasure. In the type of exchange which is for the sake of exchange (trading, banking, and other speculations), the purpose of exchange is not the consumption of products but the satisfaction of the passion for money. Similarly, when the principle of the relationship between people became alienated and was transformed into God's existence, then love toward God was placed before love toward neighbors and God's existence became the highest purpose of human existence.

Because of the aforementioned characteristics of money, Marx calls money a

---

[7]Ernest Bloch, *Atheismus im Christentum* (Frankfurt a/M: Suhrkamp Verlag, 1968), p. 67.
[8]Ibid., p. 256.

god among merchandise, the heavenly existence of merchandise, and the real object of passion (because it can buy all pleasures).[9]

God's person is analogous to money also, because on God just as on money one's daily life is fundamentally dependent. And, God and money willfully reign over human life and relate to a human being as a subject toward an object. The subject is mysterious in both cases. Money is general merchandise, and Marx noted that human products acquire a certain mystical power when they become merchandise. The mystery of the merchandizing form is that the social character of work appears to be a relationship between things, as some sort of social objectivization. Thus the world of products in its merchandizing form acquires a fetishistic character. In the process of de-objectivization of things and objectivization of people, object and subject are being substituted similarly to the effect of light upon the optical nerve, which appears as the objective form of things rather than the subjective stimulus.[10]

Both God and money represent power separated from people and superiority over people. Money represents in the sense-object manner the same thing that God represents in a spiritual-fantastic form: the goal of the highest desire or need of the human person to get some of the superior alienated power and harmoniously to connect his or her ideal and empirical existence, i.e., the spiritual and material aspects of life. This final harmony (pacification through satisfaction) would be the wholeness of personal existence achieved by ending duality and separation. Since in a conflict-ridden society there is no chance for an integrated person and for the achievement of personal wholeness, personal disalienation must appear as a social revolution which abolishes the relationship of superiority and inferiority of power and of social differences, so that the various natural powers of people flourish as does the liberation of people's natural pro-existence.

The Old Testament God did not allow the chosen people to worship the golden calf, i.e., for them to use an objectivized god-money. Similar "biblical personalism" is expressed in the New Testament consciousness which opposes the service of God to the service of wealth, and in which the God-Human Christ is overcome by great anger because the merchants are dealing with money in the Temple, which is a place only for the worship of God. These are indications of attempts for personhood to avoid objectivization, although de-personalization is not expressly mentioned.

The superiority of god-money over people is shown in that all serve it and worship it, both those who lack it and those who have it in abundance. Money buys everything, even a human being as a slave or the labor of a worker. This means that this "god among merchandise" shows "heavenly" superiority above

---

[9]Karl Marx, *Grundrisse der Kritik der politischen Okonomie* (Berlin: Dietz Verlag, 1953), pp. 132–137.

[10]K. Marx and F. Engels, *Dela,* vol. 21 (Belgrade: IMRP-"Prosveta," 1972), pp. 73–84.

humans who are merchandise. This reification of human personhood is not restricted to Marxist critical cognition, for others have recognized it, too.

Léon Mazeaud, commenting on John XXIII's encyclical *"Mater et Magistra"* (1961), supports the designation of a worker's income according to the number of hours worked rather than to the law of supply and demand, because he considers that by nature "work is not merchandise, and the worker is neither a machine nor an animal."[11] Mazeaud tries to preserve the personal dignity of workers and, as a means against depersonalization in trading and monetary relations, he recommends that workers share in the profits and achievements of the enterprises.[12] Without making a value judgment about this approach, it is worth noting that its goal is not to substitue (and devalue) human personality with material values. The Christian motive in resisting reification which Mazeaud finds in the encyclical is "to defend the dignity of man as a creation who has a soul made in God's image."[13] A Christian believes that a person should not be reduced to an object (merchandise, thing) because a person has something of God's nature. It is unworthy to objectify that which is of the absolute subject.

The believer does not think that an almighty God ruling over people brings into question their personhood, but does consider that the domination of objects over persons definitely destroys their personhood. Consonant to this is a warning by Paul VI (encyclical *"Populorum progressio"*) that human development should not be reduced to mere economic growth, by which is implied that a person is only an economic being. Paul VI underlined the personal atributes of humans and considered humans to be responsible for their progress in humaneness and for their salvation, but that this progress is foreseen also in "God's plan."[14]

Within the bourgeois critique of Marxism one frequently finds the charge that Marxism is too much of an economic doctrine which has no "ear" for non-economic values and determinants of human life. The Christian writer P. Bigo thinks, too, that Marxists compromise their most beautiful discoveries of human dignity when they ascribe transcendent values to the economic infrastructure. Instead of the traditional religious absolute and transcendence, the religion of Marxists deifies production and producers.[15] Those Marxists who had truly absolutized the primacy of the social "basis" over the "superstructure" are guilty of causing erroneous notions about Marxism. Marx himself recognized this primacy only for heretofore–existing social structures.

Characteristic for Marx is the critique of the "pre-historic" enslavement of

---

[11]Léon Mazeaud, "La doctrine sociale de 'Mater et Magistra': droit du travail et droit des societes," in *Etudes juridiques* (Paris: Dalloz, 1964), p. 388.

[12]Ibid., pp. 388–389.

[13]Ibid., p. 382.

[14]Paul VI, *Populorum progressio. Enciklika o razvitku naroda* (Zagreb: Hrvatsko društvo Sv. Ćirila i Metoda, 1967), p. 13.

[15]Bigo, *La doctrine,* p. 152.

people to things, not because humans are made in God's image, but only because they are human. The critique is directed to the transcendence of natural and economic needs and the emancipation of human values from economic values toward a true human history or the conscious creation of history according to human designs.

In Marx's *Contribution to the Jewish Question* the biblical divine anger because Jews worship money or because they place business above the cult of God is replaced with a human critique of "Jewishness." It is "Jewishness" that is criticized—not the religion or nationality of Jews, but rather that selfishness which bourgeois society continually creates "out of its own intestines." That is the "general contemporary anti-social element." Trade is the "worldly cult" of egoists; money is "its worldly god." He further says of money that:

> it demeans all human gods and transforms them into merchandise. Money is the general, for itself constituted *value* of all things. Therefore it has deprived the whole world, the human world as well as nature, of its specific value. Money is the alienated essence of human work and existence and this alien essence rules over him, and he bows down before it.

Hence basic human emancipation consists in emancipation from "Jewishness," i.e., from trading and money. And this means "the organization of a society which would abolish the prerequisite of trading."[16]

For Marx, as for the Bible, "greed for money is the source of all evil." For the biblical religious consciousness, money is primarily evil from God's viewpoint because monetary value is a dangerous competitor to the divine value in that "it demeans all human gods and transforms them into merchandise." For Marx, money is primarily evil from the human viewpoint because it deprives humans of their unique value, i.e., because it devalues one as a person and changes one into merchandise.

According to religious transcendence God is a superhuman, supernatural, imaginary refuge of people possessed and degraded by the "anti-social elements" of economic values. According to the gospels' communism, it is the opposite. Transcendence is the human empirical surmounting of the conflict between egoism and altruism, and therefore God resides with people as their love or the living principle of pro-existence. However, this communism of consumption, isolated from production, did not abolish the alienation of labor and could not reproduce itself from its own source. It vanished under the domination of private property, succumbing to egoism as the maxim of human relations. Its altruism evaporated from earth to the heaven of moral ideals. Christianity remained only the faith in a heavenly divinity with the hope for a heavenly (afterlife, post-historical) salvation. The human being still must be crucified between two lords: the lord of tangible god-money and the unreachable God in heaven,

---

[16]Karl Marx, "Prilog jevrejskom pitanju" in K. Marx, *Dela,* vol. 3 (Belgrade: IMRP-"Prosveta," 1972), pp. 145–148.

between egoism and altruism, between contra-existence and pro-existence, between empirical life and moral principles, between body and soul. As a way out of the pain of this crucifixion, religion offers Christ's example: the crucified God-Human was freed of torment at death, i.e., when the divine spirit abandoned the human body.

In contemporary Christianity transcendence does not mean exclusively a supernatural, heavenly, trans-historical, or purely spiritual way out of the contradictions of life. According to a Catholic priest, transcendence is primarily the continuous human activity of negation and transcendence of the present so that the human being may reach the wholeness which is appropriate to him or her. Only secondarily is transcendence "transition to the other side of life" into a trans-historical "reality."[17]

Christian writers who take into consideration only the human meaning of transcendence are no longer rare. They neither mention superhuman transcendence nor even reject it. Thus, the radical Christian modernist John A. T. Robinson decisively claims that God is not "outside" nor on the borders of life but in its midst. God exists in our relations and especially in our relations with other people. Citing New Testament texts (1 Jn. 4:8, 16), Robinson concludes that it is more correct to say that "God is love" than that "Love is God."[18] Transcendence is nothing but life for others to the greatest possible extent. It is the maximum of love or pure love, which Jesus was, and this is why Jesus is one with God the creator who is Love.[19] In other words, one who gives oneself to others to the point of sacrifice for their existence transcends his or her own existence. According to the interpretation of Marxist Roger Garaudy, transcendence for Robinson is a human, and not a divine, attribute.[20] That is the dimension of experience which constantly requires transcending.[20]

Having related the notion of transcendence to the notion of original sin and redemption, Pastor Dumas thinks that sin is not the loss of transcendence or of heavenly nature, but, according to the biblical text, it means disarrangement of earthly reality. Thus salvation is not some ascent of the soul into a transcendent abode but, to the contrary, an orientation toward incarnation, engagement, and obedience to history.[21]

Henry de Lubac noticed that from the beginning of this century there is a constant renewal of "doctrines of immanence" and that especially today there is an "historical" immanence which excludes all that is supernatural.[22] This theologian asks for at least some acceptance of the notion of transcendence and finds that each temporal development has in its heart "that which is Eternal," "truly Present" (le véritable Present), which inspires and directs it. That belong-

---

[17]*L'homme chrétien et l'homme marxiste* (Paris, Geneva: La Palatine, 1964), pp. 18–19.
[18]John A. T. Robinson, *Dieu sans Dieu* (Paris: Nouvelles Editions Latines, 1964), p. 70.
[19]Ibid., p. 102.
[20]*L'homme chrétien*, p. 174.
[21]Ibid., p. 42.
[22]Henri de Lubac, *Le Mystère du supernaturel* (Paris: Aubier, 1965), p. 15.

ing to the other side (*l'au-delà*) is infinitely closer both to the future and to the present (*le present*). Contemporary people are tragically absent from one another and from themselves when they give up "that Eternal" which is rooted in their being and which enables them to communicate with one another.[23]

Wolf-Dieter Marsch replies to the question about the meaning of the "Kingdom of God" that it is the "designation of ideal social awareness and responsibility" differently conceived and differently desired in various historical conditions. *"Regnum dei"* is antipodal for "the kingdom of this world" as the reign of Satan.[24] The Protestant theologian Jürgen Moltmann identifies transcendence as a qualitatively new future history which means the change of conditions of history and the abolition of present conflicts.[25]

Among "theologians of revolution" we find the view that Christianity, more than any other tradition, is preparing the power of transcending for the new revolutionaries. By that they do not mean a metaphysical transcendence, but a step from the present into the future, or from the future into the present. If this transcendence is designated as the "Kingdom of God," then the Kingdom of God is the highest reality in history. Related to this, the noted "theologian of revolution," Richard Shaull, agrees with the statement of the Marxist Ernest Bloch, "That which *is,* cannot be true." Shaull defines transcendence also as the translation from the existing into the open future. In his interpretation, the biblical God is an active, overthrowing, and revolutionary God.[26]

The transcendent "Kingdom of God" (*Regnum Dei, Civitas Dei,* heavenly paradise) in our time is obviously losing its meaning as the supernatural and extra-historical life. It loses its power to convince through its religious meaning, i.e., as a superhuman or divine transcendence of the "kingdoms of this earth" (*regnum huius mundi*). But people can accept it if it directs them to the human overcoming of the existing inhumane (de-humanized, alienated, reified) conditions or the emancipation of the person from being made into an object. Thus the Christian differentiation of the temporal (historical) from the eternal (trans-historical) being changes fundamentally and comes nearer to Marx's differentiation of the heretofore "pre-history" and the true human history. The Kingdom of God, in the sense of ideal social consciousness, starts to mean a thisworldly condition of realized humanism.

Religious contraries such as heaven-earth, transcendence-immanence, God-human being, spirit-nature, and eternity-temporaneity emphasize the primacy of the first segment which is also the source and destiny of the second. So also God the Son comes from and returns to God the Creator. The immanent soul is given to the human being by a transcendent God and receives it back after bodily death.

---

[23]Henri de Lubac, *Catholicisme: Les aspects sociaux du dogme* (Paris: Cert, 1965), pp. 241–242.

[24]Wolf-Dieter Marsch, *Die Freiheit erlernen* (Olten, Freiburg i/B: Walter-Verlag, 1967), p. 10.

[25]Jürgen Moltmann, "Die Zukunft als neues Paradigma der Transzendenz" in *Dialog,* no. 1 (1969), pp. 12–13.

[26]T. Rendtorff and H. E. Tödt, *Theologie der Revolution* (Frankfurt a/M: Ed. Suhrkamp, 1968), pp. 23–26.

Today such dualism is increasingly recognized as a tension between existence and (alienated) essence of man/woman, between the individual and society, between the private and public person, between "is" and "ought to," between the given and the necessary (and possible) life. Thereby the necessities of life grow out of the living reality, and they cease through satisfaction in a new living reality, which is the opposite of the religious perception of dualism.

Judging by all evidence, antithetical dualism does not disappear by the destruction of one and the triumph of the other opponent, but in the abrogation (surmounting, transcendence) of both in their dialectical synthesis.

Ecclesiastical Christianity engaged in a crusade against Marxism and Communism until it came to feel, in more recent times, that it will slowly vanish if it does not adapt to the contemporary world which has Communism as one of its component parts. That was the policy of anti-Communism which has now been replaced by the policy of co-existence with Communism. Political (party and state) Communism replied in the same manner, the policy of war being followed later by the policy of co-existence. Each side in co-existence retains its ideology with the hope of a proselytized end of the other side, because each side conceives of the future of the world as its own world with no opponents. Thus co-existence is a tactic, but the strategy is still some sort of quiet contra-existence.

It was already mentioned above in the discussion of evangelical communion of "bread and wine" that communism has no basis as long as the use and disposal of wealth are separated from the production of wealth. Similarly, communism remains a mere slogan if "for the time being" it utilizes (and adapts to) methods and institutions of bourgeois society while postponing communist relationships into the unforeseeable future. This is not the way to abolish the dualism of "heaven" and "earth." The ghostly transcendence remains and continues to rule over people. Communism cannot be affirmed as a true human emancipation by a vision of a future communist society nor with a present alteration of the system of exploitation and domination, but with the present practical abolition of alienated labor in all its forms of reification and domination. Simultaneously (through this very act) it means the establishment of the community of free individuals which has no purpose or existence apart from free individuals.

Transcendence can have a real meaning as a revolutionary way out to "the other side" of present antagonisms into a true human (humane) community or pro-existence of persons. Pro-existence could become a way of life acceptable to all people if, like oases in the desert, human communes would emerge and spread throughout the bourgeois society, until the desert is flooded with oases which would become refuges for all who are suffering the deprivation of personhood, regardless of whether they come under the sign of the cross or the sign of the hammer and sickle.

Translated from the Croatian by Paul Mojzes

THE PLACE OF IDEOLOGY IN THEOLOGY

James E. Will

To think seriously about theology of culture and theological ethics in our day requires taking the problematic of ideology seriously. The possible ideological distortions in the formulation of belief and the tensions between belief and practice, which long have been a concern of Christian ethicists and theologians, have become more urgent in the 1960's and 1970's, because: (a) The churches from East European communist societies came into the World Council of Churches beginning in 1961; (b) Pope John XXIII "opened the windows" of the Roman Catholic Church through Vatican Council II, allowing for a new response to Marxism, which in turn has led to the development of Latin American liberation theologies under Roman Catholic auspices; and (c) The civil religion of the U.S.A. suffered a long decline during the Vietnam War, losing much of its culture-forming potency at Watergate, just short of the nation's 200th birthday.[1] The recognition of these factors, especially by western theologians, should lead to a new appreciation of the necessity of the *oikumene* for doing theology in our epoch. General Secretary Philip Potter, in his "Introduction" to the Report of the Central Committee to the recent Fifth Assembly of the W.C.C., expressed a judgment which both reveals his sense of the ideological factor in theology and betrays, in my judgment, too negative an attitude toward ideology as such. After reflecting about the programs of the W.C.C. which have "strained every nerve of faith and obedience" to meet the challenges of the seven years since the last General Assembly, he concluded, "There is no way back for us into an escapism either of disengagement or of setting up ideological or dogmatic walls of defence."[2] To speak of these rejected possibilities as a "way back" suggests that the immediate past of the church was in some way buttressed by such "ideological or dogmatic walls" that this ecumenical leader from the Third World is determined shall no longer be the case.

Though I have no quarrel with the substance of Dr. Potter's judgment, I do

---

[1]That Robert Bellah has taken his scholarly flight with civil religion just at this point in American history confirms Hegel's insight in his Preface to the *Philosophy of Right* that the "owl of Minerva" takes its flight "only when the shades of night are gathering." Professor Bellah's most recent book, *The Broken Covenant* (New York: Seabury, 1975), indicates how much he also shares the perspective of this essay. See especially his Chapter V, "The American Taboo on Socialism."

[2]David Johnson, ed., *Upsala to Nairobi* (New York: Friendship Press, 1975), p. 17.

James E. Will (United Methodist) is Henry Pfeiffer Professor of Systematic Theology and Director of the Peace Institute, Garrett-Evangelical Theological Seminary, Evanston, IL. He received his education at North Central College, Evangelical Theological Seminary, and the Ph.D. degree from Columbia University/Union Theological Seminary. He is member of the Faith and Order Commission of the N.C.C., director of the Division of Ecumenical and Interreligious Concerns of the Board of Global Ministries of the United Methodist Church, and the Vice Chairperson of Christians Associated for Relationships with Eastern Europe. Among his recent publications is "From Rejection to Employment: The Christian Use of Marxist Analysis."

not think we take the relation of theology and ideology sufficiently seriously if we evaluate ideology only negatively, and seek only to protect theology from its baneful influences. If this were the dominant perspective informing this essay we might only analyze some historical instances where theology has been misused for ideological purposes, and call upon the churches to sin ideologically no more. But since this is not the controlling perspective, we have dared to suggest that ideology, rightly considered, has an inescapable place in theology. That place, to put it succinctly, is principally in articulating the relations between Christology and soteriology.

Reflection about the positive value of ideology was suggested as a new possibility to me when Professor Paul Ricouer of Paris, in a balanced and thoughtful analysis, defended the necessity of the ideological oversimplification of any society's history to project those unifying values which bind it together.[3] Many of us have since had opportunity to observe this process in the bicentennial celebration of the history of the U.S.A. My own reflection about that part of the history of this society which I have consciously experienced has focused on with what difference the bicentennial would have been celebrated during the Eisenhower era of the 1950's, with a fatherly conqueror of evil in the White House, the Marines landing without opposition in Lebanon to protect democracy under the umbrella of our nuclear monopoly, and the Soviet Union suffering its post-Stalinist malaise of coming to terms with the havoc that that dread dictator's despotism had wrought. The thought of that is enough to make loyal critics of our nation's previously excessive and naive ideology thank providence that our revolution did not occur twenty years earlier. Nevertheless, I affirm that we must and will have some ideology, or we shall not long endure. It appears that the concern to resymbolize American ideology is a major and proper preoccupation of the new Carter administration.

Karl Mannheim's now classical analysis of *Ideology and Utopia* was done during the late 1920's under conditions not unlike our own at this point in our history—the chaotic and conflictual conditions of the Weimar Republic, when all that Bismarck had ideologically nailed down in the nineteenth century had broken loose.[4] In that creative interlude of a decade and a half before Hitler nailed it all down again in what proved to be the shape of a coffin, Mannheim gave a mature form to the insights which Bismarck's contemporary, Karl Marx, had injected into German thought eighty years before in his *Poverty of Philosophy*. If Gladstone's epigrammatic judgment of Bismarck is true, that "he made Germany great while making Germans small," it must be recognized in our century that Marx was one dynamic genius whom Bismarck could keep in exile but not fully reduce in stature.

The insight that Marx expressed in 1847 could not be put down or sup-

---

[3]Public lecture, University of Vienna, Fall, 1974.

[4]Karl Mannheim, *Ideology and Utopia,* tr. Louis Wirth and Edward Shils (New York: Harcourt, Brace and World, Inc., 1936), Harvest Book Edition.

pressed: "The economic categories are only the theoretical expressions, the abstractions, of the social relations of production. . . . The same men who establish social relations conformably with their material productivity, produce also the principles, the ideas, the categories, conformably with their social relations."[5] Eighty years later, Mannheim generalized Marx's insight into ideology so clearly that it now should be recognized that all thought is a social process, which to be fully comprehensible must be viewed not only logically and psychologically, but also sociologically:

> Strictly speaking, it is incorrect to say that the single individual thinks. Rather, it is more correct to insist that he participates in thinking further what other men (sic) have thought before him. He finds himself in an inherited situation with patterns of thought which are appropriate to this situation and attempts to elaborate further the inherited modes of response or to substitute others for them in order to deal more adequately with the new challenges which have arisen out of the shifts and changes of this situation.[6]

Given this insight, we may no longer think in terms of a transcendent ego of pure consciousness, but we must conceive consciousness as relational, dynamic, and in a constant process of becoming. We should, therefore, consider every social, political, and *theological* analysis as closely connected with the evaluations and unconscious orientations of the analyst, and seek the critical self-clarification of theology in part through the critical self-clarification of our orientations in the everyday world.[7]

We may no longer hope to enhance objectivity, therefore, by reducing our participation in the social process, which is a tactic frequently and unsuccessfully tried by both churchpersons and academicians. The usual result of such abstraction is only a dulling of our sensitivities to many of the dimensions of the living matrix in which we have our being.[8] We shall not understand our theological object, the God revealed in Israel's history and the total event of Jesus the Christ in our history, if we do not seek fully to understand ourselves in all the complexities of our historical situation as we respond existentially and conceptually to this living God.

Such understanding makes increasingly clear that our thinking is profoundly influenced by the degree of our power and privilege in any stage of the history of

---

[5] Karl Marx, *The Poverty of Philosophy,* trans. H. Qualch (Chicago, 1910), p. 119.

[6] Mannheim, *Ideology and Utopia,* p. 3.

[7] Cf. ibid., p. 45.

[8] Mannheim illuminates this point: "Man (sic) attains objectivity and acquires a self with reference to his conception of his world not by giving up his will to action and holding his evaluation in abeyance but in confronting and examining himself. The criterion of such self-illumination is that not only the object but we ourselves fall squarely into our field of vision. We become visible to ourselves, not just vaguely as a knowing subject as such but in a certain role hitherto hidden from us, in a situation hitherto impenetrable to us, and with motivations of which we have not hitherto been aware. In such moments the inner connections between our role, our motivations, and our type and manner of experiencing the world suddenly dawns upon us," ibid., p. 47.

a given social structure. The concept of "ideology" in its most specific sense must be defined in relation to political struggle:

> The concept "ideology" reflects the one discovery which emerged from political conflict, namely, that ruling groups can in their thinking become so intensively interest-bound to a situation that they are simply no longer able to see certain facts which would undermine their sense of domination. There is implicit in the word "ideology" the insight that in certain situations the collective unconscious of certain groups obscures the real condition of society both to itself and others and thereby stabilizes it.[9]

Clarity in analysis is also better maintained if we do not try to express precisely the opposite meaning with the same term. Mannheim designated only that complex of attitudes, evaluations, and ideas which direct activity toward the maintenance of the existing order as "ideology," while naming that which drives toward changing the prevailing order "utopian."[10]

One more subtle insight from Mannheim is useful to theological reflection. That is, that certain kinds of formally utopian thinking can become ideological in fact and in effect, tending toward stabilization rather than change. When we are in the midst of mutually conflicting ideas, it is extremely difficult to determine which are genuinely utopian—that is, which will really contribute to the transformation of the society toward something genuinely new. Mannheim suggested that here only adequate historical realism could provide the criterion:

> If we look into the past, it seems possible to find a fairly adequate criterion of what is to be regarded as ideological and what is utopian. This criterian is their realization. Ideas which later turned out to have been only distorted representations of a past or (purely) potential social order were ideological, while those which were adequately realized in the succeeding social order were relative utopias.[11]

Which is to say, only that thinking is genuinely utopian which in the midst of struggle is oriented to real potentials in contrast to both pseudo potentials and pure potentials. Utopian thinking related to abstract or pure potentials is really ideological, and thus much utopian theological thinking, from the standpoint of historical realism, must be seen as ideological.

These insights from the sociology of knowledge provide a necessary preface

---

[9]Ibid., p. 40.

[10]Ibid. His own words are: "The concept of *utopian* thinking reflects the opposite discovery of the political struggle, namely that certain oppressed groups are intellectually so strongly interested in the destruction and transformation of a given condition of society that they unwittingly see only those elements in the situation which tend to negate it. . . . Their thought is never a diagnosis of the situation; it can be used only as a direction for action."

[11]Ibid., p. 192. I have found Whitehead's ontological distinction between real potentials and pure potentials useful in thinking about this issue. See *Process and Reality* (New York: Macmillan, 1929), esp. pp. 101–104. The emergence of novelty is only possible within, and is necessarily conditioned by, a general scheme of relationships.

to a discerning essay of Paul Lehmann.[12] Professor Lehmann's major vocation as a Christian theologian has been to seek a christological basis for ethical thought and action in a realistically discerned context. He wrote this revealing essay in 1962 just after the Third General Assembly of the W.C.C. in New Delhi in 1961, and just before the opening of the already-called Second Vatican Council in 1962. Metropolitan Nikodim—who at its Fifth General Assembly has become one of the seven presidents of the W.C.C.—had just then led his church into the W.C.C. after four decades of isolation in the Soviet Union. That 1961 Assembly was also marked by the uniting of the International Missionary Council with the W.C.C. Professor Lehmann discerned the paradigmatic significance of the conjunction of these two events—a significance which has grown in the intervening fifteen years to the present.

At the very time that the ecumenical church was structurally expressing the necessary relation of the unity and mission of the church, it would, by extending its unity, also feel for the first time the full impact of the communist movement upon the whole church. The ecumenical frontier was no longer coincident with the ideological and political frontier between "East" and "West." Thus, Professor Lehmann concluded, "the paradigmatic character of the decisions taken at New Delhi exhibits the encounter between ideology and incarnation as the critical focus of the dynamics of the ecumenical situation today."[13] What a prophet he has proved to be as we recall some of what has emerged since: the European Christian-Marxist dialogue; the explosive 1966 Conference on Church and Society in Geneva; the ensuing, hotly-debated Program to Combat Racism; the establishment of the Commission on the Church's Participation in Development, largely staffed by Third World churchpersons guided by the liberation theologies developed among the underprivileged; and the attempt to hold together the two major soteriological motifs—liberation and reconciliation—guiding the churches' life today in the recent Nairobi Assembly theme, "Jesus Christ Frees and Unites"!

All of this indicates that the church catholic has been regaining its ecumenical balance in response to the challenge posed by communism's messianic heresy. Another way of putting it is that the church is finally becoming willing to learn from Marxism's utopian reproof of most of the churches' excessively ideological stance. We are at last learning from Marx's assertion in *Zur Kritik der Hegelschen Rechtsphilosophie* that (at least for us religious people), "The beginning of all socio-political criticism is the criticism of religion,"[14] which is to say

---

[12]Paul Lehmann, *Ideology and Incarnation: A Contemporary Ecumenical Risk* (Geneva: John Knox Association, 1962); delivered as the Seventh Annual John Knox House Lecture in June, 1962, in that historic place where John Knox ministered in Geneva, while developing genuinely utopian plans for the reformation of Scotland. Though published immediately in English, French, and German, this essay has not yet received the resonance in the ecumenical theological community which I think it deserves.

[13]Ibid., p. 11.

[14]Karl Marx, "Toward the Critique of Hegel's Philosophy of Law," in *Writings of the Young Marx on Philosophy and Society,* ed. Easton, and Guddat (New York: Doubleday Anchor Book,

that theology is a locus of fundamental criticism. Paul Lehmann concluded his 1962 lecture with the confident words: "On the boundary where the Communist and Ecumenical Movements meet, where the struggle between ideology and incarnation is most acute, just there the reality of the incarnation makes available a perspective and a power through which the brokenness of humanity is exposed, and the fragments of a shattered humanity are being made whole again."[15]

The thesis of this essay is that the inescapable place of ideology in theology is the intersection of Christology and soteriology. Soteriology is the theological locus where our reason is always conditioned, and sometimes corrupted, by our personal and social interests; and these soteriological interests have always conditioned the formulation of Christologies in the history of the church. In the early church the hellenistic anxiety of death took Christology out of its New Testament historical, apocalyptic context and restructured it in ontological categories which supported and interpreted the existential possibility of divination—that is. of participating in God's eternal essence in a way that delivers us from the temporal flux's perpetual perishing. In the medieval church the anxiety of guilt, which was nourished in a penitential system and compounded in the perfectionism of the monasteries, created a Christology which could meet their felt need to satisfy God's feudally conceived honor. And in our emerging pluralistic and conflicted world society, which suffers anxieties of meaninglessness because of our oppression within technocratic structures and/or our alienation in the conflictual processes of a capitalistic society, we have elaborated our dialectically-polarized soteriologies of liberation and reconciliation.[16]

Those theologians who understand well the historical character of our faith and the historical form of our theology are in the best position to recognize the place of ideology in theology. From his study of the history of the transmission of traditions, Wolfhart Pannenberg has concluded:

> . . . a separation between Christology and soteriology is not possible, because in general the soteriological interest, the interest in salvation, in the *beneficia Christi,* is what causes us to ask about the figure of Jesus. . . . However, the danger that is involved in this connection between Christology and soteriology has emerged at the same time: Has one really spoken there

1967), pp. 248–251. The truth of this is perhaps nowhere better known than in the Christian Peace Conference, that ecumenical structure which has its base in the communist societies of Eastern Europe and the Soviet Union. Though it, of course, has its own ideological/utopian vectors, it is aware of their problematic. Its Theological Commission, in their meeting in Bangalore, India, Sept. 13–19, 1976, drafted a proposal to the other organs of the CPC of the theological foundations of peace work of the CPC, which stated this issue clearly: ". . . we see theology not as an isolated and academic enterprise, but as a critical theoretical reflection on our active and concrete response to God's liberating action in history. We must guard ourselves from ideological distortions by allowing for full ecumenical participation in the process of thinking theologically and scientifically about such complex issues."

[15]Lehmann, *Ideology and Incarnation,* p. 27.

[16]My obvious dependence upon some of Paul Tillich's insights is here gratefully acknowledged. Cf. his *Systematic Theology,* Vol. II (University of Chicago Press, 1957).

about Jesus himself at all?... Do not the desires of men only become projected upon the figure of Jesus, personified in him?... The danger that Christology will be *constructed* out of the soteriological interest ought to be clear. Not everywhere is this so unreservedly expressed as by Tillich: "Christology is a function of soteriology." However, the tendency that is expressed here plays a part, more or less consciously and to a greater or lesser extent, in all the types of Christological thought considered here.[17]

Jürgen Moltmann, methodologically Pannenberg's colleague, but more sensitively attuned to the economic and political struggles of our day, discerned the ideological dimensions of those Christologies which ignore or eliminate the political dimension from their understanding of Jesus. A major case in point is Rudolph Bultmann's assertions about Christ's death: "What is certain is merely that he was crucified by the Romans, and thus suffered the death of a political criminal. This death can scarcely be understood as an inherent and necessary consequence of his activity; rather it took place because his activity was misconstrued as a political activity."[18] Moltmann asks us to remember that "in the societies of Jesus' time there was no politics without religion, any more than there was religion without politics."[19] When we do, we are able to discern the ideological character of Bultmann's Christology at this point:

> The simple distinction between religion and politics which Bultmann introduces when he speaks of Jesus' activity "being misconstrued as a political activity" is nothing less than the projection back of the separation of religion and politics—"religion is a private matter"—from the bourgeois world of the 19th century....[20]

Through such analysis the ideological dimensions of much of existentialist Christology in our day becomes apparent. It is the latest mode by which the comfortable middle and upper classes privatize their faith, so that faith's impact upon the economic and political structures which are the basis of privileged social position may be ignored. James Luther Adams, social-ethicist of Harvard, put this insight sharply in his introduction to Paul Tillich's essays on *Political Expectations:*

> The emphasis of Bultmann is conducive in the main to the privatization of piety.... One must say that his notion of authenticity is in the main a transcendentalized subjectivity, a highly organized withdrawal from history.... Is Bultmann's kind of self-understanding possible without the at-

---

[17]Wolfhart Pannenberg, *Jesus—God and Man* (Philadelphia: Westminster Press, 1968), pp. 47–48.

[18]Bultmann, "The Primitive Christian Kerygma and the Historical Jesus," in Carl E. Braaten and Roy A. Harrisville, *The Historical Jesus and the Kerygmatic Christian* (New York: Abingdon Press, 1964), p. 24; quoted in Moltmann, *The Crucified God* (New York: Harper and Row, 1974), p. 137.

[19]Moltmann, *Crucified God,* p. 36.

[20]Ibid., p. 137.

tendant support of a social order? Bultmann's theology pre-supposes a stable society, a pietistic bourgeois existence with a regular paycheck, everyone minding his own vocational business, always open to spontaneous, concrete decision for the neighbor—surely false securities. In face of pervasive social, economic, and political realities and responsibilities, in face of the massive, demonic forces that harrow up the soul, Heidegger and Bultmann offer pietistic escape from history, estrangement from *civil* authenticity.... their concern, in its effect, is what Tillich repeatedly speaks of as ideology—a concealed defence of the status quo so long as it does not disturb inner and individual freedom.[21]

This form of ideology requires attention by white, middle-class congregations because it is the one they are least prepared to discern. Both the tradition and the social position of many North American congregations tend toward so close an identification with this ideology as to be ill-equipped to differentiate it from the faith which it helps formulate for them. Black theologians, however, have less trouble sorting out Bultmann's form of ideology from their faith. James Cone, for instance, wrote, "Black Theology can agree with some aspects of Bultmann's interpretation. The idea that revelation changes my own self-understanding is crucial for Black Theology and biblical revelation," but then went on to say:

Our major difficulty with Bultmann's view is that it does not take seriously the irreducibly historical character of revelation.... Revelation is not only my own individualistic self-understanding; it is the self-understanding of a community which sees God at work in history. Equally important, Bultmann's view fails to express the idea of *liberation*. Revelation is a historical liberation of an oppressed people from slavery.[22]

Most white North American congregations, however, have little trouble discerning the utopian element in Cone's black theology as he rages against his discernment of the ideological element in theirs. Consider Cone at his black-power worst, or best, depending on your *sitz-im-leben:*

Black Theology cannot create new symbols independent of the black community and expect black people to respond. It must stay in the black community and get down to the real issue at hand ("cutting throats" to use Le Roi Jones' phrase) and not waste too much time discussing the legitimacy of religious language.... That the God-language of white religions has been used to create a docile spirit among black people while whites aggressively attacked them is beyond question.... The white God is an idol, created by the racist bastards, and we black people must perform the iconoclastic task of smashing false images.[23]

[21]James Luther Adams, "Introduction," Tillich, *Political Expectations* (New York: Harper & Row, 1971), pp. xiii–xiv.
[22]James Cone, *A Black Theology of Liberation* (New York: Lippincott Co., 1970), pp. 104–105.
[23]Ibid., pp. 113–114.

Confronted with the utopianism in the soteriologies of liberation, whether in the black communities of North America and South Africa, or the marxist communities in Latin America and Asia, the white North American church often turns the more completely to the ideology within its soteriology of reconciliation. An able social ethicist said to the American Society of Christian Ethics almost a decade ago: "We may assume, therefore, that there is a *fully adequate* basis in the New Testament for understanding our vocation in terms of reconciliation— and this by contrast with the *total absence* of any inclination to interpret Christian vocation in terms of political messianism,"[24]—his term for what has since come to be called liberation theology. It is no longer possible, however, for any of us to ignore the judgment of Third World theologians such as Jose Miguez Bonino, who is also one of the new presidents of the W.C.C., when he wrote:

> The ideological appropriation of the Christian doctrine of reconciliation by the liberal, capitalistic system in order to conceal the brutal fact of class and imperialist exploitation and conflict is one—if not *the*—major heresy of our time. The explanation for its almost uncontested predominance is no doubt to be found in the insertion of ecclesiastical and theological structures in the oppressive class, in the consequent exclusion of the oppressed as agents of ecclesiastical leadership and theological reflection, in the hold of the system on the minds and interests of the churches. Significantly, this ideology begins to be challenged as a "Church of the oppressed" emerges and begins to find a voice.[25]

The East-European-based Christian Peace Conference's written contribution to the preparatory materials for the W.C.C.'s General Assembly theme—"Jesus Christ Frees and Unites"—also spoke with great clarity to this issue:

> The biblical understanding of justice and peace forbids Christians to misuse the main biblical message of God's reconciliation with humankind through Jesus to endorse or tolerate in the name of the Gospel the continued existence of unjust power structures, by pretending to reconcile irreconcilable systems. The service of reconciliation imposed on us makes it our duty to help change the unjust relations which alienate human beings. . . . The CPC study projects have revealed that reconciliation can be biblically and correctly understood only in the framework of justification. . . . Jesus Christ is our justice. He puts us in the service of reconciliation and peace. . . . We are called in his name to enter the struggle against the structures of injustice.[26]

---

[24]Theodore Weber, "Reconciliation as Foreign Policy Method," ASCE, Jan. 20, 1968, mimeographed manuscript, p. 2, emphasis added.

[25]Bonino, *Doing Theology in a Revolutionary Situation* (Philadelphia: Fortress Press, 1975), p. 121.

[26]"Peace and Justice: The CPC Contribution to the Fifth Assembly of the WCC in Nairobi," mimeographed document, p. 13. I was a participant in the ad hoc group of CPC participants who prepared this statement in Prague, CSSR, Feb. 10–13, 1975, under the direction of Dr. Karoly Toth, General Secretary. Does the adequacy of this theological insight mean that the CPC is free from ideology in its own soteriological understanding and commitments? No! Its theological formulations often have a discernible ideological component, but its social context delivers it from the ideological interest of the bourgeoisie in the soteriology of reconciliation.

If we accept the evidence for the place of ideology in our contemporary soteriologies of liberation and reconciliation, what then shall we do? The first paradoxical answer must be "nothing"! This is the human condition. There is no methodology, sociological or theological, which will allow us fully to transcend it. Professor Gibson Winter has shown that ideology is as real and pervasive in the social sciences as it is in theology. He has examined recent controversies between such sociologists as Talcott Parsons and C. Wright Mills to try to identify the scientific aspects which are common to a variety of "objective" considerations of society, rather than, as he says, "excluding some of the scientific perspectives by bringing them under a rubric of ideology." But he concluded:

> They follow to differing degrees the procedures of empirical sciences, and they attempt, so far as possible, to give a reliable interpretation of their findings. So far as these scientists suffer ideological strains, and all to varying degrees undergo such strain, this is perhaps the human condition.[27]

Ideology is a dimension of the human condition, because we are finite, social, incomplete, and estranged selves. If it must be recognized even as a dimension of the processes and results of a more relatively abstract social science, why should we hope to exclude it from soteriology and Christology, which are constituted precisely by the ultimately concerned thought of estranged persons about the ground of their salvation?

The implication of this first paradoxical answer of what we are to do is, secondly, to cease doing what some neo-orthodox theologies thought were antidotes to ideology. We must give up the specious hope that a transcendent theology, on the one hand, or a pragmatic ethic, on the other, will allow theology to escape ideology. We should accept the insight of a liberation theologian such as Hugo Assmann that a transcendent theology which does not "speak in the language of the fulfillment of love in historical action for the neighbor, inevitably falls into idealization and ideologizing. . . . the way of ideologizing has always been the way of dehistoricizing (*entgeschictlichung*).[28] Though dehistoricizing may not be "the way," it has clearly been a prevalent way of ideologizing among those who hoped to overcome all ideology, as the ongoing controversy among Barthians about the relation of religious socialism to the master's theological corpus reveals.[29]

---

[27]Gibson Winter, *Scientific and Ethical Perspectives on Social Process* (New York: Macmillan, 1966), p. 54.

[28]Quoted in Dwain Epps, "Über Ideologische Theologie," *Dialog,* 4/1972, p. 329.

[29]Cf. F. W. Marquardt, *Theologie und Sozialismus. Das Beispiel Karl Barths* (München/Mainz: Kaiser Verlag, 1972); and Helmut Gollwitzer, *Reich Gottes und Sozialismus bei Karl Barth* (München: Kaiser Verlag, 1972). Gollwitzer argues strongly against those who thought Barth's concentration on theological work per se could be interpreted as *"selbstgenügsame Denkarbeit"* or *"blosses Interpretieren,"* rather than the strenuous effort to show the integral relation of the gospel to socialist political practice, which Gollwitzer understands it to be. See especially pp. 10–12.

A similar word needs to be addressed to those who thought they learned from Reinhold Niebuhr, among others, that one may speak the language of historical action without ideology if one restricts Christian ethical decisions to the purely pragmatic. After the "brightest and best" of the Kennedy era, one should be able to recognize that the logic of pragmatism has a clearly conservative ideological vector. Paul H. Nitze, who has had a long public career in the State and Defense Departments of the U.S.A., has said this clearly in an essay on "The Recovery of Ethics" published by the Council on Religion and International Affairs:

> My particular orientation has been toward action and policy making in the business, military, and political fields. . . . Our first instinct is to leave to others the discussion of ultimate aims and principles. We tend to feel that common sense gives us a firm enough grasp on proximate aims and principles, and that our job is to get something done and have it work as we intend it to work. We recognize that these proximate aims and principles derive from and are geared into a deeper and more basic system. But we are apt to feel that our forefathers did a very good job of thinking through that more ultimate system and that there is not much use in tinkering with it. We will give it our full respect, and will be guided by the related precepts for action which have been handed down to us by tradition.[30]

Pragmatism ideologically presupposes systemic continuity in a way which makes it inevitably conservative.

Bonhoeffer and Tillich, among the theologians formed within the dynamics of the Weimar Republic, are able to provide the more positive theological direction for those who recognize this inescapable ideological or utopian dimension in human thought. Though Bonhoeffer was not directly addressing this issue, his insistence that we live and think in "correspondence with reality" provides important insight for those trying to come to terms with the ideological and utopian dimensions of theology:

> For action which corresponds with reality the world remains the world. . . . The world remains the world because it is the world which is loved, condemned and reconciled in Christ. No man has the mission to overleap the world and to make it into the kingdom of God. Nor, on the other hand, does this give support to that pious indolence which abandons the wicked world to its fate and seeks only to rescue its own virtue. . . . The "world" is thus the sphere of concrete responsibility which is given to us in and through Jesus Christ.[31]

We are to take responsibility in precisely this incomplete and alienated world which God in Christ is creating and redeeming, even though we are given no capacity fully to transcend it. In the very midst of its ambiguous dynamics we

---

[30]Paul H. Nitze, *The Recovery of Ethics* (New York: CRIA, 1960), p. 10.
[31]Dietrich Bonhoeffer, *Ethics*, ed. Eberhard Bethge (New York: Macmillan Co., 1962), p. 202.

must accept the risks of developing and expressing our inevitably human soteriologies.[32]

The risk inheres in the inescapable "correlation" which links our theologies with our ideological or utopian social contexts. Despite Tillich's tendency to "universalize" this context, at least for a given society in a given epoch, his insights expressed about the "method of correlation" are profound. Our existence in a given socio-cultural situation at a given time will predispose us to feel and articulate our existential questions in a way conditioned by that situation. The form of our existential questions in turn will condition the way in which we articulate our theological answers, as Tillich has shown:

> If theology gives the answer, "the Christ" to the question implied in human estrangement, it does so differently, depending on whether the reference is to the existential conflicts of Jewish legalism, to the existential despair of Greek skepticism, or to the threat of nihilism as expressed in twentieth-century literature, art and psychology.[33]

The same insight applies to those who are articulating soteriologies of liberation in response to the existential questions of the oppressed, or soteriologies of reconciliation in response to the existential questions of the privileged.

The risk of ideological and utopian distortion in the thought and action guided by soteriologies correlated with finite existence in conflictual contexts may be limited if we preserve the wisdom in the church's ecumenical tradition, which has refused to declare any soteriological formulae to be dogma even though it early created dogmatic christological formulae. By so doing, the church has guarded itself against any ideological or utopian fixations in the realm of praxis. Daniel Day Williams' appreciation of this crucial point is beautifully expressed: "It is as if at the centre of the Christian faith the redemptive action of God explodes all theories and formulas. The spirit breaks and creates many forms, and no one of them can contain it."[34]

If we are to stay open to this rightwising action of the Spirit, we must remain resolutely engaged ecumenically. This does not suggest that the *oikumene* is a place where ideological and utopian theology will not be expressed, but rather that it is the universal context where all theological perspectives may engage each other as the *whole* Body of Christ seeks to fulfill Christ's redemptive mission in the *whole* world.[35] There is no ontological or mystical universal which allows us to transcend

---

[32]Cf. Charles West's word to the American Society of Christian Ethics in 1974: "This is a risky business. It is quite frankly the risk of becoming an ideologue in the name of Christ" ("Religion, Revolution and the Task of Ethics," mimeographed manuscript, p. 9).

[33]Paul Tillich, *Systematic Theology,* Vol. 2, p. 15–16.

[34]Daniel Day Williams, The Spirit and the Forms of Love (New York: Harper & Row, 1968), p. 39.

[35]See the Spring, 1976, issue of *explor,* Vol. 2, No. 1 (Evanston, IL: Garrett-Evangelical Theological Seminary). The whole issue is devoted to the theme of "Beyond the Western Captivity of the World Council of Churches." My essay, "From Rejection to Employment: The Christian Use of Marxist Analysis," articulates the influence Marxist perspectives now exercise in the oikumene.

our ideology, but there is the concrete universal of Christ's church where no western "ear" may say to an eastern "eye" or southern "hand": "we have no need of you."[36] It is in the *oikumene* where we overcome our forgetfulness of Christ's intention to save the *whole* creation. Those who ideologically work for reconciliation are required within the *oikumene* also to seek reconciliation with Christ's zealots in a way which joins them in recognizing and overcoming the injustices which require their revolutionary zeal. Those utopians, whose recognition of how far the rich man or the white man or the male man is from the Kingdom of God requires their revolutionary hunger after righteousness, are ecumenically also required to intend the liberation of those who, perhaps for good reason, have been defined as "enemy." In the *oikumene* we learn that there are real enemies of God's oppressed who must be loved precisely as enemies for the sake of their liberation.

The crucial new possibility given to many today in the emerging concreteness of the *oikumene* is the recovery of relation to universal history. We cannot escape or transcend the necessity of receiving and interpreting an incarnated revelation historically. In this epoch, if not in all epochs, the traditioning of this revelation will be in part through the historical dimensions of class, race, nation, and culture which affect us all. We should not seek to escape or deny the ideological and utopian dimensions this will give to all of our theologies. But we can offer these dialogically to each other in the confidence that Christ is present and active in varying ways and degrees in all of the histories which make up the universal history taking form in the struggle of the *oikumene*. Only in such a concrete universal may we take confidence in anything like Wolfhart Pannenberg's more or less Hegelian assertion that, ". . . Christological research finds in the historical reality of Jesus the criterion for the critical examination of the Christological tradition and also the various soteriological concerns that have determined Christological presentations."[37] For as yet we have not sufficient participation in or grasp on universal history so as to be able uncritically to trust any one hermeneutic to define the universal meaning of the historical reality of Jesus. Thus we must stay open to the transcendence of the Spirit in the whole Body of Christ by keeping our methodologies orthopractic, provisional, and dialogical. Even as we are committed to doing that part of the universal truth given to us, we must remain open to the rightwising action of the Spirit in the unspeakably valuable *oikumene* which increasingly is open to us today.

---

[36]This is, of course, a paraphrase of 1 Cor. 12:14–21.
[37]Pannenberg, *Jesus—God and Man*, p. 49.

A CHRISTIAN/MARXIST DIALOGUE ON FREEDOM AND NECESSITY

Russell B. Norris

Alexis de Toqueville states in his *Recollections:* "The more I study the former condition of the world and see the world of our own day in greater detail . . . the more I am tempted to believe that what we call necessary institutions are often no more than institutions to which we have grown accustomed, and that in matters of social constitution the field of possibilities is much more extensive than men living in their various societies are ready to imagine."[1]

Today, more than ever before, there is a need to reexamine our preconceptions and presuppositions concerning the social order, in the light of both the Marxist critique and the Christian hope. We live in a world divided, grouped around differing ideological and sociological perceptions of how human beings should relate to each other. Tied to these perceptions are what appear to be radically opposing views of freedom, justice, and human dignity. Are these different understandings, with their myriad social, political, and economic structures, simply institutions to which we have grown accustomed, as Toqueville surmised? Or are they in some fundamental sense mutually exclusive?

This paper proposes to deal with but one aspect of the dialogue between these divergent worldviews: the nature of freedom in the so-called "humane society." The dictionary defines "humane" as compassionate, tender, merciful. Is freedom a necessary condition for these qualities to blossom, and if so, what sort of freedom are we talking about? Freedom, in the negative sense, could be defined as the absence of restraint. Positively, one might define it in terms of fulfillment, the enactment of an individual's true being. In other words, there is "freedom from" and "freedom for."

The western democratic tradition has tended to see these two forms of freedom as somehow interdependent. In order for the individual to find personal fulfillment, he or she ought to be as free as possible from external constraint. Thus western society has evolved a complex system of checks and balances to safeguard individual liberty, a system which has often been interpreted theologically as an expression of God's Will.

The question posed by Marxism is whether this individual freedom as it is understood in western democracy is truly the condition *sine qua non* for a

---

[1] Alexis de Toqueville, *Recollections,* Part 2, Chapter 2.

Russell B. Norris (Lutheran Church in America) is the pastor of the Mount Union Lutheran Parish in Pennsylvania. He received his education at M.I.T., University of Illinois, Lutheran School of Theology in Chicago, and received the Docteur es sciences religieuses from the University of Strasbourg, France. Dr. Norris published *God, Marx and the Future,* as well as a previous article in *J.E.S.,* "Transcendence and the Future: Dialogue with Roger Garaudy," Vol. 10, No. 3 (Summer, 1973).

humane society. Marxists have justly pointed out that the institutions of a democracy are meaningless to someone who is starving.[2] Without the basic necessities of life there is neither society nor humanity. The recent Broadway play, *The Ik,* piercingly describes the disintegration of social relationships in the face of absolute poverty and want. The members of the obscure African tribe slowly starving to death no longer seem even human, finding their only meaning and satisfaction in meeting the most basic animal needs: "When we eat, when we shit, that is good."[3]

Marxism affirms that in the last analysis, it is the economic and material factors that determine whether or not an individual or a society is truly free. Freedom, from this point of view, is found not in elections, representative government, or parliamentary democracy, but in the control of one's destiny in the most fundamental sense: the economic. For it is from the economic conditions of a people that all other forms of social interaction spring. Engels says in a letter dated 1894: "We regard economic conditions as the factor which ultimately determines historical development . . . Political, juridical, philosophical, religious, literary, artistic, etc., development is based on economic development."[4]

Engels argues that the apparent freedom of western society is but an illusion. On the surface the random nature of events in a capitalist economy appears to insure a high degree of individual freedom. In point of fact, from the Marxist perspective the result is just the opposite. Since such a chaotic and unplanned economy makes it impossible to project the future with certainty, it is in reality absolutely unfree. Human beings then have no real control over their destiny; they remain enslaved to the fluctuations of the market place. On the other hand, participation in the construction of socialism, while acknowledging the profound necessity of the laws of historical development, is in fact the highest form of freedom, since it liberates us from our helplessness before the capitalist "law of the jungle" and allows us to participate in the creation of our own history.

The clearest exposition of the Marxist view of freedom is found in Engels' polemic, *Anti-Dühring,* wherein he writes:

> Freedom does not consist in the dream of independence of natural laws, but in the knowledge of these laws, and in the possibility this gives of systematically making them work toward definite ends. . . . Freedom of the will therefore means nothing but the capacity to make decisions with real knowledge of the subject. Therefore the *freer* a man's judgment is in relation to a definite question, with so much the greater necessity is the content of this judgment determined; while the uncertainty, founded on ignorance, which seems to make an arbitrary choice among many different and conflicting

---

[2]Roger Garaudy, *Pour un modele francais de socialisme* (Gallimard, 1968), p. 20.
[3]*Newsweek,* October 25, 1976, pp. 99–100.
[4]Letter to Heinz Starkenburg, in Marx and Engels, *Selected Correspondence* (New York: International Publishers, 1942), pp. 516–517.

possible decisions, shows by this precisely that it is *not* free, that it is controlled by the very object which it should itself control. Freedom therefore consists in the control over ourselves and over external nature which is founded on knowledge of natural necessity; it is therefore necessarily a product of its historical development.[5]

The question at issue here is whether that individual freedom so cherished by liberal democracy and "baptized" by the Protestant ethic is real or illusory. Dialectical materialism views historical development in terms of necessity. The dialectic of history is like a tremendous river flowing through time, into which the individual initiative disappears like ripples from a stone skipped across the water. Only by conforming oneself to the historical dialectic is real freedom possible, say Marx and Engels. But it is possible only through the submerging of the individual's freedom of choice in the flow of the historical process. True freedom is attained only when human beings recognize the contradictions in the political, social, and economic structures of society, and take effective action to overcome them. The more "necessary" this decision appears, the higher the degree of freedom realized. In *Capital,* Marx asserts that "the realm of necessity and external utility is required. . . . The freedom in this (latter) field cannot consist of anything else but the fact that socialized man, the associated producers, regulate their interchange with nature rationally, bring it under their common control, instead of being ruled by it as by some blind power."[6] "But," adds Marx, "it always remains a realm of necessity."

Freedom to the Marxist, then, is essentially economic. It is the possibility for us collectively and rationally to control the forces of production, rather than being controlled by them. When this control is exercised by and for society, freedom is achieved. Marxism thus poses an interesting solution to the problem of freedom and necessity. Our historical initiatives must correspond to the internal laws of social development, if they are to have any assurance of success. Only when our actions conform themselves to the dialectic of history can we speak in any meaningful way of human freedom. Of course, this dialectic or paradox is by no means the exclusive discovery of Marx. In fact, the Marxist dialectic of freedom and necessity is but a secular form of a theological affirmation, the roots of which can be traced back to the New Testament, through Augustine and Luther, to our own time.

The idea is most clearly presented in the letters of Paul, although it is present in germ throughout the Bible. Basically, the idea is that true freedom is found only in conforming my will to the Will of God. When I reject that supreme Will, I become the "slave of sin," tossed about by the dark forces of chaos whose end is death. "But," says Paul, "now you have been set free from sin and are the slaves of God; as a result your life is fully dedicated to him, and at the last you

---

[5]Engels, *Anti-Dühring* (New York: International Publishers, 1939), pp. 125ff.
[6]Marx, *Capital,* Vol. III (Chicago: Kerr, 1906), p. 955.

will have eternal life" (Rom. 6:22). True freedom is not found in the willful assertion of human autonomy; as arbitrary choice it remains as illusory for the Christian as for the Marxist. In reality, the individual is always captive to some force, be it God or Satan, capitalism or the dialectic of history. Authentic freedom comes only in fusing my will with the Will of the One who is pure freedom, just as for the Marxist freedom is found in the identification of my individual initiative with the movement of the historical process. "Freedom is what we have—for freedom Christ has set us free" (Gal. 5:1).

Augustine continued and developed this paradoxical and dialectical notion of free will. In the *Enchiridion,* in the course of a discussion on the necessity of grace, he reiterates the Pauline argument that the sinner is a slave to sin, unable to choose the right. True liberty, for Augustine, is "the joy that comes in doing what is right."[7] But this freedom, analogous to the Marxist concept of freedom as the recognition of necessity, is only possible for one liberated from bondage to sin, a liberation that comes only through the gracious action of God. "We are then truly free," he says, "when God orders our lives, that is, forms and creates us not as men—this he has already done—but also as good men, which he is now doing by his grace, that we may indeed be new creatures in Jesus Christ."[8]

Luther's vigorous attacks on the notion of free will—particularly in the debate with Erasmus—arose no doubt partly out of polemics, partly from the centrality of grace in his theology (*sola gratia*). If grace were to carry any real assurance to the sinner, he reasoned, then God's will to save must be absolute and irresistable. The logical consequences of this position have often been criticized, but Luther felt such differences were a small price to pay for the positive assurance offered the sinner. Thus Luther sometimes appears to reduce the role of the will to virtually nothing. The paradoxical content of the Pauline and Augustinian concept of free will is not lost, however, and is well illustrated in the famous passage from Luther's treatise on *The Freedom of a Christian:* "A Christian is a perfectly free lord of all, subject to none," while at the same time, "A Christian is a perfectly dutiful servant of all, subject to all."[9] Luther goes on to explain that the Christian, although freed from bondage to sin through the effective action of the grace of God, finds the working out of that freedom in following the example of Christ by loving service to others. Thus the paradoxical assertion that freedom is found in obedience to the Will of God is as true for Luther as for Augustine and Paul.

When we turn to contemporary theological attempts to deal with this question, the work of Paul Tillich becomes extremely enlightening. Tillich sees the tension between "autonomy" and "heteronomy" synthesized in a new

---

[7]Augustine, *The Enchiridion,* Chapter IX, Paragraph 30, Library of Christian Classics, V. VII (London: SCM Press, 1955), p. 357.

[8]Ibid., Paragraph 31.

[9]Luther, *The Freedom of a Christian,* tr. W. A. Lambert, Luther's Works, V. 31 (Philadelphia: Muhlenburg Press, 1958), p. 344.

"theonomy." Here autonomy does not mean the freedom of an individual to be a law unto oneself; rather it is "the obedience of the individual to the law of reason, which he finds in himself as a rational being."[10] Autonomy is the law of subjective-objective reason. In other words, it is the law implied in the common structure of thought and reality; it is basically a structural quality of the human mind. Heteronomy is always in conflict with autonomy, for it represents the effort to impose an external authority on autonomy. It should not be taken as a totally external phenomenon, however, since it also represents the "depth" of reason: "The basis of a genuine heteronomy is the claim to speak in the name of the ground of being and therefore in an unconditional and ultimate way."[11] The tragedy of the struggle between autonomy and heteronomy is thus that it represents a battle between the structure and depth of reason; that is, a conflict within reason itself.

Finally, autonomy and heteronomy are grounded in theonomy. Theonomy here is not meant in the sense of an external, divine law imposed on reason; this would simply be another form of heteronomy. Rather, theonomy means "autonomous reason united with its own depth."[12] Here the structural laws of reason are reconciled with the power of its inexhaustible ground in the unity of God. Of course, there is no perfect theonomy under the conditions of existence, and the struggle between autonomy and heteronomy results in the quest for reunion; this quest is the search for revelation.

A number of salient features in Tillich's theology are readily seen. First of all, the entire construction, although built on a static, "logos" concept of reason, lends itself to a dialectical and historical interpretation. Autonomy, or human historical initiative, can be related to the common dialectical structure of thought and reality as understood by Marxism. For Tillich, the mind is able to grasp reality because both share the same "logos" structure; for the Marxist, it is the *dialectical* nature of thought and reality that makes this possible. Thus for both, autonomy refers to the structural character of mind. Heteronomy, which for Tillich is identified with the "depth" of reason, could be reinterpreted in Marxist terms as the irresistable dialectical movement of history, welling up from the depths of reality. An attempt to assert human autonomy in a willful and arbitrary manner would necessarily conflict with the movement of history. The historical process would then impose itself as an external and heteronomic force. On the other hand, the dialectical overcoming of autonomy and heteronomy would represent a Marxist equivalent of the Tillichian idea of "theonomy." This would occur only when my individual historical initiative (my autonomy) was in conformity with the movement of the dialectic of history (heteronomy).

The problem with this approach is that it does not really offer a synthesis of the two poles of the dialectic. The thesis is indeed present in the form of human

---

[10]Paul Tillich, *Systematic Theology*, V. I, p. 84.
[11]Ibid.
[12]Ibid., p. 85.

autonomy, or historical initiative; the antithesis of historical heteronomy, or the dialectic of history, is also present. But unlike a true dialectic, there is no final synthesis, no "negation of the negation." On the one hand, Marx sometimes appears to call for total conformity of the individual initiative with the dialectic of history. This would, in effect, collapse the dialectic into an identity, and it is difficult to see how human autonomy could be preserved in such a case. It would be nothing more than a return to the Greek concept of freedom as the accepting of one's destiny. On the other hand, if we accept the Marxist claim of a genuine dialectic, this interaction of autonomy and heteronomy continues indefinitely into the future with no hope for a final synthesis. Even the "classless society" represents not an end to all alienation, but simply another step in the endless dialectic of freedom. In the words of Marxist philosopher Roger Garaudy,

> Authentically human history will begin with Communism. It will be a history which is no longer made up of class struggles and war, . . . *Contradictions will not be abolished,* but they will no longer be bloody contradictions among human beings. Then, starting with questions which will no longer seek in alienated answers a coward's response, *the endless dialectic* of freedom made one with creation will flower.[13]

The lack of a final synthesis to the historical process leaves us with an interesting dilemma. Either the freedom of the individual is totally submerged in the objective laws of history—in which case the dialectic collapses into an identity—or the interaction of freedom and necessity is never resolved. In the first instance, the question of freedom becomes moot. In the second, any ultimate significance to history is lost. In the end the historical dialectic demands that we hope in the future of humankind without offering an object for that hope. The individual is asked to render up his or her freedom to the Moloch of history, with no assurance that history has a purpose or a meaning. Moltmann has observed that for Marx the theoretical meaning of history is recognized "to the extent that men make themselves ready to perceive this significance practically . . . ." This means that "the makeability of history itself becomes the goal of the making of history,"[14] and we find ourselves in an infinite regress.

One way out of this impasse may be suggested by the work of certain theologians in the so-called "School of Hope." A rephrasing of the concept of the dialectic of freedom and necessity in the language of the Absolute Future might provide the necessary dynamics for a truly Christian approach to the problem. The essence of God might then best be described as "pure freedom"—that freedom that comes to us from outside ourselves, in the ever-arriving future of God. From this perspective, freedom is best characterized in terms of an open future. If I am truly free, then my future is open, unlimited,

---

[13]Roger Garaudy, *From Anathema to Dialogue,* tr. Luke O'Neill (New York: Herder and Herder, 1966), p. 91.
[14]Jürgen Moltmann, "Hoping and Planning." *Cross Currents,* Vol. 18, No. 3 (Summer, 1968), p. 58.

uncircumscribed. But the future belongs to God, so that my freedom is rooted and grounded in God's future, the Absolute Future (to use the phrase coined by Karl Rahner).[15] This way of speaking about God in no way limits my freedom to go beyond my present existence or historical situation, but rather liberates me from the present for a new and open future in God. In other words, I am free to the extent that I can transcend the present moment. Futurity conditions, or rather *is* the condition for human freedom. But at the same time, the future remains beyond our grasp or control. It is that which comes *to us* from beyond ourselves. Our freedom consists in our assent to that new future, offered to us through the graciousness of God.

This means that the Christian is called to hope in a radically *new* future—a future in which all creatures will be set free from bondage. "Behold, I am doing a *new* thing," says the Lord (Is. 43:19). In this hope, personal freedom becomes intertwined with political, economic, and social freedom. The Christian is freed in order to serve, thus hearkening back to Luther. Or, to put it another way, freedom is contagious. Those who have been freed from "the powers and principalities of this dark world" will want to share that freedom with those who are still in bondage.

This approach to the problem of freedom and necessity is not bound by the same difficulties as the Marxist approach. The future can be said to be *our* future precisely because it belongs to God. It is more than simply the result of our own will and effort. So that from this point of view, we can say that we are only ever really free when the horizon of our personal future merges with the horizon of the future of God; for only a future that is more than a projection of our own latent possibilities can really call us to a transcendance of ourselves.

Here the cross and resurrection of Jesus Christ become paradigmatic for our freedom in God. Wolfhart Pannenberg seems to understand this when he asserts that for the Christian "the end of history is present proleptically in Jesus of Nazareth."[16] Thus, with the resurrection, the end of history is already upon us, and the future of God breaks into our world through the Christ-event. With the resurrection, a radically new possibility opens up for us: the possibility of freedom from every form of bondage and limitation—even the ultimate limit of death itself. Since for Christ death is already a past event, for our future to be one with Christ's future means that we are freed from the finality even of death. Jesus Christ is the rupture point at which the future breaks into the present.

Jesus has been called the "Messiah of Freedom," for in him the Christian faith sees the beginning of a previously unknown freedom: not merely the freedom to resist oppression (which is certainly not unique to Christians), but the freedom to give oneself wholly and completely for the sake of the other, since God in Christ has already been given wholly and completely for us. As one

---

[15]Karl Rahner, "Christian Humanism," *Journal of Ecumenical Studies* 4 (1967): 378.
[16]Quoted in Carl Braaten, "Toward a Theology of Hope," in M. Marty and D. Peerman, eds., *New Theology Number 5* (New York: Macmillan, 1968), p. 105.

theologian puts it, "Christian faith not only believes in freedom, but is already freedom itself."[17] Of course, this freedom is not yet fully realized, and Christians must continue to long for the day when the powers and principalities are overthrown and the Crucified One reigns over all. But here within history we are impelled by our expectations for the coming future of God to resist oppression and slavery wherever it exists, and under whatever form. The proclamation of Christ becomes a reality through the hope and action of the Christian community: "The Spirit of the Lord is upon me, because he has anointed me to preach good news to the poor. He has sent me to proclaim release to the captive and recovering of sight to the blind, to set at liberty those who are oppressed, to proclaim the acceptable year of the Lord" (Lk. 4: 18–19). The hope for a final salvation at the *end* of history becomes the driving force in our struggle to liberate men and women from bondage *within* history. This struggle takes the form of concrete efforts to end racial, political, sexist, and economic exploitation; the horror of war; the evil of disease; and technological dehumanization.

But the divergences between Marxism and Christianity in their understandings of human freedom ought not prevent us from recognizing their common concern for liberation and human dignity. Both Christians and Marxists suffer under the oppression of the human race, and this suffering is but the reverse side of their hope for the future. Marxists, with their economic bias, see humanity's misery centered in economic and political slavery. Freedom for them means the abolition of human exploitation and the glorification of a united humanity in which persons are masters of their own destiny. Christians, while perhaps willing to use the Marxist critique as a tool, see human misery not so much in terms of our unrealized possibilities, but more as a result of our very real *im*possibilities. In a sense, each individual could be defined as "possibility limited by finitude."[18] There is something within us that drives us toward freedom, but that drive is limited by our slavery to sin, death, and the law. Freedom for the Christian means liberation from fear and death through the gracious action of God. This freedom is anticipated in hope and actualized in faith.

Christian freedom, it must be added, is not a private matter, but is always freedom *for others*. Christians share a common hope for the universal liberation of human life from all forms of bondage—even those of finitude and death. But while we wait with anticipation for the final revealing of the future of God promised in Scripture and assured by the resurrection of Christ, we are continually driven to demonstrate this freedom in the struggle for human liberation in history. This struggle cannot be identified with any political or ideological system, for no system can contain the fullness of the hope for which we wait.

---

[17]Jürgen Moltmann, "The Revolution of Freedom," *Motive,* Vol. 29, No. 3 (December, 1968), pp. 41–42.

[18]Carl Braaten, "The Gospel of the Kingdom of God and the Church," in V. Vajta, ed., *The Gospel and the Ambiguity of the Church* (Philadelphia: Fortress, 1974), p. 24.

Neither Soviet-style socialism nor western liberal democracy stands as an ultimate type. Knowing that the future belongs to God enables Christians to be critical even of the structures within which they live.

There is, for instance, nothing particularly sacred about capitalism, or even the hybrid form of capitalism and socialism that prevails in America, that earns it a divine benediction. In point of fact, Marxists may well be correct in condemning the exploitation and dehumanization of western liberalism. No less a person than Harry Truman points out in the book, *Give 'Em Hell, Harry,* that the chief problem with Americans is that they worship money! The capitalist system, with its emphasis on individual achievement through private enterprise, leaves little space for the kind of communal concern exemplified in, say, the Sermon on the Mount. And while, certainly, no one would go so far as to make the Reign of God a paradigm for any particular economic or political system, there is ample evidence that some systems are farther from the ideal than others.

But while western democracy and the Christian faith are not simply the opposite sides of the same coin, there is nevertheless a strong connection between Christian freedom and political freedom. This is not to say that one cannot be a Christian in a totalitarian society or that the Gospel cannot survive even under the worst forms of human degredation. After all, the church had its beginnings under a military dictatorship, when women were considered chattel, and slavery was universally accepted. And yet, there is a character of protest in Christianity, a tension between the eschatalogical promise of freedom and the struggle to realize that freedom here and now. No one, for instance, would say that St. Paul had attacked the system of slavery head on, but by introducing the concept of "spiritual freedom" he uprooted the justification for slavery. "There is neither Jew nor Greek, there is neither slave nor free, there is neither male nor female; for you are all one in Christ Jesus" (Gal. 3:28). Jaroslav Pelikan puts it this way: "Early Christianity did not require the abolition of slavery, but it did unleash spiritual and moral forces that finally found slavery incompatible with the Gospel."[19] Even if the structures of slavery were left intact (for the moment), their *meaning* was changed. Persons began to be seen as equal before God. And from there it is only a step to the generalization of that equality to the political arena: "We hold these truths to be self-evident, that all men (and women!) are created equal . . ."

This is certainly not an apology for American democracy, or the western liberal tradition; there is no direct line from St. Paul to the Declaration of Independence. But the pressure for liberation that springs from the Gospel has an impact on the political and social structures in which the Gospel is proclaimed. Thus the freedom to realize one's destiny, so much a part of Marxism, is intimately bound up with the negative sort of freedom, the freedom from restraint, intrinsic to the western tradition. There is, in fact, a dialectical relationship

---

[19]Jaroslav Pelikan, "Eve or Mary," *The Lamp,* June, 1971, p. 13.

between the freedom of the individual and the common good. From time to time it may happen that individual initiative must be subordinated to the needs of the community. Without freedom from fear, hunger, or economic deprivation, the finer points of parliamentary procedure pale into insignificance. But to collapse the dialectic into mere economic or material security, at the expense of individual liberties, means the ultimate demise of any hope for a "humane society."

There is no ideal society, either Marxist or democratic. The Reign of God remains beyond our grasp. But Christians are freed by the Gospel to explore new models of human interaction, based on the sober recognition of the dual nature of freedom: "freedom from" and "freedom for." Such an exploration may profit from the Marxist critique, and it may well utilize the tools of parliamentary democracy; but it must never allow itself to be seduced by any self-styled utopian solution to the search. Until they find their final rest in the realm of God's freedom, Christians are called to live as continual troublemakers and revolutionaries in every age and society.

THEOLOGICAL REFLECTION ON THE ENCOUNTER OF THE CHURCH WITH MARXISM IN VARIOUS CULTURAL CONTEXTS*

Aarhus Workshop

Introduction

The rise of Marxism as a political power has confronted Christians with the need to look at themselves—the church—and their task from a new point of view. It has not been, nor is it, easy, partly because Marxism has historically presented so antagonistic an attitude, partly because the church has tended to find itself comfortable in the traditional social structures, but most of all because the task of working out the consequences of the Gospel for human society is a never–ending and never fully soluble problem.

The pages that follow are intended to be of help in the task. They say something about how churches have reacted in the encounter with Marxism and about the complexity of the encounter, for neither Marxism nor the church is a monolithic movement. They present some theological judgments on the nature of the encounter and suggest some criteria to guide us to a more Christian response to Marxism than the churches have sometimes adopted.

One need not comment here on the paper's genesis, for that is given within the text. The paper is written against the background of a long study process. Support for both the information given and the positions adopted can be found in other materials produced during that process—particularly in the volume, *The Encounter of the Church with Movements of Social Change in Various Cultural Contexts* (Geneva: Lutheran World Federation, 1977), to which frequent reference is made.

In spite of occasional evidence of the specifically Lutheran theological tradition that has formed most of those who contributed to the paper's composition, we believe that it is an ecumenical document which comes out of the experience of, and speaks to, the whole church. It is offered to the church as a sort of way-station on a long road of theological reflection and research—a process which must engage all who are concerned for the Christian mission in the modern world.

Mr. Gerd Decke has carried major staff responsibility in the program which

---

*This is the Report of a theological workshop held in Aarhus, Denmark, April 19–22, 1977, under the sponsorship of the Commission on Studies of the Lutheran World Federation. It is issued under the authority of the Commission. However, it is not to be regarded as an official position of the Federation, but rather as the articulation of a stage in an ongoing process of reflection. The general line of argument has been accepted by all workshop participants, but not necessarily the exact wording of each statement. Since the Report has been edited and somewhat abbreviated for this *J.E.S.* version, the original paragraph numbering has been retained.

culminated in the Aarhus Consultation. In addition to Mr. Decke, the participants included:

Prof. Dr. Anna Marie Aagaard, Theological Faculty, Aarhus (Denmark) University (member of LWF Commission on Studies)

Rev. K. C. Abraham, Presbyter of St. Mark's Cathedral (Church of South India), Bangalore, South India

Dr. Héctor Borrat, Uruguayan jurist and church journalist (Roman Catholic), Barcelona, Spain

Fr. Parig Digan, Pro Mundi Vita (Roman Catholic Research and Information Center), Brussels, Belgium

Dr. Ulrich Duchrow, Director of LWF Department of Studies, Geneva, Switzerland

Rev. Béla Harmati, pastor and lecturer in systematic theology, Lutheran Theological Seminary, Budapest, Hungary

Prof. Dr. Karl Hertz, Hamma School of Theology, Springfield, OH, USA; moderator of the workshop (chairperson, LWF Commission on Studies)

Dr. Jonas Jonson, director of Stiftsgården, Rättvik, Sweden

Dr. Martti Lindqvist, associate of Research Institute of Lutheran Church, and docent at Theological Faculty of Helsinki, Tampere, Finland

Dr. Arne Sovik, Project Director, LWF Department of Studies, Geneva, Switzerland

Arne Sovik

1. The Ineluctable Encounter

1.1.　We live in a time of reform and revolution. The values, institutions, and practices of the past are being questioned and attacked, because many of them endanger the future of society and of humanity as a whole. No people and no individual anywhere is unaffected. No aspect of life is exempt.

1.2.　*A major protagonist in the struggle for the future of the world is the complex of designs for economic, political, and social order associated with the ideology that we call Marxism.* Scarcely a hundred years old, the fruit of currents of thought and social upheavals that shook nineteenth-century Europe, Marxism has with almost incredible rapidity spread its influence through the establishment of political systems that now govern nearly half of the world's population and influence more. The first Marxist state was established only sixty years ago. A generation later communist governments took power in Eastern Europe and the People's

Republic of China was founded. In many other Asian nations Marxism exercises a crucial influence in their search for a new social order. In the last fifteen years much of Africa has turned to Marxism and indigenous kinds of socialism. Harsh repression may be the only reason that some other Latin American countries do not follow Cuba into a Marxist revolution. In Latin Europe the Marxist parties have recently become serious competitors for national power. This is one of the facts which now threatens to drive Northern Europe to the right.

1.3.   For many outside the orbit of Marxist power, its rise poses a disturbing threat to their way of life and vested interests. Even in many non-Marxist countries the emerging strength of these historical movements and of Marxist thought compels changes in the structures of education and culture. In view of the history of Marxism in power there is fear of the totalitarian character of Marxist political authority and of the serious difficulties that confront any dissenter under Marxist governments.

1.4.   Meanwhile, doubts grow both within and outside Marxist countries about the capacity of Marxism to fulfill its utopian claim to usher in the ultimate social order, the communist society. Yet there is no indication that the influence of Marxism as a political and intellectual force will wane.

1.5.   One reason for the strength of Marxist influence is the apparent theoretical weakness and the fundamental economic inequity of the non-Marxist social systems. While the welfare state is an attempt to solve the problems of inequity, at least within the wealthy countries, the socialist approach seems to many impoverished peoples the only one radical enough to end their misery and injustice eventually and to provide security and social justice. In addition Marxism is not only an effective instrument for revolution, but it also has well-developed means for maintaining its power and resisting further revolution. Perhaps most important, Marxism shows a considerable ability to change, to adapt itself to local cultures and historical exigencies.

1.6.   *For these reasons, the encounter between Christianity and Marxism is not only urgent, but inescapable.* The encounter assumes different forms in different situations, each bringing in a new set of challenges and problems for the churches' life and witness. In Eastern Europe, for example, the church has been challenged to find a new orientation and to make changes in its organization, its self-understanding, and its witness to society. In China, the traditional church institutions have disappeared, and the tiny minority of Christians has been forced to evolve new ways of living its faith and carrying on its witness.

1.7.   Throughout the world the impact of the Marxist call for justice has been a factor in the awakening of the Christian conscience to the need for identifying with the poor and the oppressed in society. The Christian dialogue with Marxist thought pervades much theological writing and Christian practice, often unconsciously.

1.8.   However, the church's response to Marxism is too often without an adequate base of understanding of its presuppositions, its aims and its methods. Frequently the response is based on limited experience with a particular type of Marxism and denies any possibility of significantly different expressions of Marxism. Misconception and prejudice result, fully reciprocated from the Marxist side. This situation poisons the encounter and distorts our recognition of both the affinities and the conflicts inherent in Christian-Marxist relations. The church has also failed to recognize the extent to which it has denied its very nature through its assimilation to the unjust systems in which it has found itself comfortable and accepted, in which its institutional interests and privileges are secured, and to the values of which, in turn, it offers legitimation.

1.9.   *In general the affinities between Christianity and Marxism appear to lie in a commonality of social ideals. Their conflicts are found in their different understanding of ultimate meaning, of human nature, and of the methods by which the goals of human life together are to be sought.* More specifically what are these affinities and conflicts?

1.10.   Many have noted at least the following *points of affinity:*

- Both Marxism and Christianity have strong traditions of moral passion in their social teachings. They reject all forms of moral nihilism or indifference.

- Both give only relative value to the right of private property; property is not to be "owned" by persons for their own selfish purposes.

- They also agree in stressing communal values. Both see possessive individualism and extreme forms of pluralism as threats to the well-being of the human community. Solidarity, especially with the poor, weak, and exploited, but finally with all human beings, is an expression of unalienated humanity.

- Christians agree with Marxists on the need for fundamental change in economic and social relations among people.

- They are both supra-national and world-encompassing in their concern. They stress the social and material rights of all, regardless of ethnic or cultural divisions.

- Both believe that history has a goal for which human beings must strive. There can be no ultimate meaninglessness.

1.11.   But there are also *points of disagreement.* Christians believe that:

- In most cases Marxists overstress the importance and value of life's economic and political dimensions.

- The Marxist view of history is anthropocentric, exclusively focused on human autonomy and emancipation.

- The Marxist view of human nature is optimistic, ignoring the deep moral ambiguity of human life. Its belief in an inevitable human moral progress in history denies the pervasiveness of human sin.

- The materialistic world view, both as naturalistic, historic, and economic determinism, does not give space enough to life's spiritual dimensions.

- The Marxist critique of religion fails to see the ultimate positive meaning of the Christian faith and its progressive social implications.

1.12.   Christians disagree among themselves on social issues. At some points they are divided in their approach to Marxism. Some of these points are stated in the following questions:

- To what extent can the Marxist social and economic analysis be used as a "neutral" tool for evaluating social phenomena?

- To what extent is the public (common) ownership of the means of production and of other material goods useful, beneficial, and acceptable?

- What is to be the status of the church in a Marxist society? What structural safeguards does the church need for the free exercise of religion?

- What is an adequate Christian approach to the question of the use of violence?

- How far can Christians accept the implications of class analysis and tolerate or participate in the class struggle?

1.13.   Through these and other issues placed before the church by Marxism, Christians are continually challenged not only to review their understanding of society, but also to examine their faithfulness to the Gospel and to the mission which the Lord has entrusted to the church.

2. The Varieties of Encounter

The Study Program

2.1.   Since 1971, the Department of Studies of the Lutheran World Federation has been engaged in a study program on the subject of "The Encounter of the Church with Marxism in Various Cultural Contexts." The overall program included as a major element a study on "The Implications of the New China for the Christian Mission in the World."

2.5.   In September, 1975, a planning seminar was held at Bossey near Geneva, and in July, 1976, a major international consultation took place at Glion near Montreux, Switzerland.

2.6.   The papers prepared for Bossey, originally published separately, are now included, together with the papers and group reports from Glion, in a book called "The Encounter of the Church with Movements of Social Change in Various Cultural Contexts" (available from the Department of Studies, Lutheran World Federation, Geneva).

2.7.   The amount of material and the complexity of issues made it impossible for the Glion consultation to finish its task, especially in the area of theological reflection. A follow-up meeting was therefore scheduled for April, 1977, in Aarhus, Denmark. Most of the eleven participants from nine countries had participated in both the Bossey and Glion meetings, and all of them had followed the entire program closely. Their task was to give systematic order to the analysis of the variety of encounters, to point out the theological and other criteria that may help guide the churches in their encounter, and to reach a clearer formulation of the many recommendations made at Glion.

2.8.   This paper is the product of that meeting.

Limitations in Evaluating the Encounters

2.9.   *The empirical evidence is so varied and complex that no clearcut judgment on the encounter of the church with the one Marxism is possible.* In fact, we have considered many different kinds of churches and Marxisms, including non-Marxist socialisms (e.g., in Tanzania) and situations where no open encounter of any kind is possible at this historical moment (e.g., in Indonesia and South Africa), but where nevertheless the issues Marxism raises for the church are present as they are elsewhere.

2.10.   There are Christians who reject Marxism in all of its aspects (cf. the studies from the USA and the Federal Republic of Germany). Others hold that a Christian who takes the political implications of the Gospel seriously must necessarily become a socialist, even a Marxist socialist (cf. studies on Latin America and Western Europe). There are Marxists who have come to appreciate religion as part of their people's cultural tradition (cf. study from Hungary). Others continue to attack religion as a reactionary political force (cf. studies on China and the German Democratic Republic).

2.11.   What is said here about the church and Marxism is by analogy true for Christian and Marxist groups that may be in conflict with their institutional church or party. There are borderline cases where in the course of the encounter both Christians and Marxists may acquire a mixed identity (as has happened in Latin America or Latin Europe). And there are still other situations where both Christians and Marxists seem to become increasingly marginal in relation to the social change that other groups in society are trying to bring about (as in India recently).

2.12.   The encounters described included situations in Latin America (Chile and Mexico), in Africa (Tanzania and South Africa), in Asia (China, India and Indonesia), in Eastern Europe (GDR and Hungary), in Western Europe (FRG, Finland, Italy), and in the USA. Encounter situations in Argentina, Brazil, Uruguay, Ethiopia, France, and Norway were also discussed.

2.13.   Although this range of samples was quite broad, it was still limited. Important situations were dealt with insufficiently or not at all, such as those in Latin Europe where the Catholic Church is by far the largest or those parts of Eastern Europe where the Orthodox churches are predominant. The majority of case studies came from areas where Lutheran churches, often rather small minorities, are present, but were mostly written from a wider point of view.

2.14.   Despite such limitations, a sufficiently wide range of experience was discussed to allow us to obtain a certain overview and draw some conclusions. In any discussion of Christianity and Marxism it must be kept in mind that the two are not strictly comparable, because they are not in the same category of social entities. To overlook this fact confuses the discussion.

Variables in the Encounter

2.15.   *The shape of Christian-Marxist encounter is determined by a number of factors* which vary from situation to situation. These variables can be classified under the following headings: the context of the encounter, the particular situations of the Christianity and of the Marxism involved in it, and the level at which the encounters take place.

2.16.   Context:

          - The *geo-political context* comprises, for example, the relative political and economic dependence in regard to a superpower, and the degree of development, dependence, interdependence, or self-reliance relative to other societies;

- the *cultural context* is determined by religious, ethnic, linguistic, and other factors;

- the *national context* varies greatly according to such factors as the relative presence or absence of pluralistic patterns, the degree of a general scientific and technological tradition, and historical experiences (war, peace, revolution, colonization, civil war, rapid social change, etc.);

- the *local context* may, among other things, be urban, highly industrialized, rural, homogeneous, highly differentiated, etc.;

- the *class structure* may be extremely polarized or show a differentiated stratification with many intermediate steps between the extremes of lower lower and upper upper class;

- the *situation with regard to revolution* may range from non-revolutionary and counter-revolutionary to pre-revolutionary, revolutionary, and post-revolutionary (without necessarily implying any progressive or chronological sequence among these).

2.17.   Situation of Christianity:

- The *types of Christianity* can be differentiated in various ways, and we must therefore take many different kinds of churches into consideration; e.g., majority and minority folk (ethnic) churches, transplanted churches, denominations, mission churches, individual congregations, small groups of Christians within all of these, and even intellectual currents in non-Christian groups originating in the Christian tradition.

- In all of these cases, the *degree of dependence* of the church or Christian group in question is decisive, whether on state institutions or on other overseas churches. The ecumenical relationship among churches is also a factor.

2.18.   Situation of Marxism:

- The *types of Marxism* can be differentiated according to their orientation to a particular center of policy, power, and authority, such as Moscow or Peking, with varying degrees of dependence. There are varieties of independent, indigenous, Marxist or Marxist-influenced socialisms merged with other movements for social change such as nationalism, populism, and indigenous communalism. Some kinds of socialism are decisively non-Marxist, but nevertheless take up many Marxist elements in terms of analysis and policy. And, finally, all over the world elements of Marxist thought are adopted, consciously or unconsciously, by many intellectuals, politicians, etc.

- In terms of *power status,* Marxism may be in power, in opposition (either emerging or marginal), or underground.

(a)   Concerning Marxism in power, one may distinguish among the Soviet Union and China which are in one category of independence, the Eastern European people's democracies, and the socialist societies in developing countries.

(b)   As am emerging force, Marxist parties may be in coalition governments (e.g., Allende's Chile, Finland, Iceland), may be in working agreement with non-Marxist government (e.g., Sweden, Italy), may be in permanent opposition (e.g., France), or may be coopted by authoritarian governments which pursue or claim to pursue socialist policies (e.g., Peru, India). Marxist groups may also be extremely marginal (e.g., FRG, USA) and split up into numerous mutually-antagonistic groups.

(c)   It is difficult to assess the strength of underground Marxism. Where there is a sudden change from pre-revolutionary to revolutionary situations (as in Ethiopia) or from revolutionary to counter-revolutionary situations (as in Chile), the relative power and influence of the Marxist groups can change very rapidly.

2.19.   Levels of Encounter: The encounters take place at the *levels of institution, practice, and theory.* The encounter is most obvious in its institutional form. The institutions engage in a certain type of practice; their theories interpret, legitimate, and at times direct their actual practice.

- at the *level of institution,* we need to distinguish between the institution's center and the periphery, between the top and the grass roots, between formal and informal institutional relationships.

- at the *level of practice,* we need to differentiate between short-term tactics and long-term strategies.

- at the *level of theory,* we need to analyze the differences between the content of theoretical formulations and their social function. If theoretical statements are used, consciously or unconsciously, to cover up and further a group's interest, their function becomes ideological in the negative sense.

2.20.   The encounter may take place at all three levels simultaneously, or at only one or two, and not necessarily consistently. For instance, there may be positive encounters among small groups at the level of practice, while there is an impasse at the level of relations between institutions. Similarly, practical cooperation may coexist with ideological non-cooperation. Intellectual dialogue may take place while opposition prevails in practice and between institutions.

2.21.   The paramount variable in the encounter appears to be the power relationship.

3. Theological Bases and Criteria for the Encounter

3.1.   In his treatise on "The Freedom of a Christian" (1520), Luther insisted that service of the neighbor in his or her needs was the primary norm for Christian living in all spheres of life. In the same year, Luther (in his "Sermon on Usury") rejected the monopoly capitalism of his time and, in accordance with criteria based on Christian faith and reason, he called on the political institutions (emperor, kings, princes, lords, and diets) to exercise public control of capital.

3.2.   In spite of the obvious historical differences between Luther's time and ours, is not Luther's condemnation of the capitalist practices of his time equally relevant today? Does this mean that basically we are to support socialist systems and reject capitalist ones? If, on the other hand, we deny the validity of Luther's argument for us, what are our reasons? What are our criteria of evaluation?

Theological Bases

3.3.   *The proprium of the Church is Jesus Christ.* In his life, death, and resurrection he has overcome sin, death, and the powers of evil. He has thus reconciled us with God, who calls us out of the world and at the same time sends us into the world to participate in the struggle against the powers of evil that keep people in false dependencies; Jesus Christ liberates us from idolatry, meaninglessness, and injustice.

3.4.   *The theological bases for developing criteria for the church's encounter with political and economic systems must therefore be rooted in our understanding of the struggle of God for the good of creation and its salvation and welfare against the powers of evil.* The way both Christians and the church and political and economic institutions participate in this struggle is called, in traditional (Lutheran) theological terms, the problematic of the "two kingdoms" or "two regiments," i.e., of the two ways God governs the world.

3.5.   The decisive point of departure of the biblical message is that God is establishing sovereignty over the power of evil, against the sin which destroys creation. Human beings have received limited power from God which they can use for mutual destruction or for mutual welfare in cooperation with God's love. That is why Jesus summarizes the divine law in the unity of love of God and love of neighbor (Mt. 22:37–39).

3.6.   *The "spiritual regiment" of God through the Spirit of God itself liberates people from false gods.* They receive forgiveness and are enabled to begin anew. All of life is renewed through the Holy Spirit (metanoia).

3.7.   Wherever people are forced into open or hidden idolatry, Christians and the church have to resist and, if necessary, accept suffering for their faith. In extreme cases such idolatry may force people to deny God and profess atheism. This can happen wherever Marxism makes a claim on all of human life and exerts total power institutionally, practically, and ideologically.

3.8.   In other cases such idolatry may be more difficult to detect. For instance, most Christians and churches fail to recognize the veiled idolatry inherent in capitalism which expresses itself in the expansion of private property and profit at the cost of all other considerations and brings with it destructive effects on nature and the quality of life (exploitation of people at the power peripheries, waste of natural resources, and disregard of ecological needs).

3.9.   The preaching of the Law and Gospel must therefore be directed not only to the individual. In order to set the Gospel free, Luther attacked the social structures of his day that had in fact become corporate idolatries, beginning with the institutional church itself (see "The Babylonian Captivity of the Church," 1520). Today we must continue to strive, for the sake also of the individual, to uncover and attack corporate idolatries, the conscious and unconscious dependencies of people, groups, and classes.

3.10.   It is the Holy Spirit which enables the church to renounce its idolatries, to repent and renew itself, and to judge individual and corporate spirits and exorcise the demons among them.

3.11.   *The "worldly regiment" of God makes people cooperate with God for the good of creation, whether or not they accept the Gospel of Jesus Christ.* All human institutions and all persons are called to shape human life and God enables them to do this. In principle, God's law, God's will for the good of the whole creation, is written into the hearts of all human beings (Rom. 2). And in principle, human reason, in its consideration of the long-term effects of action for others, has the same perspective for the good of all which love for the neighbor implies. However, in actual human life both reason and love are always jeopardized by the power of sin and by individual and corporate self-centeredness and self-aggrandizement at the cost of others.

3.12.   Since the power of sin permeates and perverts both Christian and non-Christian thought and action equally, Christians and the church have as such no guaranteed insight or prescriptions for what is best for people. Therefore primary and direct responsibility for shaping human life must rest with the economic and socio-political institutions where Christians and non-Christians live and work together. The church itself must not assume the executive power to carry out this responsibility; rather it must call upon these institutions and their leaders to meet theirs.

3.13.   The church and the Christian need to and normally can express their political responsibility in cooperation with other partners in society. They can therefore work together critically in any political and economic programs whose approach does not produce negative consequences for people. This holds true, even if a state or social order is avowedly atheist (as are some Marxist governments), or if a scientific, technological, and industrial system operates "as if God did not exist" (as is the case in all "modern" societies).

3.14.   *Signs of a church faithful to the mandate of its proprium, the Gospel of Jesus Christ, therefore are: public proclamation of the Word, celebration of Holy Communion, and suffering the "cross of Christ" by embodying love of God (against idolatry) and love of neighbor (against injustice).* This implies that the church must suffer violence itself and minimize violence for others; therefore,

- as the *community of those who follow Jesus,* the church is called to see beyond its own interests and the political and economic interests of its own class, race, nation, or culture;

- as the *people of God,* the church is called to reject all false claims to authority and domination (whether these are expressed by nationalism, Marxism, capitalism, or imperialism);

- as a *"community liberated to be human,"* the church is mandated to establish signs of a new, reconciled community through its order, structure, and life.

Criteria for an Intermediate Political Ethics

3.15.   *In order to be able to know where and how to engage itself, the church needs to make use of all available intellectual, scientific, and empirical resources.* It cannot simply deduce its practical-political decisions from motivations of faith or from such general Christian or human values as love, reconciliation, freedom, justice, equality, brotherhood, or security. As general concepts these values can be interpreted in many, sometimes contradictory, ways. They are to be translated into action through the mediation of the social sciences and historical and political analyses which reveal the dynamics of institution, practice, and theory in the churches, the various expressions of Marxism and in the Christian-Marxist encounter. In this way the disagreements between Christians about the particular ways of practicing love, reconciliation, etc., can be more easily understood and evaluated.

3.16.   The encounter of the church with Marxism is always a particular encounter in a specific place and time. To evaluate this encounter, we therefore need to find out what type of institutional organization is combined with what hierarchy of values or set of goals by each particular form of Marxism; and we need to know what concrete political measures are taken to achieve such goals. What are the priorities of goals and methods of action, what organizational instruments are used, and what are the anticipated and unanticipated consequences for people?

3.17.   Very often, and this is also the case in the Marxism and China Study, general values and overall political goals are directly linked with observations about very specific pragmatic political actions. It is, however, extremely hazardous to claim that a specific action will lead to the realization of a general goal such as ''justice,'' unless we make use of intermediate political ethics which would allow us to compare alternative options and to answer the basic question, *what order of social priorities should be put into practice by what institutional arrangement, and what possibilities of action exist*—taking into account particular situations, cultural contexts, socio-political circumstances, and levels of economic development—*for reaching a maximum improvement without paying too high a price in social and human costs?*

3.18.   For such an evaluation the following *areas of goal and policy priorities* are important (not necessarily in the order given): distributive justice, control of power, limitation of force and violence, efficiency of production, participation in vital political options, people's self-determination, respect for human rights, and non-discrimination against individuals and groups.

3.19.   Depending on the particular historical context, each priority area may be seen more as a means, and in other cases more as an end; the priorities obviously include both goals and methods and imply certain institutional arrangements for their realization. The balance among them will again depend on the special characteristics of each historical situation. In practice, Christians (and others) will often disagree which combination of policies is the best.

Critiria for the Church's Institutional Integrity

3.20.   The *proprium* of the Church, the Gospel of Jesus Christ, can express itself only through the existing structures of life, in interaction with cultural, social, and economic factors. In the past, the church has often failed to embody this *proprium,* and the credibility of the church has been damaged, especially by its assimilation into the dominating classes. Must the church therefore participate in the struggle of the oppressed classes—and, if so, how is this to be done?

3.21. At the very least, the church is called to engagement in society, i.e., to conscious encounter with movements of social change and to critical differentiation in these encounters. Neither assimilation in order to gain institutional security nor estrangement in order to keep institutional purity will correspond to its mandate. Conflict with its society through engagement for it will lead into suffering (theologically speaking, "the cross"), which is a mark of the church.

3.22. If the church is to develop an intermediate political ethics with politico-ethical criteria permitting decisions about priorities for action, it must first of all develop similar criteria for its own life. Too often there have been both a lack of sober analysis and an absence of self-criticism. The church has sometimes tended to use two types of analysis. It has used very idealistic concepts when describing its own teachings, goals, and institutions. It has used quite a different method when speaking of Marxism; here it has stressed empirically-observable negative facts and short-comings. The use of politico-ethical criteria in determining the church's constructive critical engagement on behalf of the whole of society, including its encounter with Marxism, will therefore only be effective and credible if they are based on the church's own institutional integrity.

3.23. *At the level of institution, the theological criteria* for critical engagement in the encounter should *include shared exercise of power and decision-making*.

3.24. The institutional integrity of the church as an institution of repentance and renewal depends first and foremost on the work and presence of the Holy Spirit in the community of believers, which enables the members to be the body of Christ engaged in a common task and life (1 Cor. 12). This community of life includes participatory sharing in power and in the making of decisions under the perspective of the common good "in Christ."

3.25. Does the leadership of the church itself allow critical involvement in its exercise of power and decision-making? Does it allow a variety of views to engage in non-repressive debate—or does it repress, marginalize, or exclude views and people that challenge the established powers? Only if the church has participatory exercise of power and decision-making will it have the internal and external authority to engage in critical involvement with Marxism. It will then create a publicly visible example which will set a criterion for the whole of society. It will witness in its life to the reality of "the universal priesthood of the baptized" it professes.

3.26.   *At the level of practice, the theological criteria* for engagement in the encounter should *include solidarity with the oppressed.*

3.27.   The members of the body of Christ are to practice self-giving in order to strengthen and honor the weaker parts of the community. This means that for the sake of the common good they must be partisans of the weakest, those who have no chance and are voiceless. There can be no engagement for the whole, no true reconciliation of opposing interests, unless there is a primary concern for redressing the injustices done to the persecuted, the disinherited, and the poor. Love is the supreme criterion (Rom. 13:10 and 1 Cor. 13). Otherwise the traditional theological-ethical criterion of the "common good" will always be misused by the most powerful.

3.28.   The consequences of solidarity with the oppressed will depend on whether or not Marxism is in power. Without involvement there is no way in which solidarity can be expressed, and without critical evaluation an expression of solidarity may easily degenerate into tolerating new oppression. Conformity with those in power runs the danger of overlooking the oppressed which the Marxist system produces, while opposition to Marxism tends to forget the oppressed who were produced by the old system. Solidarity with the oppressed means taking part in the struggle of classes, races and groups, regardless of who are the oppressed and who the oppressors. Such partisanship will always lead into all kinds of ambiguities and into suffering.

3.29.   *At the level of theory, the theological criteria* for the church's critical involvement in the encounter should *include ideological self-criticism,* a critical distance from one's own situation and self-interest.

3.30.   Solidarity with the oppressed implies that the church reject its identification with the ruling political and economic powers. The danger of such identification with anti-Marxist political forces is common because they are often able to use Christianity as an integral part of their anticommunist ideology. Identification is less likely with Marxist forces because it has been stereotyped as nothing but an atheist attack on religion. Wherever this type of simplification and demonization of Marxism—sometimes of all socialism—occurs, there is a false dependency on anti-Marxist political systems which becomes idolatry through the identification of these systems with Christianity (the "Christian West").

3.31.   Only the acceptance of justification by faith through grace (Rom. 3) can liberate us from the need to justify ourselves by "Christian" political action against "anti-Christian" groups. On the other hand, it is faith in God's justifying grace that alone can relieve Christians in Marxist societies of a temptation to continuous self-flagellation for past errors and the abdication of a critical position vis-à-vis the new regime.

3.32.   The above criteria may help orient the church in the encounter in two ways:

- *internally,* the church that lives up to these criteria in its life as the community of believers has a paradigmatic, sometimes even a representative, function for society;

- *externally,* the church that lives up to these criteria in its life for others as a public institution has an anticipatory and advocacy function for society.

4. Types of Encounter

4.1.   In the encounter of the churches with various forms of Marxism and socialism, the variety of encounter types is at first glance overwhelming. It is difficult to use a general typology for all encounters. However, it seems possible to summarize them under *four main types,* which are descriptive, but also have normative, prescriptive overtones: withdrawal, opposition, conformity, critical involvement.

4.2.   Whether *assimilation, estrangement, or engagement* of the church in society emerges in the encounter will largely depend on the specific variables described above and on how they interact in each particular case. It will depend especially on whether Marxism is in power, in opposition (emerging or marginal), or underground.

Withdrawal

4.3.   Withdrawal from Marxism happens when the church takes an avowedly apolitical stance and favors an individualistic piety, rejecting any institutional involvement and discouraging any personal engagement in politics.

4.4.   When Marxism is in power, this essentially sectarian position leads to estrangement from society. It is not acceptable to the historic traditions (see studies on Hungary, GDR, Ethiopia, and the case of non-Marxist socialism, Tanzania[1]), although there are groups within the churches which tend to withdraw.

4.5.   Where Marxism is not in power, the church's withdrawal from encounter is often justified as a position of neutrality vis-à-vis all political forces

---

[1]This and similar references refer to materials in the volume "The Encounter of the Church with Movements of Social Change in Various Cultural Contexts" (See 2.6.).

(e.g., in Finland or FRG). Participants in the Marxism study interpreted this as a far-reaching assimilation to capitalist society.

Opposition

4.6.   Opposition to Marxism usually takes the form of anti-communism. It can originate in sharp disagreements on economic, political, religious, or philosophical questions and usually ends in a general antagonism against all Marxist and often also non-Marxist socialist movements and ideas.

4.7.   In situations where Marxism is not in power, even if publicly present as an opposition, to be anti-communist generally means to be assimilated to the dominant forces of society and culture (e.g., FRG, USA, Finland, Mexico). In some situations, anti-communism seems to be nothing but the defense of the status quo (providing the enemy image needed for social cohesion, as in the case of South Africa).

4.8.   However, there are situations (as the case of Indonesia) where the communist attempts to take over power and the geopolitical threat this presents make it impossible for the churches not to be outwardly anti-communist, although there seems to be some interest in a more differentiated response.

4.9.   There are more differentiating forms of opposition, such as "anti-Sovietism," "critical-intellectual approaches" willing to engage in dialog, or preferences for non-Marxist socialisms or indigenous radical movements competing with Marxism.

Conformity

4.10.   Sympathy with Marxism and unreflected partnership is the natural consequence where the lower classes, castes, or races have no other political force on their side (as in India, Ethiopia, South Africa). Here the church remains assimilated to a particular class culture but is estranged from the dominant strata of society, as long as Marxism is not in power.

4.11.   Conformity is especially widespread when Marxist governments are in power. In the case of Marxist types of socialism, the churches may adopt an attitude of ideological non-coexistence and practical cooperation (e.g., in Hungary). In the case of non-Marxist types of socialism, conformity can lead to virtual ideological and practical identification (e.g., Tanzania). In both cases close assimilation to society takes place.

4.12.   Where Marxism is emerging as opposition, there are cases of "Marxist Christians" or "Christian Marxists" who accept the Marxist analysis or who "convert" to a Marxist "religiosity" (e.g., in Latin America and Latin Europe, but also in other parts of the West).

4.13.   Where churches had previously conformed to anti-Marxist systems, they have also tended to conform to Marxist governments where these have taken over. Their lack of critical involvement under systems which produced injustice (capitalism, feudalism, etc.) may have undermined their credibility and destroyed their ability to involve themselves critically under a new system.

Critical Involvement

4.14.   Critical involvement first of all takes the form of open dialog, without which there can be no genuine cooperation. It evolves into reflective partnership when Christians and Marxists join to achieve a common goal while recognizing the differences in their worldviews (e.g., Italy, France, Norway).

4.15.   Where Marxists are in power, critical involvement is discouraged by the party and may therefore lead to estrangement. It exists, however, in most situations where Marxism is not in power, and especially where Marxism is marginal. Reflective partnership becomes more apparent where Marxism is emerging as a power with some political weight. Critical involvement may then represent acceptance of political changes in society, though it may also imply engagement.

4.16.   ''Christians for Socialism'' in Western Europe and Latin America is the strongest, but also the most ambiguous, form of critical involvement possible. It can become either identification with or opposition to a specific type of Marxism. Especially where Marxists are in power, they discourage a Christian viewpoint on socialism and prefer the response of conformity. In such situations theological terms such as ''church for others'' denoting ''critical solidarity'' with the building of socialism may describe a similar tendency. (e.g., in the GDR).

4.17.   One special case is that of Chile after Marxists, socialists, and other political groups were driven underground. There significant parts of the church showed solidarity with the persecuted who happened to be Marxists and with whose political views they did not identify. This led to estrangement from those in power, but must be seen as engagement for the society at large.

4.18.   The indirect and unilateral encounter of the churches outside China with the People's Republic of China is an attempt at critical involvement with this form of Marxist challenge, and also with the churches' own tradition and mission history.

4.19.   Contributors to the Marxism Study tended to favor critical involvements both in situations where Marxism is in power and where it is not. Its central criterion must be solidarity, the existence for others. It must mean transcending the "socio-centric thinking" that identifies with the point of view of one's own group, class, or church institution. It thus corresponds most closely to the theological criteria outlined above under Part 3.

5. Critical Issues

5.1.   *In the encounter with Marxism the church cannot evade facing the discrepancy between its theological self-understanding and its institutional interest.* The churches, and Lutherans among them, like to think that their position on all important issues, including the encounter with Marxism, is determined by their theological self-understanding and confessional stance. However, in the analysis of encounters in the Marxism Study it becomes clear that the churches' institutional hierarchy tends to oppose Marxism when the latter is not in power and tends to conformity when it is, although there are some significant exceptions to this rule.

5.2.   Thus, whether willingly or unwillingly, the church performs the function of providing or strengthening the prevailing political or civil religion. This may be the reason why the churches in non-Marxist societies display an extraordinary unwillingness and even fear of recognizing the reality of class conflicts. They realize that such recognition would imply the need for partisanship in a class struggle against the powerful. This denial of class divisions may be the greatest obstacle for a fruitful encounter with Marxism.

5.3.   The more the emotional "fear of communism" and the concomitant demonization of Marxism are used as an antidote to social change before Marxism is in power, the less is critical involvement possible afterwards. Rather, the overemphasis on institutional interests will most probably lead to a new conformity. Therefore under Marxist governments, too, the churches are inclined to defend the newly established order as being the only legitimate one; here, too, they often deny the existence of class conflicts and the class character, though significantly changed, of the new society.

5.4.   *We therefore need to raise the following critical issues:*

- Called by the Word of God to be an eschatological sign of the new earth and thus by its very vocation and identity an agent of social change, the church needs to reconsider those of its theological statements which can be used to legitimize the existing social order.

- Knowing that it is supposed to be "in the world" but "not of the world," how can the church provide an alternative culture and at the same time adapt itself creatively to each particular context for the sake of its message?

- In checking and judging its institutional interests by its faith affirmations, the church needs to use the available instruments of social science, being willing to listen to the criticisms coming from Marxism or Marxist-inspired ideology criticism.

- How can we, through the theological criteria that shape our faith, help each other understand and eventually overcome the differences in our political and value judgments that are due to our different positions in the encounters?

- While acknowledging that ideologies such as Marxism are in part needed for setting social goals, raising awareness, and activating people to change, the church must reject the all-embracing claims of such ideologies. It must judge whether they still have their revolutionary dimension or have become status quo ideologies opposing social change. In the latter case the church needs to call them back to their own task of advocacy for the oppressed.

5.5.   *The catholicity of the church as well as the dimensions of current problems demand a global insight and concerted action of each local Christian community on those problems that affect the whole earth.* The domination of southern developing countries by northern developed powers in some way affects every local Christian community. Power is concentrated in the capitalist and socialist superpowers (and under their aegis in a few states of the northern developed areas). Within the capitalist system the transnational corporations (now increasingly active in socialist areas) have become independent and largely uncontrolled political factors; they represent the highest privatization of power. Although the countries situated on the power periphery are especially dependent on capitalist powers, the industrialized countries in the so-called "socialist camp" also raise objections to the establishment of a new international economic order as soon as their own interests seem touched.

5.6.   *We therefore need to raise the following critical issues:*

- How can the churches, together with other concerned and responsible groups, work toward the achievement of socio-political systems which would allow everyone to share equally in both natural resources and social freedoms?

- How can the churches in their task of advocacy strengthen the independence and self-reliance of the countries at the power periphery whose natural resources and cheap labor are being exploited by the transnational corporations of the rich industrialized countries and by parallel structures of the socialist powers?

- How can the call for a new international economic order raise consciousness and provoke appropriate action in each local Christian community, whether in capitalist or socialist, dominant or dominated, areas of the world?

5.7.   *The world views of both liberal capitalism and Marxism see human freedom as the final goal. The church claims to hold the key to full human liberation.* Both capitalism and Marxism claim that human freedom is possible when the basic economic needs of people are satisfied. While this is certainly a fundamental presupposition, freedom (understood as the possibility for loving, creative, participatory and mutual human relationships) is at present endangered by the excessive concentration of power—political, economic, and cultural—which characterizes both capitalist and Marxist societies. This concentration of power brings with it imposed consumption patterns, bureaucratic pressures toward formalization and centralization, and technological complexity and control, and does not in fact liberate people to community.

5.8.   Once basic needs are satisfied, people will ask for more participation in the important decisions affecting their lives, and the demand for human rights and freedom will become intensified. The liberation from sin, death, and the powers of evil which happens in Jesus Christ also implies consequences for human liberation from natural constraints and historical oppressions. It is, therefore, an integral part of the church's central message and existence to defend all human rights.

5.9.   *We therefore need to raise the following critical issues:*

- What kind of religious freedom, i.e., what safeguards for its internal autonomy and for its public existence as an intermediate institution in society does the church need for the public proclamation of the liberation through Jesus Christ and its existence as "church for others"? To be sure, the church must not stress religious freedom simply because of its own institutional interests. But a defense of its own rights may directly or indirectly help secure the human rights of other groups in society, too.

- In order to protect and further human freedom and limit the power of the powerful in both capitalist and Marxist societies, there seems to be need for two complementary efforts:

   a) decentralize power through the strengthening and furthering of intermediate institutions within each society, therefore creating more freedom of movement for individuals and small groups;

   b) centralize power at the international level in order to control new particularistic powers that further their own interest at the expense of others and prevent an equitable distribution and use of resources.

5.10. *Structural changes in the world will challenge both the church and Marxism and lead to new forms of encounter at the institutional, practical, and theoretical levels in the near future.* The worldwide energy and food crises and the continuing impoverishment of two thirds of the people of this world increase the potential of control and oppression which the industrialized socialist and capitalist nations of the northern regions of the globe have at their disposal.

5.11.   However, there is growing awareness of the ecological interrelatedness of all living things, of the limitation of natural resources, and of the need for a balanced relationship between humankind and nature as a condition for survival. This poses an increasing challenge to both capitalist and Marxist technological production-oriented systems.

5.12.   The question of atheism will acquire new urgency in the face of the all-encompassing threats to human survival. The practical atheism in all of us, which causes us to live "as if God did not exist" and manipulate creation for our own short-sighted goals, needs to be taken as seriously as the attacks of theoretical atheism on the Christian faith. This latter can only be countered convincingly through a witness that belies the alleged, and often only too real, link between faith in God and politically reactionary positions.

5.13.   *We therefore need to raise the following critical issues:*

- In view of the obvious limits of an evolutionary conception of technological and historical progress, new theological and ideological interpretations of how people relate to the created world will be necessary.

- It is conceivable that the overwhelming threats to human survival will lead to a corresponding increase of fear and irrationalism on all sides. It is equally conceivable that this situation may provide new opportunities for a Marxist-Christian encounter which could include such questions as theoretical and practical atheism and the ultimate meaning of human life and creation as well as questions of existentially experienced love, joy, suffering, and death.

- For the sake of human survival, it will be imperative for churches and Christians to find bases for cooperation with groups that profess atheism. It will, however, be necessary to examine the consequences of such atheist world views both for the style of political struggle (minimizing the use of violence in the struggle for justice), and the ideological tolerance of different partners (accepting in love also the person of another ideology). Ultimately, the question needs to be asked: Are both sides ready to undertake ideological self-criticism of their complicity in human self-glorification?

Appendix: Recommendations of the Glion Consultation

The recommendations of the Glion consultation make it clear that the participants desire their own churches and the LWF:

1. *to continue the program and style of studies of "the encounter of the church with Marxism in various cultural contexts";*

2. *to include in this program complementary studies of the encounter with capitalism, transnational corporations, and connected phenomena;*

3. *to expand this program of studies to include general questions of the church and the social order and of the churches' public responsibility, especially in relation to political, social, and economic power structures;*

4. *to engage in studies of the churches' adaptation to and witness in their socio-economic and cultural environment, including the questions of self-reliance, dependence, and interdependence of the churches in the rich and poor parts of the world;*

5. *to emphasize those areas of self-study and exchange between churches that up to now have not been sufficiently promoted or have seemed too difficult to undertake;* e.g.,

5.1.   That within the churches dialogue be encouraged among groups of various political and theological views, and

5.2.   That the LWF help to reduce the prevalent ignorance and prejudice (in non-Marxist countries) concerning the position of churches in socialist countries;

6. *to produce pedagogical study guides and materials in this area of concern, especially for the level of the congregation and the training of church workers;* e.g.,

6.1.   That the churches engage in a "pedagogy of the oppressor" program. (Note: "If middle and working class American Christians are in need of a 'pedagogy of the (relatively) oppressed' vis-à-vis the power of corporate business, and a government whose policies—taxation, defense, spending, etc.—favor the rich, all American Christians need a 'pedagogy of the oppressor' which sensitizes them to their complicity in global structures of injustice" [Regional Group: USA]);

7. *to provide for structures of action and studies that allow for advocacy in matters of public responsibility;* and

8. *to help develop more adequate theological positions, worship, and general liturgical forms and church structures for the witness of the church in this area.*

SOCIO-POLITICAL THESES FOR THE
CHRISTIAN-MARXIST DIALOGUE

Udo Bermbach

I. The Current State of the Dialogue

The current development of the socio-political systems, especially in the southern and southwestern European countries, is characterized by the fact—among others—that the traditional socio-political structures largely can no longer cope with the social problems and their required solutions. The contradictions are becoming ever greater between the religious, theoretical, but also concrete social and economic traditions and the emerging tendencies. At the same time it is obvious that a reorientation of politics in the broadest sense cannot consist in the radical elimination of such traditions, that is, in a revolutionary break, but neither can it go on in an unbroken continuity.

The present global political situation which has found meaningful expression in the signing of the Helsinki Agreements permits and forces political and social corrections only within a framework which relates on the one hand to the basic principles of existing structures, but on the other hand has to be investigated as to the degree to which acceptance and reworking of basic changes is permissible. Especially for countries like Italy, France, and Spain, and even many countries of the Third and Fourth World (though under different aspects and circumstances), the problem is posed as to how much Catholic tradition and Catholic consciousness can be combined with political solutions, which in turn are related to the traditions of socialism in the broadest sense. This problem exists on two levels—first, in the theoretical discussion, that is in the area of anthropology (in the European usage of the word) and philosophy, and secondly, on the level of practical politics under the aspect of the convergent possibilities of mutual recognition of political systems and organizational structures, which can guarantee for the historical European political culture a continuing existence and further development, along with the varying expressions of the nation states.

In this connection two facts are of special importance: first, the Second Vatican Council with all its consequences for the self-understanding and the political praxis of the Catholic Church, and, second, the development of a West European socialism-communism [Eurocommunism—translator's note] which, since the events of 1968, feels stronger than ever before in a concrete relationship to the individual national development problems of European states, and which

Udo Bermbach (Roman Catholic) is professor of political science at Hamburg University, Seminar für sozial-wissenschaften. From 1975 to 1977, he was the president of the German Political Science Association, of which he is currently the vice president. The fields of the theory of direct democracy, pluralism, party politics, and civic initiative groups are covered in his recent publications. This article was prepared as the main discussion paper for the European Congress of the Paulus-Gesellschaft in September, 1977.

interprets its Marxist foundation and orientation as a general, even though still binding, theoretical matrix for action. It does not dictate a structure of organization binding for all times, but suggests rather basic principles for possible political organization, which are quite open to national traditions.

In the following an attempt will be made, albeit sketchily, to outline where, on the basis of the above-mentioned facts, points of contact between two positions can emerge. This could be of importance in various ways for further historical developments, especially in the West European states. Prior to this, however, I will report very briefly the results relating to the basic issues which have emerged in past contacts between Christians and Marxists sponsored by the Paulus-Gesellschaft. They, as well, form the basis for a new beginning of the dialogue for both partners.

1. As a result of the dialogue up to now, it is perhaps basic for the dialogue between Marxists and Christians that both—in contrast to scientific-relativistic value systems—insist on an emphatic "concept of truth." They strive for human truth and true humanity (Metz, 1968). In the course of the discussion, or in situations of concrete dialogue, Christians and Marxists tend typically to be on one side facing on the other side the natural scientists and increasingly society itself, which is becoming ever more scientifically oriented. Since the Second Vatican Council, it is clear for Christians that God's revelation in Christ does not release them from the difficult search for human truth and true humanity, that both must be realized in the given social situation in which the individual exists and has to act. But this means that the truth, in a most inclusive sense, develops historically as well. In the last analysis, only human praxis can decide what true humanness demands. The faith that God is involved in this process of search after historical truth does not release the Christian from basic uncertainty in dealing with concrete socio-political plans for action. Karl Rahner dealt with this issue at one of the first congresses of the Paulus-Gesellschaft (1965) by suggesting that:

> The Christian faith knows a unity between spirit and matter from their origin, since he professes that this origin is one and the same, namely the infinite and absolute and the reality of the one whom we call God... spirit and matter have a unity in their history... Accordingly, the climax of the History of Salvation *(Heilsgeschichte)* is not the de-secularisation of man as spirit, as a way to reach God, but the descending and irreversible secularity of God, the coming of the Divine Logos into the flesh (incarnation), the acceptance of the material, so that it remains God's reality in which God, through his Logos, reveals himself to us forever, really and truly.

This recognition of the historical process, and its structural openness, is certainly an aspect of convergence. For the Marxist truth is also realized in the movement of human history (even though in a more exclusive sense), which has to determine and fulfill human life. Of course, the danger is that Marxists absolutize this historical process. That they find in this process the meaning of life itself has repeatedly become obvious in the dialogue. Marxists have pointed this out themselves and noted it as "theory deficit." For instance, Machoveč (1968) admitted that Marxism has "till today not solved the question of the meaning of human life, in spite of significant efforts." But this also makes it clear that the narrowing of human existence in society to a primarily economic-technocratic context of action cannot be a Marxist position. For the Marxists the historical process also remains fundamentally open. The concrete movement, the organizational development of human societies, including socialist ones, are in themselves not yet an answer to the question of truth (*Wahrheitsfrage*). Machoveč stated, "The solution cannot be to make a fetish of the idea of progress or of the god-like collective, nor a party mechanism, even if non-Marxists could believe this today. The solution will rather lie in a dialectically understood humanness." Both positions have the conviction in common that human beings are not yet what they could be (Rahner), but that these "not yet beings" (Bloch) perform their social positions. Under this aspect Rahner (1965) discovered "parallels in the structures" between Christianity and Marxism, without, however, covering up the differences. But just as Marxists did not want to be held solely to imminence (Congress, Munich, 1964), Christians did not want to be held solely to transcendence. And it is at this point that the dialogue has reached a first decisive narrowing of the gap between the positions.

2. As a basic result of the dialogue between Christians and Marxists up to now, it has been accepted by both sides that the principles of ethical values derived from the Christian faith do not have to be necessarily or exclusively connected with one particular social system—in this case the capitalist one. To the contrary, on the level of orientation toward practical actions, values such as love, justice, and solidarity are quite compatible with socialist values. The Marxist partners in the dialogue therefore have not rejected the historical, cultural, and especially the humane, achievements of Christianity, but supported them rather forcefully (especially at the Congress in Marienbad), and they have also emphasized that under this aspect Marxist atheism has to be made historically relative. It has to be interpreted basically in the context of the contemporaneous discussion and, therefore, does not have to be a necessary and inevitable element of Marxist social theory.

Milan Prucha has pointed out that Christianity and Marxism do not have a strict reciprocity since neither position is a complete universal system of interpretation. When on the one hand Rahner points out that the revelation does not offer a concrete, inner, worldly utopia, that there is no statement within Christianity which describes the socio-political human order once and for all, and when on the other hand Marxists have said repeatedly that the problem of transcendence is present within the Marxist frame of reference only as a problem at best and was largely underestimated, then it becomes clear why both sides can engage in a meaningful dialogue. This, of course, is true only when the Christian life derived from the spirit of revelation does not bind itself one-sidedly to a particular social system and, vice versa, when Marxist thinking leaves room for Christian motivation of individual orientation for action. The sentence of Machoveč (1968), "I would not be sorry at the demise of religion as such, but if I should live in a world which could forget totally the "Jesus event" I would not want to live at all," points out how much a socio-historic theory needs a structure which explains its meaning. If this is missing, the danger arises that images of organization (which can be explained historically)—for instance the role and structure of a party— become an ontological substitute, take on a life of their own, and lose their original instrumental character. If, on the other hand, these structures become one-sidedly absolutized, the danger arises that the practical life and the daily needs of people are only of secondary importance, and in a case of doubt they would be neglected. It is this "Dialectic" which forces Christianity to free itself from a close tie-in with one particular form of social structure and to remain open for differing social blueprints as long as they can be combined with basic Christian concepts. In this connection the following thoughts are of importance:

—The Marxist theory originated out of the critique of the bourgeois-capitalist social order, and is therefore primarily a critical theory. That means that it has developed as a scientific system, a definite scientific-theoretical and philosophical basic conception. Out of this arises a method of analytical procedure which, of course, is of such a quality that it includes the possibility of a structural transformation of the results of the analysis.

—Out of this it follows that neither Marx nor Engels has formulated a closed model of a future socialist economic and social order. Both were rather concerned with the historical systematic explanation of social developments and a resultant projection of certain tendencies, always subject, however, to historical confirmation or rejection.

—Differing ideas of organizational structures of society can rightly claim to be based on Marx and Engels, as long as they remain in the categorical frame of reference of Marxist theory. The problem of revisionism is resolved in large measure in the demand to find solutions to real problems in the concrete social situation, which are in accordance with the humanistic emancipated claim of Marxism, based on the theoretical basic positions of Marx and Engels.

—This humanist-emancipatory claim of Marxists' thinking (not only of the early Marx) remains embedded and indebted to the western Christian tradition and also to the ethos of liberty of early bourgeois society. The relationship to this position has only again become obvious after the experience of two world wars, not only because the more enlightened separation of these positions has shown the dangers for humankind which can arise out of the hypostasis of partial aspects of a total tradition. As far as Marxism understands itself as a "dissolution" (in Hegel's sense as preservation and further development) of the totality of European tradition, it should be possible to make room for, rather than merely tolerating, Christians who live in a socialist society.

—If the experience of misery (in an inclusive, especially also in an individual, psychological sense) has taught Christians that fundamental Christian attitudes can be realized only with great difficulty in differing social systems, then a one-sided identification with the capitalist economic and social system can be justified at best historically, but not in principle. For the dialogue with Marxists it must be possible for Christianity to say farewell to capitalism as an exclusive option and to open itself to organizational solutions which might possibly be more in harmony with the Sermon on the Mount. What specific forms these solutions might take remains open at this time.

3. One of the most important problems of the dialogue up to this point has been interpretation of Marx's formula of humanity as an ensemble of social relations. Especially here the dialogue has tended to make the Marxist position more precise. Schaff emphasized again and again that humans have "an individuality in the sense of uniqueness," "an unrepeatability," which is a self-contained "microcosm," not only the creation of society, but also its creator. Prucha speaks of the "eternal open dialogue between the individual existence and the social being of man," and concludes that human beings cannot "work a mutual reduction or transfer from one to the other." Under the impression especially of the early writings of Marx, the social determination of human life is at times given up (misunderstood as Marxist) in favor of the individual's activity, articulation of needs, and responsibility. To be sure, man and woman remain bound to social structures. They are, almost in the Aristotelian sense, *zoon politikon,* but they remain in this situation with all of their subjectivity and "inner being" (Schaff). Illies has formulated this in a similar way: "Christians know the very Christian and very heavy commandment of loving one's neighbor. This is nothing else but a command to form society." Schaefer (a natural scientist) agrees with this in certain respects: ". . . man does not relate to himself, but as an individual is in relationship with groups of people, whose structures emerged historically in a way about which we cannot say anything definitively" (1966).

With this singular emphasis on the uniqueness of individual existence an expanded interpretation of the understanding of freedom goes hand in hand. In bourgeois societies and by non-Marxist social scientists the social aspect of human existence is ever more strongly emphasized, and with it also the tie-in of freedom in social structures and restrictive stipulations. The reverse tendency is developing in Marxism. The individual is interpreted as a being determined toward freedom, as "creator of the basis and the superstructure as well as the intermediary in their mutual relationships" (Schaff). In relation to this it is stated clearly, that a positive anthropology which could offer a systematic development of a socialist understanding of freedom can, for various reasons, not be found in Marx. It is exactly this which has to be developed by Marxism in its current phase. The experiences which have been made in the meantime in socialist societies should be among the important guidelines. On the other hand, it has to be stated emphatically that Christians often are satisfied in pointing to an incomplete socialist concept of freedom—namely a collectivist-oriented society—without taking a concrete position at the point where the bourgeois concept of freedom has sunk to a mere pathetic claim because of the class structure of capitalist society. The connection between the individual possibility of freedom and class structure of society remains central for Marxists. Garaudy (1968) has expressed this as follows:

> Marxist humanism understands itself as an integration of two antithetical traditions—the Greco-Roman and the Judeo-Christian, in as much as it supersedes both. It is in full control of the two ends of the chain, the autonomy of man and the identification of freedom with creativity, freedom and necessity. Human beings, Marx wrote, take control of their own history but not arbitrarily: they make history on the basis of existing conditions. It would impoverish Marxism greatly if one were to reduce it only to the Greek tradition, to the Hegelian formulation accepted by Engels: freedom is insight into necessity . . . the class consciousness is the necessary condition for gaining freedom . . . The problem of freedom is therefore for Marx not only an individual problem, but also a historical and social problem—a class problem.

Some thoughts can be added which could be of importance for both sides for fruitful dialogue. In light of the concrete experience in socialist societies, how do the Marxists perceive the relationship of the socialist concept of freedom to the bourgeois understanding of freedom? Can we proceed from the assumption that individual development, formulation of individuals' needs, and the development of creative possibilities shall be limited through social restrictions only as much as absolutely necessary (and what would that be?), in order to do justice to the uniqueness of the life of the individual? Perhaps one could say that the synthesis of the Marxist and non-Marxist concept of freedom can be realized on the level of material freedoms if both acknowledge that freedom of the individual can only be realized when it is combined dialectically with equality and fraternity (i.e., solidarity). If freedom is not to lead to the destruction of its own requirements, it has to understand itself bound to the demand of the recognition of the other human being as partner with equal claims on a human life with dignity and the comradly concern for the long-range common interest. If equality is to characterize a relationship in which one meets the other as equal, then this has to be an equality which offers the possibility of real development and therefore real freedom, and which is based on the knowledge of a solidarity which binds all together. If solidarity is to be the acceptance of the priority of common interests over short-sighted self interests, it has to be based on the free acceptance of each other as fully recognized partners and has to be expressed in the freedom of all to secure the future of the whole. Such an understanding of freedom cannot only be related to the concrete material conditions of human realization. It has to include simultaneously the possibility of transcendence, namely to include also the freedom of faith, including a faith or an expression of faith which feels responsible to society.

II. Theses for Discussion in a New Dialogue

All theoretical and conceptual plans for society today must begin with the presumption that the material future of humankind will be secured only when the problems of "limited growth" are correctly understood and resolved. Whether society is capitalistic or socialistic, these problems result from the shortage of natural resources—virtually ignored in Marxist theory—and from the increase in total number of human beings, whose survival must be secured.

Concerning natural resources and their shortage, solution of a two-fold task is urgent. First of all, it must be clearly established that particular necessities of life are finite and nothing can be substituted for them. Even if the development of technology creates some further satisfaction of elementary needs, such a process is limited by the scarcity of natural resources. Secondly, the fact is that technical development in highly industrial western Europe and North America has already gone so far that the ecological bases of human existence are severely threatened.

These problems cannot be solved on a national level or on a level of neat division between capitalist and socialist systems. They are international by their very nature and consequence and, therefore, require international cooperation and unanimity if they are to be solved. Such a requirement is no longer an ethical imperative; it is the *conditio sine qua non* for the survival of an existence worthy of human beings.

The following inquiries which result from these factual considerations could be central to a new dialogue:

1. Rejecting Marx's expectation, today's Marxists can and must agree that the transformation of capitalism for which they are working cannot be justified by reference to the goal of increasing material wealth. It is true "that without assurance of greater prosperity for the masses, any philanthropy or humanism remains idle talk" (Jozsef Lukács, 1968). But equally significant is another consideration, that "biological-hedonistic individualism, making a fetish of wealth" (Jozsef Lukács) can no longer be accepted as a goal for the formation of society, if the human species is to survive.

2. However, development of productive capacity by means of science and technology does not by itself guarantee a society worthy of human beings. The developmental dynamics of the tension between the productive forces and the conditions of production do not suffice to steer independently the developmental process of society, either in an evolutionary fashion in highly industrialized countries, or in a revolutionary fashion in the third and fourth worlds. What is required is, instead, an international solidarity in which national and international problems can be accepted and overcome.

3. In order for such solidarity to become a reality, Christians too must come to see that the structures of western, capitalist, industrial societies oppose this solidarity in essential points and thus must change. An economic system that, despite many cases of governmental regulation, is primarily oriented toward profit-making is ill suited to the solution of the problems we are discussing.

Therefore, social changes must be undertaken which encourage not only ethical conviction but also ethical practice.

4. Marxists and Christians agree at one point. The problem of alienation so much discussed in Marxist theory and philosophy in recent years—and apparent in capitalist as well as in socialist systems—has shown that material satisfaction is a presupposition but not in itself a solution of this alienation. Thus it should be debated whether more equal distribution of wealth would alleviate alienation and how far the Christian faith can and should make a meaningful contribution to this end.

5. Just as critical as production and distribution of wealth is the related politics of population growth. At least since the explosive growth in population in the third world it has become clear that the best laid plans fail when the population increases faster than the production of necessary goods. Christians must openly recommend a politics of population that is economically and socially defensible. It needs to be added that limitation of population growth is not only—and perhaps not mainly—an economic problem. Social communications, solidarity among people, development of a humane society—all these are empty postulates, if they do not take place in an environment wherein human beings can realize their individual potentialities.

In view of the rapid growth of technically usable knowledge and the resultant problems which threaten humankind as the result of conflicting ideologies and value systems, one must conclude that no permanent model for societal organization is possible. In the degree to which novel problems arise, novel possibilities for their solution must be devised and tested. The very existence and further development of threatening problem areas is sufficient proof that previous models of political organization—of both socialist and capitalist varieties—possess no satisfactory capacity for problem-solving. While in capitalistic societies governmental means of social controls are weak—and private interests may therefore win out over public—in socialist states governmental bureaucrats are often so independent that they are no longer aware of actual human needs.

If we think especially of the national state traditions of western Europe, the following principles of structure may be suggested as a politico-social model:

1. Every attempt to transform social-political institutions must have clearly in mind the actual human beings who will be involved. Inalienable values whose realization must judge the worth of any social-political system include the right to life; preservation of personal and bodily protection; equality before the law; freedom of faith, conscience and creed; freedom to propogate ideas, to assemble, and to join groups; freedom to travel; the right to work—in brief, all those human rights which are guaranteed in the Human Rights Charter of the United Nations (December 10, 1948) and in the European Convention for the Protection of Human Rights and Fundamental Freedoms. Those basic human rights won by the bourgeois revolution must never be surrendered, which means they must be further developed in the direction of social equality and solidarity. But the legal obligation of state and society to maintain civil rights and the responsibility to

guarantee them and unceasingly to bring about their actualization must never be abrogated, when far-reaching structural changes, are made in any society.

2. This means that the state must not be assigned a controlling function over ideological questions. A post-capitalist society, wherein problems of production and distribution are no longer determined by antagonistic class interests, must be characterized by plurality and public debate of ideas, opinions, and political attitudes. This pluralism cannot be postponed—by pointing to the fact that western Europe is still capitalistic—to a later stage of societal development which may have overcome the basic antagonisms of capitalism. Pluralism today must be the ineradicable constitutent of political attitudes and actions, for every stage of social change postulates pluralistic exchanges of opinions and activities. Lombardo-Radice has given the systematic basis for this view: "If one applies Marxism to Marxism, one comes to the conclusion that Marxism too has its deficiencies, its unavoidable one-sidedness, and thus that Marxism can and must be completed and developed by other complementary truths, themselves also one-sided and partial." This consideration, derived from the scientific character of Marxist theory and social analysis and combined with the conviction that scientific progress can only be guaranteed if every conceivable hypothesis has the opportunity to verify its truth-claim in open confrontation, must be applied to state and society without any restrictions. Since the state has the primary function to guarantee the safety of people and the satisfaction of material needs, Christians must agree with Lombardo-Radice when he says: "The state in a socialist society can make no distinction among its citizens on the basis of ideology. [Marxists] . . . believe that a Marxist return to the liberal concept of a secular (laicized) state would be very fruitful."

3. Pluralism as a principle of structure implies a definite relationship to democracy. Concepts of monistic democracy, in which one party could have exclusive decision rights in all questions of social, cultural, and scientific development, are inconsistent with the pluralistic postulate. The critique made by many East and West European Marxists of a kind of Marxism that has become authoritarian and self-justifying should find expression in the development of a new concept of social democracy.

4. In a socialist democracy, governmental positions result from open, free elections and depend upon majority vote. Violent, revolutionary changes should likewise be eliminated in highly industrialized capitalist states; they should no longer be the means of political struggle and political debate. The institution of free elections also implies that when positions of power have been won, they should later be subject again to open franchise which, of course, does not mean that every social change and every new structure of production and distribution will always require return to the old. This will hardly be a difficult question since the history of many European states shows that when important economic and social changes have been undertaken by leftist governments (e.g., nationalization by the Labor government in England), even a conservative government has not been able to go back to the old system. Nevertheless, if it is true that new

solutions are always necessary for social problems which continue to arise, Marxism too, and the political parties representing it, must not lay claim to inviolable solutions but respect the popular vote.

5. An institutionalized protection of the rights of minorities is indispensable in a socialist democracy. If freedom is always the freedom to think differently from the majority (Rosa Luxemburg), then those citizens who as the result of elections find themselves in minority positions must enjoy the possibility of their own political organization and of public expression of their opinions. Institutionally this means a pluralism of political organizations as well as the right of political opposition. It also implies, e.g., the right and possibility for Christian churches to have worship services and religious organizations. In his East Berlin speech of June 30, 1976, Berlinguer characterized the previously mentioned principle of structure as follows: "We are fighting for a socialist society which regards as fundamental the strengthening of the value of personal and collective freedoms. These freedoms should guarantee the basic principles of a non-professional, non-ideological state and its democratic formation; the plurality of parties and their ability to turn over the reins of government to new majorities; the autonomy of trade unions; religious, artistic and scientific freedom." The question how far such a position may be simply tactical will be decided in political practice, in the concrete relationship with non-socialist partners, and in the interior composition of Marxist-oriented parties.

6. This leads us to a consideration that is essential to the structure of organization in a socialist democracy. When Marxist parties give up their totalitarian claims (notably in the problem involved in the concept of the "dictatorship of the proletariat"), when these parties describe the fundamental structure of bourgeois democracy as consistent with Marxism, then the postulate of democracy must refer not only to society in general. It must also be understood as the radical principle which informs the whole society. That is, depending on the level of development of a particular national society, the organization of decision-making and finding of the public will must take place in all socially relevant groups, parties, and other organizations "from bottom to top." There must be opportunities for citizen participation in expressing opinions and in deciding issues. Those who wish to do so should have access to the political arena. In such a system there will be "open elite" (i.e., a method that makes possible the exchange of the elite by means of elections which express the public will), together with self-governing organizations in the area of commerce, culture, and science—just as in political organizations. The churches are also included in this, and they need to scrutinize their own structures. Bureaucrats, too, must be a part of such self-governing organizations in order not to become autocratic or to act as instruments of repression toward dissenting citizens. Furthermore, spontaneous organizations arising out of local need, perhaps through citizen initiative, must be possible in a socialist democracy, without their being threatened by any negative sanctions.

7. Parliamentary institutions which have grown in the soil of bourgeois

society are today sadly in need of reform and must be adjusted to changed situations in order to strengthen democratic claims. Of course socialist democracy need not always be bound to certain historical forms of parliamentarianism—it should on the contrary be open for newly evolving forms of democratic structure—but it also need not discard the parliamentarian principle as invariably antiquated. The fundamental structural principles of the parliamentary system are actually indispensable, as far as basics are concerned, since the rights of political opposition and of alternative political parties which are institutionalized in that system are useful in a socialist democracy. It is not clear what Berlinguer means when he says: "We do not suffer from parliamentarian cretonism, while others have succumbed to anti-parliamentarian cretonism. We view parliamentarianism as an essential arrangement in Italian politics, and not just for today but also for the period of transition to socialism and indeed during its construction" (October, 1973). Marxists should adopt a clear principle about combining the right of institutional opposition and the parliamentarian principle.

8. In recent years the institutionalized participatory structure of capitalist and occasionally also of socialist systems has not been adequate to satisfy the public desire to share in decision-making. New forms of local political self-management have appeared and will continue to appear in varying degrees of intensity in different countries of western Europe. These forms act in many ways like advisory councils, of course without wishing to lay claim to the organization principles of the whole society. Local advisory committees in schools, kindergartens, etc., are using community initiative in concrete planning for political issues or municipal rehabilitation, and especially for environmental protection. All of this indicates that people are becoming more aware of the importance of politics in the determination of their own destiny and that they insist on having a share in the decision-making which is so significant for them. A socialist democracy would have to accept such initiatives positively. It would have to make available in communications and in institutions the greatest possible participation by the general public in political processes. It would have to consider whether political organization principles might be instituted, similar to those of advisory councils, such as a greater dependence on actual election of public servants and the use of rotation at certain levels of political, social, and economic life, as already suggested by French Marxists, and as already in part an actuality in Italy. A stronger institutional imprint of directly democratic elements would at the same time be a significant contribution to reform in the sense of a timely adaptation to parliamentarian institutions and would be a counterweight to technocratic and authoritarian tendencies that are so apparent today.

9. Regardless of the attitude toward parliamentarianism, a socialist democracy cannot dispense with the division of power. Contrary to Marxist opinion, the liberal principle of "checks and balances" has lost none of its importance, either in the experiences of "personality cult" or of increasing centralization of political power in the hands of a few. This is true in capitalist as well as in socialist

countries. If in capitalism legal, functional, federative, and temporary division of power is (or may be) a matter of social homogenization, mostly because of the similar interests of various classes of society, division of power in socialist democracies should be established by means of various kinds of decentralization of power. Among other things, that means the independence of law courts and with it the guarantee of the principle of the constitutional state, preservation of federative traditions where these are present, and the assurance of regular elections to be held at previously announced times, etc.

III. Possible Expectations of Dialogue Partners

Since in this first sketch of suggested discussion concepts for a renewed dialogue between Christians and Marxists it is possible only to outline basic and indispensable principles of post-capitalist society, we cannot here produce a thorough treatment of the sociological "model." It is, nevertheless, important to consider what mutual expectations each may justifiably have. In dependence on the memorandum of the Bensberger group's "Anti-socialism by Tradition?" let us try to formulate the most significant expectations:

1. There is no doubt that Christians and Marxists have had negative experiences with each other. In particular, the Catholic Church has more commonly united with conservative political forces and has been more likely to be directed by an institutional viewpoint than by a socially emancipating idea. On the other hand, this ecclesiastical attitude has been greatly strengthened by the close ties between atheism and Marxism. For a new dialogue to be fruitful, it is imperative that both sides openly clarify their present positions, in order that negative experiences on both sides not become crystallized as basic positions for negotiations. Both sides must embark on such a dialogue with the firm intention to correct each other and to learn from each other.

2. Marxists can rely on the concrete proof that Christians no longer identify themselves with existing capitalist societal structures. On the contrary, Christians speak out against fascism, racism, and colonialism, and against particular consequences of capitalist economic organization. That is to say, they stand for all those who are weak, politically, economically, socially and culturally—the majority of the people in the world.

3. Marxists can furthermore expect that the democratic and pluralistic postulate to which they should feel obligated must also be an obligation for the churches. That means that the churches too not only tolerate but also promote a process of democratizing and pluralizing, together with the possibility of a "national model."

4. Lastly, Marxists can expect that the official social teachings of the churches will take definite positions on capitalism, on the critique of capitalism, and on socialism. In other words, the churches also will work out a binding analysis of society showing how future development of society must be evaluated and furthered.

5. On the other hand, Christians must insist that Marxism not function as a secularized doctrine of salvation which is so binding on all citizens in a socialist democracy that no room is left for individual or collective religious faith.

6. Instead, Marxism in a socialist democracy must be much more open to confrontation and discussion with non-Marxist partners and opponents. Theoretically and in practical politics it must be cooperative.

7. In regard to the credibility of West European Marxists, one of the decisive factors is their attitude toward the established socialist states of middle and eastern Europe and the relationship of these states to the respective churches. To the degree that ecclesiastical institutions are not free from repression and constraint in these socialist states, to that degree the suspicion grows that West European Marxism is tolerant of Christians as long as it is not in the position of political power. A necessary task for Marxists is to accept the fact that political creativity, articulation of social needs, and initiative can be nourished by Christian motivation. Such acceptance must, of course, be more than verbal.

Translated from German by Christoph Schmauch, Conway, NH
and Norman Adams, Norton Hill, NY

COOPERATION AND DIALOGUE*

Jozsef Lukács

The theoretical dialogue, the exchange of views between believers and non-believers, has actually emerged out of the needs and struggles of everyday life to which the dialogue should revert unless we want it to turn into mere quibbling or wasteful academic discussion.

The reasons for this reversion are not only our efforts in order to harmonize and complete people's everyday life, but also the needs of socialist construction insofar as these require the strengthening of national unity of both believers and non-believers. This unity has already been realized in regard to the most decisive political questions—in the struggle for peace, in the efforts made for public welfare and for the propagation of culture—in efforts to create a more humanitarian world. In the past as well as in the future, this unity must be preserved by constant work and dialogue in its support.

This naturally follows from the fact that a nation is a practical union of people with different views, having divergent motives for the same aims. Though the political agreement in the past creates both the basis of, and a real possibility for, cooperation in the future, it does not automatically make this possibility a reality. As this reality will emerge from people's conscious activity in the future—and these future people will have different ideological views—so the appropriate settling of the new tasks should be endeavored which, in turn, assumes permanent grappling with ideological factors.

Thus the dialogue has been transformed into practice, but this practice needs discussion again, or it needs a particular type of dialogue. Based on agreement on the most decisive questions, tolerant and consistent dialogue has been and is always demanded.

1

We are closely tied to our own worldviews which neither Christians nor Marxists want to loosen. This is all for the best. Nevertheless, despite this contrast in worldviews, the scope for our mutual relations has not yet been exhausted. For, even though the ideological frames of reference into which

---

*A translation from Hungarian in a revised form from *Affirmative to Man* (Budapest: Magvetō, 1973), from a chapter entitled "Dialogue."

Jozsef Lukács (Marxist) is university professor at the Eötvös Loránd University in Budapest and a corresponding member of the Hungarian Academy of Sciences. He is the director of the Institute for Philosophy of the Academy of Sciences, the president of the philosophical committee of the Academy of Sciences, and editor of the review *Világosság*. He has published *Ways of God* and *Affirmative of Man* and is the editor of *Les relations de l'état socialiste et des églises à l'Hongrie*. He participated in Christian-Marxist dialogues at Herrenchiemsee (1966), Marianské Lazné (1967), Geneva (1968), Wallersee (1974), Tutsing (1975), Rosemont (1977), and Salzburg (1977).

people are placed cannot be correlated, we live in the same country under common social conditions. Presumably, it is a common feature in the views of Marxists and of those believers who are serious and responsible thinkers that they have no right to be satisfied with the present human condition with past morality still being applied. Neither Marxism nor Christianity can be taken seriously without working for human renewal.

A Christian thinker will probably reply that the only possible radical renewal is by faith, and that it is only in Christ that human beings can really be transcended, but I wonder whether the Christian contribution to this can be reduced merely in the name of a religion that made fraternal love its categorical imperative and, according to Catholic teaching, made salvation dependent upon good deeds. On seeing the failure of the principle, "love they neighbor as theyself," in history, responsibility might as well be laid on human sinfulness. Abandoning the real concern for human improvement in the world, the world—consenting to some sort of Platonism—could be regarded as a vale of tears.

However, we have some reason to hope that after two outrageous world wars, and based on their growing historical experience, the peasant and worker believers and the most responsible thinkers and outstanding representatives of Christianity are not indifferent to our life and to the most critical questions regarding the future fate of humankind. Although our ideals cannot be reconciled under any conditions, we cannot forget about the warning given by Pope John XXIII, Pope Paul VI, and the Communist and Workers' Parties at their last meetings. These warnings have been exemplified by the preceeding twenty-five years of Hungarian history as well, namely, that there is a possibility for agreement in our *actions*. It is not some kind of petty tactics that supports this agreement, but rather something that must be created due to our responsibility for people.

2

All this is, of course, easy to say but difficult to put into practice. Unfortunately, the truth is that in each call for cooperation, the initiative was always made by the Communist side. Examples of this can be found from Lenin to the present, through Thorez's and Togliatti's politics of an "outstretched hand." In some church circles a great number of rejections and protests were provoked in response. Some years ago, Georges Marchais, secretary-general of the French Communist Party, in an interview for *La Croix* emphasized the importance of practical cooperation and of dialogue that respects the differences in ideologies. At the same time and in the same paper, he was immediately accused that all this was merely a "plot," for, it was said, those who support the Communists' politics also lend them support for their worldview. "By the virtue of the relation between Marxist philosophy and politics," wrote Noël Copin, "it is philosophy that would benefit from an active political support."

The warning was also issued in a milder form in the *Bulletin* of the Secretariat for Non-Believers:

The actual possibility to enter into a dialogue is to be distinguished from the
problem whether the conversation is intended to serve politics rather, and if
it was so, it is directly or furtively to become a means for those aims which
are far both from seeking the truth and from mutual friendship.

It was particularly emphasized in the *Bulletin* that all this should be taken into
consideration, especially when cooperation with Communists is in question.
Besides, the philosophy of communism and it; political doctrines must be kept in
the forefront in the dialogue because "for the Communists a dialogue is always a
matter of politics."

All this, of course, applies directly to the *international* dialogue. Still, such
reservations are worth a closer examination, because they naturally can be associated with the conditions of the relation between Christians and socialism in
Hungary. However, it should be realized that it is quite obviously not the only
authentic Catholic view for us. It would not be just, for instance, to forget the
concept of dialogue by John XXIII in his *"Pacem in terris."* Fundamentally, he
declared principles similar to those expressed by Marchais, which were rejected
by Copin and protested against by the *Bulletin*. In fact, what Pope John emphasized was that, while the political movements of non-Christians and non-
believers cannot be identified with their fundamental viewpoints, some "beneficial or benevolent elements" can be found in their endeavors. It can well be
appropriate for the Christians to base their practical cooperative program on
these, even if the difference in worldviews still exists.

As for the question of what Communists think the purpose of the dialogue is,
of course, they never denied that they expect practical political results from this
discussion. On the other hand, Communists are not to conceal the connection
between their worldview and their political program. There is no contrast between politics and ideology for them, since their primary principle is to start from
the *objective* needs of a real social development in the first place, and not from
people's worldviews. This is the basis which determines their tasks and their
search for unity, because they are convinced that people formulate their ideological postures first of all on the grounds of their life experiences formed by the
effects of great social changes. Their program for the improvement of social
democracy means that, in the cause of realizing the great aims of social development, they extend and strengthen the unity of people with different social positions and worldviews. The ideological debate, of course, may have a part in the
course of this cooperation insofar as it is necessary to polemicize with views
impeding or retarding cooperation, without respect to their emergence in either a
religious or a non-religious form.

For Christians the question may be raised in other ways. If some of them
impose religiousness upon the partner as a *pre-condition* of political cooperation,
the dialogue with non-believers will seem to be very difficult, "almost hope-
less." But if they seek the solution, as John XXIII does, in the *practical* political
field, sooner or later they have to take a position on the question of whether there

is only *one* possible given social orientation issuing out of Christianity or, to the contrary, whether under different conditions Christianity may accept different "models." Moreover, can they claim incompetence with regard to the sanctioning and criticism of the worldly systems?

As far as we can survey the changes in the political and social attitudes of Christianity, it can be asserted that the church had already affirmed different social forms throughout history without losing essential Christianity in such views. As it is known, there have already been some prevailing opinions in churches both tending to consent to the established order, and criticizing this consent. Lastly, the forces of commitment and non-commitment to different systems are also presented in the Christian theology and philosophy in our time.

Even when the essentially transcendental mission of the church is being emphasized, the political importance of Christianity cannot be neglected. The Aristotelian thought, "happiness is action," was not alien to the classics of Christianity. Consequently, it is not impossible, at least in principle, to formulate and represent a view which is both Christian and practically committed to socialism. In my personal view, this standpoint—and there are many examples of it—is much closer to the original spirit of Christianity than those conscious or unconscious, subtle and indirect apologies of the capitalist relationships and class society which can be found in most documents published under the name of "Christian social doctrine" at all times.

But the question still to be answered is whether these Christian "affirmations" provide an opportunity to use Christians as a means for objectives otherwise not acceptable to them. No Marxist will, of course, deny an expectation of the withering of religion when the classless society, communism, has been achieved. Nevertheless, Marxists in theory base decisions *upon history* itself (this, perhaps, is not objectionable to believers). One is not a Marxist who strives against Christianity, if he or she is not also seeking a real opportunity for humankind to get rid of the conditions of its "infancy," the oppression and exploitation of working classes, women, and different races and nationalities; to eliminate privation, ignorance, relentless self-interest, distressing loneliness, war, and hatred.

Another question is whether or not the *"cui prodest"* (the question, "for whom is it beneficial?") is predominant in the definition of the Christian political attitude. Since it was the Marxists themselves who emphasized the importance of consequences in contrast to a purely deontological ethical approach, the problem cannot be neglected. Marxists judge the rightness or wrongness of a decision in the light of its likely social consequences. Hence, the only question is: Who or what are those historical subjects which provide the dividing line in form of their interests?

For Marxism the interests of a single social institution—even if it is the socialist state or the Marxist party—cannot be determinants, but are only *determined*. They are not the ultimate purpose, but only a means for the progress of humankind. (This can readily be accepted by Christians, for they also regard the church as a "means" provided for human salvation.) The only determining factor for Marxists is the objective interest of people, and the progress of human-kind. Although it may be due to the merits of the Marxist theory that this interest, which today coincides with the interests of the modern working class, is rightly expressed by the Communists, it does not mean that the genuine factors of human progress have become less objective.

Now, it is not our task to answer the further question of whether or not a Christian theoretician admits the objective interests of the great masses of people as the primary and determinant basis for the actions in this world. These interests today demand a resolute struggle against the capitalist agressions of war and against the world of moral decay of capitalism. They also demand an endeavor in order to replace all this by an order which is developing into modern Com-munism. On the other hand, if Christianity, consciously or unconsciously, iden-tifies its interests with those of a social order based on conflicting classes, this necessarily means that they are opposed to progress.

If a Christian theoretician is favorably oriented toward socialism, and one can find a number of such instances in our world, it is only evidence of the fact that he or she could realize these objective interests based on his or her own worldview as well. It is not an evidence of his or her being "manipulated." Of course, the Christian hopes that the ideological consequences will be different from those expected by Marxist participants. This means simply the acceptance of the ancient principle, *salus rei publicae suprema lex,* and, by starting from this, the preference for the alternative of peace and socialism to the inhumanity of the capitalist world.

3

Joint political activity, of course, does not mean that there is no more need for debate, since the common purposes have been laid down on different consid-erations of ideas. We should say that in Hungary the dialogue has already been surpassed, inasmuch as the believers' and non-believers' identical aims are being realized in practice. And, from time to time, differences of ideas are followed by praxis which transforms the dialogue into cooperation. Of course, the dialogue has not been ended. It just appears in particular and new forms. There is still much to debate, even today.

The discussion will hardly produce anything if it is directed toward the ultimate questions of our worldviews. All that could be obtained through such discussion is that the concept of human autonomy, in other words, atheism, is just as important and necessary an element of Marxism as the belief in God is for Christianity. I doubt whether the discussion would be fruitful enough if we started from András Szennay's proposals. He suggested that "the intellectual-spiritual acquisition . . . of the fundamental truths" could be "a common task for both believers and non-believers."[1] Szennay referred to questions such as "what

---

[1] Andrew Szennay, *Hidden Deity* (Budapest: Saint Stephen Society, 1969), p. 307.

is the meaning of life?''; the problem of right and wrong; the social value of natural consolation; consolation based on belief; etc. Rather, I am in full agreement with Professor Istrán Király who, when referring to a person who is seeking the final objective and meaning of life in the transcendental, and to one who does so in this human world, assumes the necessity of a debate between the two. He suggests that it is only through this polemic that progressive Christians can see the actual values of life in the world in the proper light, and that they can attribute appropriate significance to the realization of these values, rather than getting involved in some conservative or antisocialist political alliance.

The confrontation on ultimate questions cannot be eliminated by the debate, since a Christian answers the problems of life from different viewpoints than does a Marxist. Nevertheless, basically, the debate is concerned with the given scope of human opportunities, and meets the immediate reality of human responsibility. It is not the sources of our values, but the values themselves, that have to be discussed. It is a discussion of ideas too, but its main points are provided by the issues of our life, which are expressly devoted to serve this socialist life. At this point we can agree with Szennay, who says, ''Both for believers and atheists the dialogue seems to start with an exchange of thoughts, but it turns toward our common actions. This action is bound to become political in the sense of serving a community—*politeia*.[2]

Now if we are going to cast some theoretical light on the values of the human world, the outcome still remains contradictory. Although it will turn out that Marxism and Christianity are dealing with the same question, still their answers given to this question differ in many important respects. It would be misleading if the dialogue participants were convinced that beyond the ultimate ideological questions there is the promised land of convergent ideas which are directly suitable to be the foundations for cooperation. This is not so, and it could not be so; the Christian view of humanity and society and Christian ethics have different contexts of analysis from those of Marxism.

In spite of all the differences between our views, there has always been a tendency within Christianity from its very beginning that in its utopian form it attacks social injustice, inequality, and suffering, and that it believes in a radical changing of the world. Engels could rightly say about the first Christians' anti-Rome attitude that indeed their ''socialism, as far as it was possible at that time, was really settled and it came to power.'' It was to be realized not only in eternal life but soon also in the emerging millenarian concepts. Thus Engels could state about Thomas Munzer and his Anabaptists that they challenged the institutions, views, and ideas which were characteristic of all social formations based on class conflicts. These utopian schemes, specifically because of their religious orientation, proved to be compatible with those relationships against which they originally protested. However, there is no doubt that their adapted secular forms from More and Campanella through Morelly and Mably to Saint-Simon and Owen objectively became the ''antecedents'' of Marxist socialism.

---

[2]Ibid., p. 311.

Why cannot Christians today follow the way their historical thoughts developed for thousands of years, when the movement of new social and ideological struggles directs their attention to the realization of the essential aspects of utopia, and to the investigation of realistic solutions? If this seems acceptable for both of us, then there is a way toward communication which is a dispute on important social and moral questions without giving up our starting point in the realm of ideas. We can communicate with the purpose of increasing each time the chances of practical cooperation through dialogue.

4

A Marxist, of course, will never expect from Christianity that it would become revolutionary, even though today there are millions of Christians who become revolutionaries due to the dictates of their conscience. But if Christians become better acquainted with Marxist aims (and Marxists, too, should get acquainted more deeply with Christianity), they will very often find some important moral or social statements which, they might think, Christians themselves could have asserted *mutatis mutandis*. A Christian might think so without accepting Marxist atheism, although Marxists do not wish to mislead others about the fact that they are atheists.

Let me give only one example. Sometimes the materialism represented by Marxism is interpreted as some wicked materialistic selfishness that worships the idols of money instead of God. Very often it is forgotten that it was the author of *Das Kapital* himself who devoted all his works and his life to shatter this idol. Sometimes the Marxist-materialist view is vindicated to put material affluence on a pedestal and to waste its virtues bolstering a consumer society. We regard as fraudulent every justification of human happiness based on the poverty of the masses, famine, and cultural and social deprivation. But the elimination of all this misery is only an obvious precondition of happiness; it is not of wealth itself. It is worth considering also what Marx himself meant by wealth:

> Thus the old view, in which the human being appears as the aim of production, regardless of his limited national, religious, political character, seems to be very lofty when contrasted to the modern world, where production appears as the aim of mankind and wealth as the aim of production. In fact, however, when the limited bourgeois form is stripped away, what is wealth other than the universality of individual needs, capacities, pleasures, productive forces, etc., created through universal exchange? The full development of human mastery over the forces of nature, those of so-called nature as well as of humanity's own nature? The absolute working-out of his creative potentialities, with no presupposition other than the previous historic development which makes this totality of development, i.e., the development of all human powers as such the end in itself, not as measured on a predetermined yardstick? Where he does not reproduce himself in one specificity, but produces his totality? Strives not to remain something he has become, but is in the absolute movement of becoming? In bourgeois economics—and

in the epoch of production to which it corresponds—this complete working-
out of the human content appears as a complete emptying-out, this universal
objectification as total alienation, and the tearing-down of all limited, one-
sided aims as sacrifice of the human end-in-itself to an entirely external
end. . . . This is why the childish world of antiquity appears on one side as
loftier. On the other side, it really is loftier in all matters where closed
shapes, forms and given limits are sought for. It is satisfaction from a limited
standpoint; where the modern gives no satisfaction; or, where it appears
satisfied with itself, it is vulgar.[3]

It is not my task to interpret these thoughts for Christians. But it seems to be
obvious that even if they disagree with Marx about the definition of wealth, on
the basis of their Christian standpoint as well they should reject that society
which makes material welfare (which is only an important aim of humanity) an
absolute aim, and where it is not the person who appears as the aim. Even if they
doubt that humans can develop a full mastery over their own nature—and that its
only presupposition would be the previous historic development—surely they
will approve it as a morally respectable endeavor. They will also see that they can
join it in spite of our different estimations on the final effects. And Christians
must also admit that this Marxist confession is anything but the devotion of human
opportunities to some hedonist idol. Christians probably do not believe that,
without God, a person can be in the ''absolute movement of becoming,'' but they
will be pleased to hear that, by these words, a person cannot survive so basely, in
a state of some narrow philistine satisfaction. And I suppose that Christians will
comprehend the pursuit of universality, or the program of shattering humankind's own created idols—the idols of race, money, and even of the Self. And
people do all this not because they want to worship new idols, but in order to
realize their own development, without being ''measured on a predetermined
yardstick,'' without ready-made patterns.

The realization of human wealth and full human development is, of course,
rooted deeply in a dialectical and materialist view by the Marxist program. But
this materialism is not the least characterized by the obvious distortions of the
accusations against it. It does not postulate the mastery of material goods over
humanity; on the contrary, it regards as the essence of history that people work
out themselves from their relations given by nature, and gain mastery over both
the external forces and their own natures. In this conception everything is subordinated to the real human wealth and many-sided development, as opposed to the
utilitarianism of capitalist profits, or to lofty idealism that is, while preaching
spiritual values, inclined to make peace with a reality of deprivation, without
being deterred from idealizing material and spiritual poverty.

Speaking of real human wealth, we must now ask the way toward it. We must
ask and answer this question repeatedly. I suppose that all agree that we are faced

---

[3]Karl Marx, *Grundrisse. Foundations of the Critique of Political Economy,* Chapter on Capital,
Notebook V.

with the common tasks of humanizing human morality and civilizing human instincts. But what makes the individual's moral development possible? We need to pose the question like this: Are there some conditions of our moral purification, embedded in the social structure, which can be created only through actions, more specifically through the common actions of believers and non-believers? Has history, the master of our life, taught us that it is not enough to accept self-interest, aggressive tendencies, and brutality merely as psychological facts, or that persuasion is not sufficient because they are grounded in particular social structures, and there is no hope for real moral improvement unless these social relations are eliminated?

The answer, given by the masses of believers, is implied in the trends of our socialist society. This is an answer given by those believers who are no longer willing to accept the identification of Christianity with a social order based on the power of financial monopolies, on the artificially-conserved powerlessness of the masses, and on fundamental social conflict of opposites. These Christians— whose number is increasing—realize (and not only due to the pressure of external circumstances, but also due to the dictates of their own conscience) that they should give active support to the formation of a socialist order. Socialism, by overcoming several difficulties, is really a precondition to the formation of the new person, even if those who inspire the formation of this social order have divergent worldviews.

After all, repeatedly, the question is whether we regard divergent ideas or the genuine and objective interests of human progress as primary, in respect to practice. This is a question that we have to answer every day. The answer, I think, can only be given collectively, and only if we follow the way of a common struggle for social progress more bravely and more consistently through a tolerant dialogue respecting the views of all participants.

CHRISTIAN AND MARXIST COOPERATION IN THE G.D.R.

Adolf Niggemeier

In the present stage of worldwide confrontation between progressive and conservative forces, the relationship of Christians and Marxists is increasingly gaining in political significance.

In a process of more than thirty years, relations have developed in the GDR between Christians and Marxists which are determined by both theoretical positions and practical experience. They are, to anticipate, close and confident relations, determined by mutual respect and cooperation. These relations have issued from the joint struggle against fascism. Few Christians in Germany consistently struggled against fascism, but together with communists, socialists, liberals, and representatives of other humanist views they suffered in the prisons and concentration camps of Hitlerite Germany, united by the anti-fascist resistance struggle. This cooperation of forces with different political outlooks was determined above all by their common anti-positions, by resolved anti-fascism, anti-militarism, and anti-imperialism. In their joint work after 1945, for overcoming the material and spiritual consequences of fascism and war, it turned out very soon that Christians and Marxists had much in common in view of the people and the future of the people—above all, in their striving for peace and social justice.

Realizing these common aims, we Christians have learned a decisive lesson: The basic contradiction of our times is not "Christianity or Marxism," as the enemies of social progress maintain. On the contrary, the basic contradiction is that between capitalism and socialism. With this statement we neither belittle the atheist component of Marxism—which we cannot accept as Christians—nor do we overlook the fact that there is an unbridgeable gulf between Christianity and Marxism in view of the so-called "last things." Syncretism is alien to us. However, two things have been confirmed; on the one hand our view as to the character of the basic contradiction in the world, and on the other hand our realization of the fact that in the social sphere things Christians and Marxists have in common are stronger than those by which they are separated.

The question in 1945 was not yet to build up socialism on the territory that now comprises the GDR. It was much more important to make a fundamental decision; namely, to replace the old, compromised system by an anti-fascist, democratic order. This aim was pursued by all progressive forces. It was the

Adolf Niggemeier (Roman Catholic) is a lawyer and has been a member of the Parliament of the German Democratic Republic since 1967, as well as Secretary of the Central Committee of the Christian Democratic Union of Germany. He received his education at the Law School of the Karl Marx University in Leipzig and served as a constitutional expert of the Commission for the Writing of the Constitution of the G.D.R. He has written articles on questions of peaceful coexistence, political consequences of disarmament, cooperation between Marxists and Christians, and on the churches and Christians of the G.D.R.

economic power that granted trusts, banks, and big landowners that political power which they had abused in such a terrible way to set up the fascist dictatorship and to unleash the Second World War. Consequently, this economic power had to be broken. This was only possible by profound socio-economic changes, such as the nationalization of industry, land reform, and educational and administrative reforms. Many Christians supported that process to the best of their abilities.

After successfully carrying through these reforms—which had the nature of revolutionary change, the Marxists submitted the proposal to declare the construction of socialism the fundamental and joint task of all democratic forces. This proposal aroused a lot of discussion within our ranks, and it took us a long time to consider and examine thoroughly whether and how far the socialist model of society that was offered to us corresponds to the social consequences of the maxims of Christian ethics. We asked whether this model was in accordance with our Christian ideas of a socialist order. In trying to develop a social model of our own, we realized that there was no specific Christian program for solving economic, scientific, and social problems. The Gospel is a touchstone for us, but it is not a guidebook for political decisions. Indeed, we were very deliberate in responding to the Marxists' offer to build socialism jointly. The Christians' acceptance and support of this offer has by no means always been without conflicts. This engagement has not always been harmonious, but there have been tensions and contradictions as well.

A quarter of a century ago Otto Nuschke, co-founder and long-standing chairman of the Christian Democratic Union of Germany, was able to explain our decision in favor of socialism which was determined by the principles of Christian ethics and which is of lasting validity. Summarizing our historic, political, and social perceptions Nuschke said:

> We stand for socialism because it provides the indispensible economic preconditions necessary for the development of genuine humanity.
>
> We stand for socialism because it corresponds with our Christian ideals. In socialism the care for the people is in the centre of all efforts thus enabling an actual implementation of charity.
>
> We stand for socialism because it eliminates the exploitation of man by man and opens up perspectives for everybody to fully display his or her talents and abilities.
>
> We stand for socialism because it ensures freedom of conscience and religious activities.

Our confidence in the new society is fully justified. In practice it becomes increasingly apparent that there are genuine points of contact between the ethical postulates of our Christian belief and the humanist concern of socialism. I should like to summarize some of them in five points.

1. The most important thing is that Christians and churches have every

freedom necessary in order to render peace service. The policy of peaceful coexistence between states with differing social systems is inherent in the socialist order and is aimed at solving conflicts by peaceful means. There are tremendous conflicts in the international arena, but they do not necessarily have to result in bloodshed. It is the success of the strategy of peaceful coexistence that there has been peace in Europe for over thirty years. We have learned that socialism and peace form a unity.

2. With the new economic system a new labor ethos has developed. Social ownership of factories, machines, and agricultural enterprises has produced new relations among the people. The new way of working has created not only material but also ethical values. Work has become more than just a means for making one's living. It has become again the most essential source for displaying human creative abilities and for shaping human life in a sensible and useful way. According to our Christian understanding work has become part and parcel of the human being. More and more Christians have recognized that only socialism is able to endow work with the dignity by which it is distinguished in the Gospel. The biblical tenet, "He who does not work shall not eat," is reflected in socialism as a unity of the right to work and the duty to work. The biblical order that humankind subjugate nature is fully realized in socialism.

3. Socialism brings about social justice and security. On the basis of social justice and security, there are developing ethical values, such as self-consciousness, self-respect, and the pursuit of education. Everyone has the opportunity of free development of his or her personality. Togetherness instead of individualism is a social principle. The free personality develops as a constructive link of a collective in which the individual traits of a personality can mature. The material and cultural living standards are merging in the socialist way of life. No one can rule over someone else because of more economic power. We have overcome those occasions when charity had to be practiced in the form of private charity or to soothe somebody's social conscience. At those times the tough reality of society, with its antagonistic class contradictions, often forced many citizens to act according to the inhumane slogan, "Charity begins at home." In our society Christians are able to transfer the love of God to personal relations marked by genuine humanity.

4. We Christians want to live according to the Gospel. This includes religious liberty and freedom of conscience. These fundamental freedoms are also inherent in socialism. All citizens are equal irrespective of their political outlook and religious confession. Our activities are by no means restricted to our parish. In our society we need not conceal our Christian motivation, but can act as Christians unrestrictedly. Christian ethics and morals as motives of social activities are not only respected in our state, but they are put into practice in accordance with important principles of our state policy. Free of state influence—in our country for the first time after centuries—are Christian testimony and service for the people by preaching and diaconate. The socialist state does not expect God's blessing for its measures, nor does it strive for guardianship over the

churches. As a Catholic citizen, for example, I appreciate that this is the first time that our confessional minority status does not entail political and social isolation or disadvantages. We enjoy full equality. The engagement of an increasing number of Christians in socialism has decisively promoted the position of our churches. The Protestant church expressed this in 1973: "We are not churches beside or against socialism but churches in socialism."

5. The new society gives Christians the possibility to take a frank attitude toward comradly cooperation with non-Christians in two ways: On the one hand, those working Christian citizens who are not members of the working class are their allies, as they are social beings in our society as well. They recognize the working class as a major force of economic and social developments and renewal for the benefit of the whole people. The interest of the working class is not egoistical, but it is in line with the basic interest of all working people. This is the basis of our social alliance. On the other hand, Christians as members of the Christian Democratic Union or other political groupings together with the Socialist Unity Party of Germany (SED), which is the communist party, are part of the alliance of these political forces. The SED develops the strategy of the struggle for peace, social progress, and consolidation of the workers' and farmers' power. Such a policy serves the fundamental interests of all citizens and forms the basis of our political alliance. The independence of the parties and their responsibility for the society as a whole remains unrestricted. In the Democratic Bloc, the organizational form of the alliance of political parties and mass organizations in the GDR, questions of political and social developments in the GDR are discussed jointly. There are no majority decisions. Out-voting others is excluded.

In some practical questions our views on problems of political relevance differ from those of our Marxist friends. For example, in discussions about the family and youth laws we considered some amendments of principles necessary in order to make these laws acceptable for Christian citizens also. There have always been ways and means to meet the demands of all political parties. This was particularly true of the discussions about our first socialist Constitution. Our Marxist friends did not turn a deaf ear to our arguments to include in the constitution, in addition to the constitutional principles of religious liberty and freedom of conscience, the explicit right of every citizen to embrace a religion. In this connection one must also mention the financial support for the churches by the state, e.g., for diaconate work, clergy salaries, the maintenance of religious buildings, and theology scholarships at state universities.

I do admit, of course, that not all of the ten million Christians in my country saw these points of contact between Christian and civic duties in socialism from the very beginning. There are still people today who have some reservations, but their number is decreasing. The majority of Christians in the GDR have endorsed the course of socialism. Therefore, we can be quite certain that there will be Christians and churches in the communist future just as there are Christians and churches now in our socialist society, because our religion does not depend on particular socio-economic relations and is therefore not connected with the downfall of a social order. And, finally, our Christian belief is not an obstacle but an encouragement to serve progress in the world, even though my communist friends hold a different view on this point.

Nevertheless, it is always our common aims which are decisive. It is they that determine our cooperation with Marxists, not the other things in which we hold different views. This is an affirmation of general validity which manifests itself everywhere. Making the majority of Christians in our country aware of this is the result of our political activities and, to an even greater extent, the result of social practice. The latter confirmed and corroborated the originally more intellectual-theoretical decision in favor of socialism.

Today there are numerous Christians in my country in responsible social positions as managers of nationally-owned enterprises in industry, agriculture, and trade; as directors of schools, cultural facilities, and clinics; as teachers at universities, colleges, and institutions of higher education; and as lawyers. Even the president of the Supreme Court is a Christian. What counts for holding such a responsible post are initiative, knowledge, abilities, and skills, not religious confessions. For example, out of a total of 110,000 members of the Christian Democratic Union, there are nearly 21,000 working in people's representations, from municipal representations to the People's Chamber. In the State Council and Government, in all councils of counties and districts, and as mayors of several hundred communities, CDU members hold positions of political responsibility. This gives public evidence that the CDU takes part in drafting and implementing the policy of the GDR.

Christians and Marxists together have built this country. It has become their common political homeland.

DIALOGUE BETWEEN MARXISTS AND CHRISTIANS AS A
PRESUPPOSITION OF COEXISTENCE IN FREEDOM

Jakov Rafael Romić

Exploring and analyzing the possibility of dialogue between Marxists and Christians based on the positions which Marx, Engels, and Lenin [hereafter MEL] maintained toward religion was undertaken in the first part of my book *De dialogo inter marxistas et christianos*.[1] The conclusion was drawn that efforts on behalf of dialogue, which is the presupposition of coexistence in freedom and out of which will ensue the creative cooperation of evolving humanity, encounter a double barrier. The first barrier is theoretical, originating in the monolithic vision of the future which the Marxists aim to bring about. The second, practical barrier is the exclusion by Marxists of believers from participation in tasks of social justice and social advancement in countries in which Marxists are in power. One could approach the problematic of the dialogue from another perspective, but those other perspectives would be no less sensitive but probably more sensitive areas than the question of religion. For a Christian there are very concrete reasons why the approach to dialogue from the perspective of the Marxist attitude toward religion is the most realistic.

The Marxist vision of the future is Platonically idealistic,[2] while the forecasts

---

[1] Published doctoral dissertation in Latin (Vicenza, Italy: Libreria Internazionale Edizione Franciscane, 1972).

[2] The meaning of the term will be clear in the text below, but here an explanation is necessary as to the purpose of its usage. I do not intend to say that the founders of Marxism-Leninism are conscious followers of Platonic idealism (though similarities do exist), but I wish to do the following: (1) point to the unreality of the Marxist concepts of the future, as well as to the unreasonableness of those Marxists who are in power, as well as those Marxist philosophers who interpret such Marxism as the only correct one and who interpret various aspects of reality with unrealistic mythologies. Thus, for instance, the Polish Marxist philosopher Lezsek Kolakowski was astonished when he attended the 1960 meeting of Yugoslav Marxists at Bled that some Yugoslav Marxists dared to venture into fields other than the mere translation of the Central Committee of the Communist Party's decisions into philosophical terminology. And (2) I wish to shock both the Marxist and non-Marxist reader with my own experience so that they will stop and think about *this* aspect of Marxism. My former professors in the High School, when they spoke about religion or about Christianity, repeated uncritically assertions from Soviet textbooks about Jesus Christ's not having been a historical figure, about religion as a priestly invention, etc. Such lessons are still being taught to students in Yugoslavia. As I prepared for the priesthood and read the texts of Thomas Aquinas and other neo-scholastics, I had a hard time understanding why Lenin considered Christianity idealistic. Then as a

---

Jakov Rafael Romić, O.F.M. (Roman Catholic), is a Franciscan friar from Yugoslavia. He received the Sacrae Theologiae Licenciatus at Zagreb and the Philosophiae Doctor at Antonianum University in Rome. He has taught at the Philosophical and Theological Franciscan School in Dubrovnik, at the Philosophical Faculty of Antonianum, and at the "Institut za teološku kulturu laika" in Zagreb. Since 1975 he has managed a Croatian TV program in New York City. He has participated in a number of Christian-Marxist dialogues, including the Florence Symposium of the Paulus-Gesellschaft in 1975. In addition to several articles, he has published *De dialogo inter marxistas et Christianos, Personalisticka etika,* and *U vremenu s Kristom.*

of the three great founders of Marxism-Leninism—which were never realized in the manner predicted—continually jeopardize individual freedoms and liberty in general. The atheism of the three great founders is a human position which abolishes God, that is, includes God's negation. This atheist aspect of Marxist humanism did not undergo significant modifications to this day except with some thinkers of those Communist parties which are not in power and hence are not relevant.

In Part I of this analysis we shall deal with the nature of Marxist humanism which emerged and presently continues to be the ideology of the so-called "dogmatic Marxists." After a brief consideration of some "reinterpretations" in the practical attitude toward religion, in Part II we shall deal with the progress in the theoretical reinterpretations of those Marxists who participated in the international congresses sponsored by the Paulus-Gesellschaft between 1964 and 1968. In Part III we shall analyze as illustrative the events of the congresses which took place in 1964–1965, as was done in the second part of *De dialogo inter marxistas et christianos,* which proved that the dialogue is possible but that the condition of this dialogue is the reinterpretation of some Marxist postulates.[3] In Part IV we shall deal with the barriers to dialogue. Basically they are the Platonic-idealistic mental structure, which is to be found in both the founders and among many contemporary Marxists, and the divisions among both Christians and Marxists into progressives and conservative traditionalists. Finally, in Part V, we shall take into consideration some contemporary manifestations which will, we hope, bring new impulses for dialogue today and lead to a more humane coexistence containing a horizon rich with new perspectives and alternatives.

Is it nonsense to write on this theme to which many others have already contributed? It might be in vain, but it is not senseless! After a longer period of inactivity after the Soviet intervention in Czechoslovakia in 1968, after which the protagonists of the dialogue were both disappointed and tired, the dialogue, because it is needed, is commencing again (e.g., the Florence symposium in 1975 and the Salzburg Congress in 1977). In order that future dialogue be more fruitful, we intend to share both our critical thoughts as well as our hopes in this short survey.

---

soldier in the Yugoslav People's Army I was surprised by the one-sided interpretation of history according to a scheme in which "everything before the revolution, i.e., before World War II, was bad and now everything is good." Among the things "before the revolution" were always Christianity and Idealism. Reading Marx I could understand this somewhat better. He rejected the idea of God, the Absolute Spirit of Hegelian idealistic philosophy. But why do later Marxists, who obviously have no contacts with Hegel, repeat uncritically something which they did not think through in this new historical situation? A critical approach to Marxism or to some Marxist themes cannot neglect or pass over this idealistic structure of Marxism. This lack of critical posture is the source of theoretical wandering and straying as well as of great practical distress. Lack of criticism is not an element of the dialogical approach to any theme.

[3] I am purposely avoiding the term "revision," because even those Marxists who are sometimes labeled as "revisionists" rely on the texts of the founders and on praxis as the sole Marxist method of viewing reality.

1. Exclusivistic Humanism Precludes Dialogue

"Exclusivistic humanism" is a concept of a human being who *a priori* denies God. It is not a human position which would within revolutionary Marxist atheism merely place God "into a parenthesis." Exclusivistic humanism represents an uninterrupted threat of this atheism and, vice versa, atheism is the uncut thread of the Marxist concept of human beings. In Marx it appears as early as his high school writings, and it is explicit in his doctoral dissertation, "Differenz der demokritischen und epikureischen Natur-philosophie" (1841). Here he says, *"Mit einem Wort, ganz hass' ich all und jeden Gott."*[4] Such atheism later gripped both Friedrich Engels and Vladimir Ilyich Lenin and most, if not all, contemporary Marxists. An exception might, for instance, be Erich Fromm who does not hate God, though he does not believe in God.

The concept of the human being is an essential determining factor in the dialogue, because the question as to whether the human being is creator or creation is to be found in the basis of every philosophical anthropology. Marxism, from its inception, accepts an anthropocentric anthropology, one which excludes God *a priori*. It is impossible to reduce an anthropocentric and a theocentric anthropology to a common denominator. Thus we shall need to turn to the concept of the future as the single possible source of a sincere and reasonable deliberation about dialogue.

In the name of the human being, the lord and center of the world, the question of God for Marx is nonsensical. This rejection of the God question would be justified only if it were really true that the human being is indeed the lord of the world and its center. Contemporary Marxists, such as Ernst Bloch, Adam Schaff, Branko Bošnjak, and some others, are aware that the human being is neither the center nor the lord of the world. In our time, it appears, many thinkers have generally lost such a naive faith. A study of the MEL critique of religion leads us to a paradoxical assertion which is valid in regard to exclusivistic humanism: the human being knows that he or she is not God, yet still wants to be God. Marxist humanism, to the degree to which it remains incapable of reinterpretation, on account of its voluntaristic *a priori* negation of God, shall remain a barrier to dialogue. In the recent past there were some attempts to overcome this exclusivism. Since these are still very marginal endeavors, only minor attention shall be given to them, though in the interest of a correct interpretation of the whole picture they must be considered.

The eminent philosopher from Zagreb University, Branko Bošnjak, has made attempts to overcome the differences between the two humanisms, the one in which the human being is a creation and the other in which he or she is a creator.

---

[4] "In a word, I hate all and every God." [All of the quoted material is translated from German or Croatian as quoted in Romić's manuscript rather than from the published English translations of the respective books (translator's note).]

He does this by means of the idea of anthropological universalism or "anthropocracy." It would seem that this is a utopian attempt to free the human being from ideologization and politicization which lead to the loss of human values. Humanism, according to Bošnjak, is a phenomenon which gets to be ideologized in history in two ways. In Christianity it gets to be politicized; in Marxism, ideologized. In practice there is neither pure Christianity nor pure Marxism. They are two cases of the same sickness, because in both instances we are not part of that which they essentially ought to be, but in that which the corresponding institutions create for us. Christian brotherly and sisterly love on the one side and the classless society on the other are the perfect ideal. But these ideals have not yet been historically realized. In order to bring about these unrealized ideals, Bošnjak proposes de-politicization or de-ideologization in order to prepare the way toward anthropological universalism which would offer the possibility of foregoing situations of general social conflicts sometime in the future. That future, he says,

> ... depends on the possibility of correcting the ideologized praxis per se in which exclusivism is being manifested. If the purpose of socialist action were to devour capitalism and vice versa then there would be no possibility to bring about a joint basis in which the human being would emerge as a true human being.[5]

Another Yugoslav Marxist, Andrija Krešić, perceives the danger of the contemporary historical situation in the two ideologies which oppress nations. He believes that the dialogue is the way out of that danger. According to him it is human nature to struggle against oppressive power by means of communicating, conversing, mutually understanding one another, and such. For this Marxist it is not important to induce people to abandon their myths in order to enter the sphere of logos, but rather to supplant coercion with dialogue. Through dialogue it will be possible to find the common human root and common interest and thereby be able to escape the present slavery to irrational powers.[6]

One may then conclude that exclusivistic humanism, on the practical level, needs to be considered as a threshold which one must step over if one is to go beyond the situation of conflict. On the theoretical level, however, it remains a basic difference between Christianity and Marxism. This theoretical difference need not be eliminated at all cost or just so that one may escape the conflict. It is needless, indeed dangerous, to hope or to hastily encourage the hope that humanity will ever achieve the point of having only one ideology or one worldview.

---

[5]Branko Bošnjak, "Ideja humanizma izmedju ideologiziranog marksima i politiziranog kršćanstva" [The Ideal of Humanism between Ideologized Marxism and Politicized Christianity], in *Praxis* (Zagreb), Nos. 1–2 (1970), p. 107.

[6]Andrija Krešić, "Nenasilje kao ljudski način opstanka" [Non-violence as a Human Way of Existing] in *Praxis,* Nos. 1–2 (1970), pp. 53–63.

II. Dialogue in the Light of Reinterpretations of the Practical
Attitude toward Religion

In 1868, in a letter to Engels, Marx said that a struggle ought to be undertaken against some clergy in Germany, in particular against Bishop Ketteler from Mainz, who were working in behalf of the rights of the workers. Marx called these priests "dogs." Before the great October Revolution of 1917, Lenin said that believers, even clergy, could take part in political life and might even join the Communist Party.[7] Lenin's view resulted from his belief that religion is a "private matter" in relation to the state in which the Marxists have not yet attained power. Marx's exclusivistic attitude toward religion can be understood when we consider that he faced a globally reactionary function of religion in the society in which he lived. Lenin's attitudes are not coherent. This became evident when he changed his views toward religion after the October Revolution by turning to persecution. His earlier intentions were tactical in nature. This tactical move of Lenin's raises the question of credibility for those Marxists who are not yet in power as they promise religious liberties.

Reading MEL, one is unwarranted in coming to the conclusion that religion ought to be persecuted or that one must deal with it by means of so-called "administrative measures."[8] Engels' texts in *Antidühring* are quite classical in this respect. Yet, in our opinion, none of these texts provides a solid ground for an affirmative, positive cooperation of Marxists with non-Marxists in general and with Christians in particular. Contemporary Marxists seem to neglect to speak about these exclusivistic aspects of Marxism. Due to all the above considerations, contemporary Marxist attitudes toward religion are characterized by frequent changes. It is interesting that Marx and Engels in their *Grundsetze des Kommunismus* (1847) left the question of attitudes toward religion open and have thus provided the opportunity for numerous interpretations and even more frequent manipulations.

III. Dialogue in the Light of Reinterpretations of Some Theoretical
Attitudes

1. The relationships between the infrastructures and superstructures were, according to the founders of Marxism-Leninism, well defined and directed. Infrastructures control the superstructures. Superstructures are derived from the economic basis. The economy is then the source of art, ideology, law, the state, religion, philosophy, and so forth. Marx's vision of history, which develops according to dialectical laws, ends with the achievement of the perfectly-ordered

---

[7]A detailed consideration of this question is to be found in Jakov R. Romić, "Predrevolucijski Lenjinovi stavovi prema religiji" [Lenin's Prerevolutionary Attitudes toward Religion] in *Jukić* (Sarajevo), No. 2 (1972), pp. 86–91.

[8]"Administrative measures" is a term which designates the use of restrictive governmental decrees to limit or curtail religious activities. [Translator's note.]

society. An end is brought to evolution by ending class struggle which served as the moving power of history. That schematic vision of history is, in our opinion, a remnant of Hegelian idealism in the Marxism of both Marx and the Marxists. According to that scheme the dependence of the superstructure upon the infrastructure is essentially determined one-dimensionally.[9] Into this clear vision Engels brought some ambiguity. In a letter to Joseph Bloch, dated 1890, he said, "The economic moment is not the only one, but only its basis. Various superstructures are influencing the course of historical struggle, especially its form."[10] And yet Engels, as well as Marx before him and Lenin after him, expected the so–called natural death of religion. The rejection of the "administrative approach" to religion was in fact based on that expectation which in turn depends on the essential dependency of the superstructure upon the infrastructure and their certainty that the expected scheme of the future monolithic society will take place.

The Anarchists—for instance, Bakunin, Kropotkin, and Landauer—already sharply criticized Marx's understanding of the dictatorship of the proletariat. More so than Marx they were able to predict the danger of a deformed dictatorship of the proletariat based on the nature of dictatorship which tends to preserve its power as long as possible.[11] In his own theory Marx was unable to include limits which would help avoid the pitfalls of deformity at the beginning and during the dictatorship of the proletariat. On this account such deformation became possible both in principle and in reality. This neglect of Marx can be understood if one remembers the eschatological element in his notion of history. In it he burdened the proletariat with too large demands upon them and with too great expectations. The concrete historical deformations of the dictatorship of the proletariat point to the vulnerability of Marx's schematic vision of history.

This schematic understanding of history became the obstacle to a deeper psychological and anthropological analysis of the phenomenon of religion on the part of the founders of Marxism-Leninism. And since, in socialist countries, religion showed greater independence from the economic basis than was expected the attitude toward religion is being changed by some contemporary Marxists. A variety of attitudes toward religion exists among them. Some Marxists persecute religion, contrary to the position of the founders of Marxism-Leninism. Others are attempting to reinterpret the duration of the existence of religion (Adam Schaff on account of his understanding of the concept of alienation; Branko Bošnjak because of existentialist considerations). The third group says that pluralism is possible, but they offer no detailed explanation of how

---

[9]Cf. Karl Marx and Friedrich Engels, *The Communist Manifesto* (1848), and many other works.

[10]Cf. Friedrich Engels, *Herrn Eugen Dührings Umwalzung der Wissenschaft (Antidühring)* in *Werke,* Vol. XIX. Also letter, "An W. Borgius," January 25, 1894, in *Werke,* Vol. XXXIX. All references are from *Werke* (Berlin: Dietz Verlag, Institut für Marxismus-Leninismus beim ZK der SED, 1960).

· [11]Cf. Künzli, "Problem moći u anarhističkoj kritici marksizma" [The Problem of Power in the Anarchist Critique of Marxism], in *Praxis,* Nos. 1–2 (1970), pp. 117–125.

pluralism works within a Marxist context (for instance the French and Italian writers). The fourth group are reinterpreting the religious phenomenon along the lines of their reinterpretation of the relationship between the infrastructure and superstructure within a new global vision of history. In our opinion only the latter can create preconditions for a useful dialogue which would be more beneficial for human coexistence.

A very valuable attempt in this respect was made by the recently deceased Marxist Ernst Bloch. According to him the infrastructure enjoys an ontological priority, but the superstructures may, in fact, have primacy. How could one otherwise explain the emergence of the Reformation in the sixteenth century or the French Revolution in the eighteenth century? Religion existed before the emergence of class society (Bloch mentions the role of the physician-magician as well as the role of the poet). This religion can also continue its existence in the classless society of the future. Bloch's "immanentist transcendence" is an attempt to save the contemporary person who suffers from an "infraproduction of transcendence," in the West on account of a boring pluralism and in the East because of an equally boring monolithism. Bloch's "utopian realism" lost its schematic certainty.

2. The concept of alienation can also not be separated from the schematic understanding of history by MEL. In this respect they are the heirs of Hegelianism. For Hegel, the Absolute Spirit enters an object (*Dingheit*) so as to be able to recognize oneself through the process of phenomenologization. Self-consciousness and its object in this alienation (*Entäusserung*) remain in the indivisible unity of being-itself. This "exteriorization" is the negative moment in the Hegelian dialectic of the Absolute Spirit. Feuerbach placed a strong emphasis upon it but did so on an anthropological level. The human person, in relation to God, who was understood by Feuerbach as a human product, losses his or her own essence. In *The Essence of Christianity* (1841) Feuerbach wrote, "Man must become poorer so that God may be richer. Man must become nothing so that God may become all." But for Marx, as he stated in *Theses on Feuerbach,* this is still too abstract. In MEL alienation is not only a figure or moment of the Absolute Spirit which is manifested within the framework of its own being, as in Hegel. Nor does it stay on the theoretical level, as with Feuerbach. For them it means getting lost in the nothingness of one's own illusion. A being which is external to the human being rules over him or her, though that very person created that being. This loss becomes evident in alienated labor.

Marx started to consider the concept of alienation at the same time that he considered the concept of emancipation, which is of some significance. He started dealing with it in 1842 in the *Jewish Question.* A Jew is, said Marx, "a practical expression of human self-alienation because one can observe a Jew seeing that an external power rules over man. The God of the Hebrew is silver, and silver is the alienated essence of human labor. Man is a slave to this foreign being and prays to him." Soon thereafter in another place Marx analyzed human labor, which in and of itself is creative, but which, in a bourgeoise society, became such that workers were being lost proportionately to their increasing poverty and the capitalists' increasing wealth.[12]

Engels, following Marx, also thought that religion dispossesses humans of value, that it empties the human being of humanity (*Entleerung*). Religious alienation is the transfer of values from the human being upon an apparition, a dream vision, a mirage of some transcendent God. God then gives the human of God's own plentitude. A vacuum of value is thus created in the human being. This vacuum will persist until the person becomes conscious that he or she revered himself or herself as God. If a person wants to be liberated, that person must reject religious illusions.[13] In another place Engels says that the source of alienation is economic exploitation. Economic oppression gets to be reflected in the form of religious alienation. The latter depends on the former. If the cause is removed the reflection will disappear.[14] Lenin, too, considered economic slavery to be the root of all alienations, including the "lie of religion." They are to be destroyed by the revolution.[15]

If religion is alienation and alienation is the loss of human qualities, is there a place for religion in the future society according to MEL? The answer, it seems, is that there is no place, because the vision of that future for the founders of Marxism-Leninism is not pluralistic. The future is brought about according to the laws of dialectic. The present (capitalistic and theological) will be negated and replaced by a new future (communistic and atheistic). Here it is clear that communism is necessarily connected with atheism just as in the past religion was necessarily tied to capitalism. After the completion of the *Manuscripts* in 1844, Marx thought that the perfect emancipation of people could happen only in the communist-atheistic society, since in such a society there is neither religion nor other forms of alienation.

Religion as a "private affair" is possible in that state which has emancipated itself from religion through separation of state and church. But in a communist state religion cannot exist even as a "private affair." The existence of religion in a communist state[16] would presuppose ideological, and even dialogical, pluralism. Such pluralism was not foreseen by MEL for the last stage of human history.

Since the discussion of pluralism of Marxists and non-Marxists (including Christians) cannot be separated from the vision of the future monolithic society, a

---

[12]Cf. Karl Marx, *Ökonomisch-philosophische Manuskripte aus dem Jahre 1844* (Berlin, 1932), in *Werke*, Vol. E, I.

[13]Cf. Friedrich Engels, *Die Lage der arbeitenden Klasse in England* (Leipzig, 1845), in *Werke*, Vol. IV.

[14]*Antidühring* (1878).

[15]Vladimir Ilyich Lenin, *Socialism i religiya* [Socialism and Religion] in *Sochinyenyiya* [Works] (Moscow: Institut Marksa, Engelsa, Lenina pri CK VKP, 1947–1957), Vol. X.

[16]Marx and Engels did not use the term "communist state."

reinterpretation of the concept of alienation seems to be the second necessary precondition of the possibility of dialogue. Progress in this respect was made by the Polish philosopher Adam Schaff from 1964 onward. He holds that Marx's understanding of alienation was true for the time in which he lived and from his perspective of the future society in which all forms of alienation are to disappear. But in our time, according to Schaff, it is impossible to think along the lines of Marx's schemes, because they contradict contemporary praxis and vice versa. In his book *Marxism and the Human Individual*[17] Schaff maintained that various forms of alienation could continue their social existence and that they might vanish from society only if the human species became extinct. Schaff's view is, in our opinion, a precondition to the dialogue. It points to the contingency of the Marxist vision of history. Having made his starting point with praxis, Schaff did not come to the same conclusions as did Marx, because he realized the persistent nature of alienation as well as the non-essential dependence of religion upon the economic base. Praxis thus demands ideological pluralism. Marx's definition of religion as the opium of the people Schaff considers to be a document of a historic era rather than a normative definition.

3. The "opium of the people" as a definition of religion is a third point which, in the perspective of the dialogue, the Marxists need to reinterpret. In 1844 the young Marx said that "the criticism of religion is the premise of all criticism."[18] Surprisingly Marx did not devote a single work to the critique of religion, unlike Engels and Lenin, but devoted only marginal attention to it throughout a number of his works. A large number of Marx's statements on religion are mere assertions made rhetorically and somewhat stridently, as was the customary manner of many other young Hegelians. It appears that Marx did not abandon this manner of writing when he ceased to be a Young Hegelian.

Two conclusions follow out of the fact that Marx wrote about religion parenthetically and without proofs, except where referring to historical forms of religion: (A) If it is true that "the criticism of religion is the premise of all criticism," then it is clear that Marx himself did not provide this foundation. Consequently, the criticism of religion in Marxism must be viewed as a "foreign body" within Marxist thought. This is to say that the criticism of religion is not originally Marxist but was taken over from its philosophical precursors, mainly from Feuerbach. And yet it was amalgamated into the total Marxian doctrinal corpus according to which religion is always something that deprives the human of his or her own worth. (B) The fact that Marx neglected the criticism of religion is indicated by his later preoccupations, especially after the famous *Theses on Feuerbach*. His efforts were directed to an admirable goal of changing society so that the human being and the world would be placed on their own feet. This "placing on their own feet" Marx accomplished on the theoretical level by

---

[17](Warsaw, 1965).
[18]In the introductory part of K. Marx, *Zur Kritik der Hegelschen Rechtsphilosophie* (1844), in *Werke*, Vol. I.

substituting the Absolute Spirit with the human being, and on the practical level by giving the human being the task of actualization of the self and of history according to Marx's own scheme which nevertheless was not freed of the Hegelian structures.

Marx's position was somewhat toned down by Engels. He did not use Marx's definition of religion and recognized in religion some human values. Moreover, in many of his writings he praised the social structures of Early Christianity. And yet Engels continued, and Lenin magnified, viewing religion in the light of Marx's definition of religion. This definition, if we are to take it as a historical description, expressed the truth partially, but today it is even less accurate. Marx's definition was never really acceptable, and it must undergo new reinterpretations if the dialogue with believers is to become possible.

Contemporary Marxists increasingly realize how fragile Marx's definition of religion is. The French Marxist Roger Garaudy wrote eloquently of the need to reinterpret it. If religion were always and everywhere the opium of the people, then it would follow that it would be necessary to find the most effective means to eliminate it at once. However, if Marxists are to adopt and adapt the heritage of values which was contributed by religion and if Marxists expect mutual enrichment from the dialogue with Christians, then persecution becomes a factor of alienation even for the Marxists.[19] This position of Garaudy appears to be a prerequisite for the beginning of the dialogue between Christians and Marxists. Having discovered true human values and riches in religion, Garaudy gave a task to both Prometheian and Christian humanism (the first in its faith in the human being, the second in its faith in the God who became a human being and who continues to live today as a human being) to create a common will for the actualization of the total human being.

IV. Dialogue Today: Barriers

The major barrier to the dialogue between Christians and Marxists is the Platonic idealism which is to be found in Marxist circles. Dialogue, it must be emphatically stressed, is not a mere Socratic method of discovering the truth, but the only possible manner of human coexistence. The second barrier is to be found in the inner division among both Marxists and Christians into so-called progressives and traditionalists. The progressives in both camps are attempting to involve themselves in dialogue. The traditionalists consider it impossible. They see in it only dangers and, what is worse, they want to reserve it exclusively to themselves. Here I am talking about attempts to obstruct and condemn various associations of clergy by the ecclesiastical hierarchies within socialist countries and the so-called normalizing of relations between these socialist countries and the Vatican. I also include here the suffering of those Christians and Marxists

---

[19]E.g., Roger Garaudy, *De l'anathème au dialogue: un marxiste s'adresse au concile* (Paris: Plon, 1965).

who entered into dialogue "without permission" by their respective establishments.

1. *The Marxist dogmatic-idealistic position is a barrier to dialogue*. In places where the dialogue actually started among both partners barriers emerged because of both excessive caution and remnants of dogmatism. It was hoped that the meetings of the Paulus-Gesellschaft would have an impact in spreading the dialogue worldwide and, after having made an impact upon the Marxist theoreticians, gradually extending it to the sphere of social practice both in respect to certain Communist parties and on the international level. But this did not take place. Thus we are forced to ask the question as to whether dialogue is possible for Marxists. The answer is affirmative only under the condition of reinterpretation of the above-mentioned views. But this leads to an even more thoroughgoing reinterpretation which consists in the total rejection of the utopian-idealistic or Platonic mode of thinking by Marxists and their return to praxis as the only criterion of Marxist truth. Utopian idealism and Platonism see, uncritically of course, the solution of all human inadequacies in the classless society. This is not a scientific view, no matter how much it claims to be. Rather, it is an idealistic view. Society without social antagonisms can be seen in Marxism only as a negation of known forms of existing society. Insofar as this future society has been at least partially realized in practice, this realization indicates the contingency of Marx's positions on the theoretical level. On the practical level, it produced all kinds of deformations.[20] Marxism should minimize its enthusiasm for historical dialectics, primarily of its historical aspect. Marx thought dialectics to be scientific. Engels oversimplified it, especially in *Dialectics of Nature*. Lenin got so carried away in his enthusiasm for dialectics that he utilized it exclusively; for him dialectics was the sole manner of thought which had the right to claim that it was scientific. Such enthusiasts still exist in large numbers. Dialectics applied to history is hardly a candidate for the kind of exact science that the natural sciences are. Dialectics too enthusiastically applied to history carried Marxism toward unachievable predictions in the period before the October Revolution and into dogmatism after the October Revolution.

Marxism should reject its *a priori* denial of the religious and other non-Marxist interpretations of human beings. The position of the founders of Marxism-Leninism and the general position of those Marxists who attended the international dialogues were *a priori* rejections. Even more dogmatic is the position of those Marxists who never intended to engage in dialogue with Christians. One ought to mention that the "revisionist" Marxists are the ones who support the dialogue most ardently. They are sometimes very popular, but they are rarely in the position to make an impact in their own societies, because they are very definitely opposed in those efforts by the orthodox Marxists. That is why dialogue as it is being carried on today can lead to only minor reduction in

---

[20]Faith in God and faith in science are phenomenologically both equally structured.

tension between contemporary ideologies (though one ought to take advantage of any degree of relaxation in tension).

2. *Is Christianity ready for dialogue?* As in Marxism, there is no lack of barriers for dialogue among Christians. Christianity, too, ails of the same sickness of inner divisions. The divisions are manifold, but we shall emphasize here the one that is of greatest consequence for the dialogue. There are two theologies. One could be named "theology in popular edition," while the other is open to the achievements of contemporary scholarship. "Popular theology" frequently proclaims a God concept which, indeed, represents an alienation of true human values. Such a concept was being rejected by theologians and philosophers over the centuries if one is to believe Erich Fromm.[21] Fromm correctly distinguishes the biblical concept of God the liberator from the idol who, tailored after human fashion, enslaves. After Bonhoeffer, the majority of theologians have opted for God the liberator. This primitive popular theology interprets Marxism in the most primitive fashion and usually insists on the rejection of the possibility of dialogue with Marxists.[22]

The so-called "progressive theology" has been attempting to reinterpret the notion of religion as well as the concepts of God, of human beings, and of history by placing them all into a new perspective.[23] Without evaluating this theology, we need to emphasize that some of these theologians have been able to find a "common language" with the Marxists. Occasionally they may find more easily a "common language" with the progressive Marxists than with their own "official church."[24] This internal division of Marxism and Christianity is the first barrier that needs to be eliminated in order to enable the dialogue to move from the theoretical into the practical sphere and in order to make it efficacious in diminishing the degree of interpersonal human and international tensions.

V. Dialogue Today: Perspectives

Certain phenomena in contemporary capitalism and socialism which make the dialogue possible need at least to be mentioned. The founders of Marxism-Leninism did not, of course, predict them, and until recently they were completely unknown. They appear in various forms and played a considerable role, for instance, at the congresses of the Paulus-Gesellschaft. These phenomena may be considered the soil in which the seeds of unpredictable possibilities for dialogue and for a more humane co-existence can emerge. Thus, for instance, the working class in the U.S.A. cannot be considered revolutionary anymore, con-

---

[21]*You Shall Be as Gods* (New York: Holt, Rinehart and Winston, 1966).

[22]G. Scatamburlo, *Perché il Concilio non ha condonnato il Communismo* (Rome: L'Apennino, 1967).

[23]Harvey Cox, for instance, in his secularized theology considers human beings as God's partners in history. See on this J. R. Romić, *U vremenu s Kristom* [With Christ in Time] (Zagreb: Kršćanska Sadašnjost, 1976), pp. 124–142.

[24]Leslie Dewart, *The Future of Belief* (New York: Herder, 1966). See the author's introduction to the Italian translation of his book, *Il futuro della fede* (Brescia: Queriniana, 1969).

trary to Marx's expectations, because this class does not wish the destruction of, or any major changes in, the existing social order. In that large country the critique of the social order and the desire for social change depends mainly on the university students.[25] Noteworthy also is the attempt by Jean-Paul Sartre[26] to enrich Marxism with existentialism and vice versa, but frequently Marxists consider him a revisionist for these efforts.

Within contemporary Marxism there is an increasing number of Marxists who openly reject every dogmatism because of their humanistic inspirations. In these circles of developed Marxism one may notice the emergence and development, though with different degrees of success, of the theoretical and practical question of "one's own path to socialism." Since this is a recent trend, it would be wise to postpone the evaluation of its success, because the criterion of evaluation in Marxism is praxis. Fortunately for the dialogue, all Marxists who participated in the formal congresses directly or indirectly belong to the progressive Marxist circles, among whom there can be, in principle at least, new possibilities for dialogue.[27]

In certain countries—some of them capitalist and others socialist—there are developments which are likely to contribute to new forms of dialogue. A longer, more thorough study is needed in order to evaluate these developments. One such new phenomenon is workers' self-management in Yugoslavia. It is a consequence of Yugoslavia's "own path into socialism."[28] If we add to this that the late French President de Gaulle spoke of certain forms of self-management as part of his notion of economic development, it will become evident that social consciousness is more creative than could be predicted.

The study of these phenomena which emerge out of humanistic tendencies has not yet been fully carried out by Marxist theoreticians, nor has it been done in practice. The social practice reveals unpredictable difficulties. Thus it is impossible for me to agree with Oleg Mandić, an official Marxist representative of the Yugoslav regime who, for instance, maintained at the Paulus-Gesellschaft Congress in Salzburg in 1965 and elsewhere that the cooperation between the believers and Marxists within Yugoslavia's self-managing system was already accomplished, indeed quite developed. In 1969 at Bonn Mandić again offered misinformation instead of information. But neither can I agree with Giuseppe De Rose, a professor at the Gregorian University and a consultant for the Secretariat for Non-Believers at the Vatican,[29] who prematurely condemns Italy's "separate path" into socialism for which the Italian Marxists have been struggling since Palmiro Togliatti's speech in 1963 in Bergamo, Italy, and even more so since his famous "testament" written from Yalta, U.S.S.R., and since the Tenth Congress of the Communist Party of Italy.

---

[25]Ivan Kuvačić, *Obilje i nasilje* [Affluence and Violence] (Zagreb: Praxis, 1970), p. 148.

[26]Jean-Paul Sartre, *Critique de la raison dialectique* (Paris: Gallimard, 1960).

[27]It is interesting that such openness was not manifested by the East German Marxist Walter Hollitscher and the Bulgarian Marxist Asari Polikarov, who did participate in the dialogue.

[28]Alfred Meyer, *Communism* (New York: Random House, 1967), pp. 177–189.

[29]This Secretariat is formally independent from the Vatican but is in reality very dependent upon it.

This is not to say that certain caution and suspicion are not justified in relationship to the "separate paths to socialism." Lenin's shift in behavior before and after the October Revolution and Togliatti's statement in Bergamo that "history can never be reversed" give cause for such caution, and so do the forcible suppression of the "separate roads" in Hungary (1956), Czechoslovakia (1968), and Croatia (1971). Similar cause for suspicion is the cruel dealing of some Communist parties toward those Marxists whom they label "revisionists." Thus, for instance, the only Marxist who in my judgment researched religion in a scholarly fashion, Esad Ćimić, was not only expelled from the Central Committee of the Communist Party of Bosnia and Herzegovina and from the membership in the League of Communists of Yugoslavia, but also had difficulties with his teaching position at the University of Sarajevo, though there was not a single public criticism against the scholarly quality of his writings and lectures.

It is a bitter experience to contemplate the downfall of the progressive movements within Marxism, especially if the suppression of several "Springs" devours or hurts those Marxists who are our friends. Despite this bitterness, which is considerable, the question of the dialogue remains an open question, because, at least on the theoretical level, the evolution of Marxism in the direction of humanistic liberalism in almost all capitalist countries favors dialogue. An evolution in the same direction is evident in Czechoslovakia (prior to its occupation) and in Yugoslavia (prior to December, 1971), especially on the part of those Marxists who gathered around the periodical *Praxis,* which has recently been suppressed.

VI. Conclusion

This discussion on the Christian-Marxist dialogue can be summed up with three concluding points. We shall also point to a few contemporary trends and manifestations which, I hope, will bring about new possibilities of dialogical coexistance, or which are, at least, seeds for possible dialogue. Not all appropriate trends will be pointed out but only those which impress me as being more than a brittle hope.

1. According to MEL, dialogue between Marxists and non-Marxists, including Christians, is not possible. The reason is their monolithic vision of the future society and their exclusion of believers from practical cooperation on creative projects. A tiny opening for dialogue among the founders of Marxism is to be found in their rejection of the "administrative" approach toward religion and in their concept of praxis as a constant source of new interpretations.

2. Dialogue with Marxists is possible as was shown, for instance, at the congresses of the Paulus-Gesellschaft from 1964 to 1968. These congresses showed that dialogue is possible but at the price of reinterpreting some of the theoretical positions of MEL.

3. Dialogue between Marxists and Christians is necessary in order to bring about a more humane society. The statement which was made by Roger Garaudy, and others, including Erich Kellner in his introduction to *De dialogo*

inter marxistas et christianos that the "future society cannot be built against Marxists nor Christians, nor can it be built without Marxists or Christians" is substantially correct. However, I wish to emphasize here that the societies of the future might be built without one or the other unless we turn jointly to look toward a common future. Former visions of the world, I think, have lost their power.

The so-called theologians of revolution—especially the ones who inspire the Third World, or more specifically Latin America, under the influence of foreign ideologies and due to their own lack of experience—speak of an illusory but not a real possibility to replace one imperfect vision of society (the capitalist) with another which is at least as imperfect (the communist). The revolutionary spirit, by which Christianity, too, is inspired, is permeated by the principle of discontinuity, which might be acceptable on the purely social or "secular" level. But the reality of the church eludes the purely temporal categories. The church's dynamic will never be explained through dialectics or purely rational schemes.[30] The future might, indeed, bring about some new types of revolution.[31] The present notions of future arrangements will not suffice.

In those countries where the Communists took power, they took control over all means of public communications, all propaganda, etc. The ecclesiastical institutions felt very threatened by this, though I think they should not have. This takeover of propaganda is an act with two consequences. The negative consequence is that the freedom of many individuals and communities has been curtailed. But the positive consequence is that the precondition for a more creative faithfulness of the church has been brought about. Namely, if the church uses the same means of propaganda as other secular institutions, including the state, in order to secure the power to rule, then it shows that the church is looking toward means to rule and not to serve people. Thereby the church would manifest the lack of belief in a God who ought to reign over all. Even clearer is the process of nationalization of church properties which took place after the "revolutions." In the past, especially in difficult times, the church has shown more concern for the privileges of some of its members than the rights of all of its members. The loss of church properties is beneficial for the church's realignment toward the rights of all.

The existing forms of Marxism are not without weaknesses. To the contrary! However it is important to recognize the historical achievements of Marxism as well as the historical cleansing elements in its antithesis, Christianity. In addition, one ought to recognize the new possibilities of a more humane future society. For instance, the self-management of workers frequently is not carried substantially beyond the ideological level. Then it becomes a mythology, an opium for the people. Regardless of the motives of those who invented workers' self-management, one must admit that the idea is capable of creating a new consciousness among the workers; namely, that workers' self-management is a

---

[30]Romić, *U vremenu s Kristom,* p. 201.
[31]Harvey Cox, *The Feast of Fools* (New York: Harper Colophon, 1969), p. 143.

truly valuable ideal and that it should be actually rather than only nominally implemented. If the working class starts moving toward this goal it will be difficult to obstruct it.

The creation of a large working class in those countries that had a "revolution" despite the high price paid for this industrialization (at the expense of the peasantry which, because of their lesser degree of dependence upon the state, were able to resist the state in masses, thereby causing them frequently to be fearfully ravaged) is also an act with two consequences. The negative consequence is that the workers in those countries are completely dependent upon the political powers. The positive consequence is that the working class became enlarged as well as more concentrated. Under these conditions it is easier for the workers to obtain knowledge and information, and, hence, it is more difficult to impose an absolute rule over them.

In connection with the creation of the working class one must not forget that the process of urbanization is accompanied by the spiritual process of secularization. This secularization is to be understood as the liberation from a spiritual "suit of armor" which retards the growth of the liberated person. Besides many negative effects, secularization is also a chance not only to liberate the person from some older "suits of armor," some former cultural values which were presented in a dogmatically unchangeable form, but from every spiritual "suit of armor." The working class is, indeed, in the continuous position to effect its own liberation.[32]

Having come to power by a revolution (or "revolution"), Marxists have created real preconditions for a new class of well-educated people. Not intending it, they created their own developed humane antithesis. It is, namely, well known that in socialist countries there are excellent educational opportunities. It is not the privilege of the rich but the possibility for the majority.[33] This, too, is an act with two consequences. The negative effect is that not all graduates can find a suitable job. But the positive effect is that they can become more creative and less open to manipulation. How else can one understand the fact that the sons and daughters of dogmatic and orthodox Marxists are mostly liberal humanists?

All of the above considerations should be coupled with the fact that throughout the whole world there is an emergence of a new class of well-educated people, a class which pays little attention to the artificially-created borders between people, nations, countries, and systems. This new class of spiritually-raised humanists will not tire in promoting the dialogue on all levels nor in the realization of preconditions of coexistence in freedom.

Translated from the Croatian by Paul Mojzes

---

[32]Romić, *U vremenu s Kristom*, pp. 124–146 (ch. 6, which is entitled "Secularization as a Chance for Liberation").

[33]For instance, there was only one university on the territory of Croatia before World War II, with fewer than 5,000 students. Now there are seven universities with over 100,000 students. This is rather typical of socialist countries.

COMMUNISTS AND CATHOLICS: FROM DIALOGUE TO COLLABORATION TO CREATE A DEMOCRATIC AND SOCIALIST SOCIETY

Alceste Santini

I

The dialogue among Communists and Catholics which is intended as a search for points of understanding through a constructive encounter at all levels for a democratic and socialist society belongs, by now, to the history of our country [Italy].

The problem of the historical relations of Communists with the Vatican and the Catholic world was already felt by Antonio Gramsci, even before the creation of the Communist Party of Italy (PCI), which took place on January 21, 1921. In March, 1920, Gramsci defined the problem as follows: "In Rome, Italy, there is the Vatican, there is the Pope. The liberal Government already has a system of balance with the spiritual power of the Church. The state of the working-class must find a similar system." On October 2, 1920, a very interesting article entitled "La Questione Romana" ["The Roman Issue"] appeared in *L'Ordine Nuovo* ["The New Order"].[1] In the article the relationship between the movement of the working classes and the Catholic world was confronted for the first time in a new and different way, with respect to the radical socialist tradition and the positivist culture. Among other things, it was stated that "Communism, being a harmonically integral doctrine, with a highly humanistic and truly realistic concept of life, does not disregard nor deny any facet of contemporary humanity. Communism—and we maintain this openly—does not want to suffocate religious freedoms: on the contrary, it intends to guarantee all of them in the best way possible."

Almost sixty years have passed since these statements were made. The theoretical elaboration of our party regarding the issue of our relationship with the Catholic world, and the Vatican in particular, has become much wider. In

---

[1]Historians call the dispute which arose between the temporal power of the Church and the national movement seeking to affirm the autonomy and independence of the Italian State "the Roman Issue" [*Questione Romana*]. The issue was settled by the Lateran Agreements (*Patti Laterani*), on February 11, 1929, but, lately, the Church has tried to reaffirm its position with the Second Vatican Council.

Alceste Santini (Marxist) received his doctoral degree in philosophy and history from the University of Rome where he remains a member of a research group for the study of church-state issues. He is an essayist on the questions of the Vatican and the Catholic world, which is also his editorial responsibility for the Communist daily *L'Unità* and the ideological magazines of the P.C.I., *Critica marxista* and *Rinascita*. He is the founder of the two journals, *Religioni Oggi* and *Qualesocieta,* in which Marxist and Christian writers enter into dialogue. Among his recent books are *Questione cattolica—questione comunista* (1975), *Il Gesù dei marxisti* (1976), *La Chiesa cattolica di fronte alla crisi del mondo contemporaneo* (1976), and *La donna della Chiesa* (1977).

fact, it constitutes not merely one of the most characteristic aspects of the PCI—as a party related to the majority of the population strata—but also one of the reasons for which we obtained many significant successes in the long years of struggle. Today, the correctness of the conduct of our party and the vital contribution given to it by Gramsci and Palmiro Togliatti clearly stand out in the evolution of the situation in Italy and all over the world, in spite of the persistence of many contradictions and risks and of the new problems that constantly arise.

Among the problems, the relationship between democracy and socialism as related to the contest between socialism and capitalism is extremely relevant. In reference to our "New Party" (founded in 1944), Togliatti affirmed, "The reality is that we—the Communists in Italy—earlier than all Communists of West Europe are confronted with a new problem, a problem which never arose in years past. We, the Communists of Italy, earlier than all Communists of West Europe, are confronted with the challenging new task of creating a Communist Party under totally new conditions, with totally new and different goals."[2]

In this way, the necessity to search beyond the traditional Communist and socialist scope of activity was deeply felt in order to develop a new and different experience in the realm of action and in regard to social and political alliances. From that time onward Togliatti was concerned with avoiding a fixed identification of the Marxist ideology with the party so that "our party" could be better identified with the working classes. Furthermore, in order to foster theoretical research and practical action, not restrained by dogmatic nor sectarian standpoints, he said:

> Marxism is not a dogma nor a catechism, rather it is a guide for action. Now, today, the action of the working classes has reached a point where, in order to evolve further, it has to follow paths not yet followed. Today, the Marxist leaders of the working-class party must be able to trace these paths, to anticipate the best way to develop them, and, finally, to follow them firmly.[3]

With this approach, Togliatti described Marxism not as a fixed philosophical and political system, totally defined so that it could be mechanically followed, but rather as a method, a science of revolution which could be enriched and continually verified in the light of experience and in regard to the results obtained by other particular sciences. This means that Marxism must constantly be confronted with other currents of thought and with new human realities to better enlighten and guide the struggle for a new world. Besides, the constant test given by experience is the only way to demonstrate the superiority and the validity of the Marxist system.

I do not intend to go over all the elaborations by Togliatti and repeatedly by the PCI up till the present with the intention to practice the above-mentioned

---

[2]From a speech given by Togliatti in Florence, on January 10, 1944.
[3]Ibid.

methodology in the sphere of political initiatives on the national and international levels. In fact, it is evident that there is the necessity to develop further a dialogue for a reciprocal recognition of values, the attainment of understanding and even agreement with the political components of Christian persuasion, and, finally, the pursuit of common goals, according to the results attained by the Second Vatican Council, in the Catholic Church and in the Catholic world at large.

In any case, I want to make it clear that the political program defined today as "Euro-Communism" is not new, even though it has been amply developed under the objective conditions created in Italy, elsewhere in Europe, and all over the world, only recently. Today, the PCI includes a constantly increasing number of members of the Christian faith due to its open character and its dynamic Marxist inclination. By the way, it should be remembered that, by a decree, since the Fifth Congress in 1945, in order to become a member of the PCI, one need only accept the program and the regulations of the Communist party, but not necessarily accept Marxist philosophy.[4] This does not mean a denial of the ideal part of the struggle. It is, instead, evidence that our party is not a philosophical academy, but rather an immense, popular organization guided by Marxism as a doctrine of the revolution. And Marxism, I repeat along with Togliatti, is not a dogma, nor a catechism; it is a guide for action. In other words, Togliatti meant that the Communist leaders still have the task to create new routes which are, therefore, different from those presently followed by the socialist countries.

So a Communist party which intends to reform society in a socialistic way does not fear confrontation; it looks for it and it promotes it. For this reason the message contained in Togliatti's Memorial, written in August, 1964, from Yalta is very important: "We have to become the supporters of intellectual freedom, artistic creation, and scientific progress. To do so, we must not abstractly oppose our ideas to other currents of a different nature; instead, we must start a dialogue with them to investigate the different cultural issues as they appear today. We must keep in mind that those who disagree with us are not necessarily our enemies nor agents of our enemy."

By carrying out this methodology, the PCI affirmed at the Eleventh Congress in 1966 that we intend to have a socialist state, which "is neither confessional nor atheist," but a laic state in every sense of the word. Later, at the Thirteenth Congress in 1972, it was declared that the PCI has the task of "promoting the free development of all authentically democratic forces. Moreover, we shall cooperate to give the proper historical manifestation to those values supported by Christian consciences to create a superior society." These directions have been confirmed by the Fourteenth Congress held in March, 1975. Furthermore, the documents subscribed by the Spanish and Italian Communist parties in July, 1975, and by the French and Italian Communist parties on November 15, 1975,

---

[4]Article #2 of the Party Constitution: All Italian citizens of 18 years of age can be members of the PCI, independently of their race, religious faith, and philosophical convictions, provided that they accept the political program of the party and bind themselves to work for its realization.

elaborated them. In the latter document we read: "Socialism will constitute the higher phase of democracy and freedom; it will be democracy achieved in the most complete way." And the two largest Communist parties of the West added: "The freedom of thought, expression, press, of meeting and affiliation, the free moving at home and abroad, the inviolability of private life, the freedom of religion, and the philosophic, cultural, and artistic freedoms must be assured and increased."[5]

The consequence is that the Catholic Church and the Catholic world would have complete freedom of expression and affiliation. In our country the latter is also guaranteed by article #7 of the Constitution. The Communist Party has given a conclusive contribution to such a commitment. In the above-mentioned document, it was also stated that, in the future socialist society and in the same PCI, there will exist no distinction between first- or second-class citizens based on their beliefs and cultural backgrounds, but everybody, with equal rights and duties, will be needed to work in different fields to construct the socialist society, which must objectively represent "the higher phase of democracy and freedom."

II

In the 1960's, the earnest dialogue between Marxists and Christians, with all its cultural and political consequences, could not have been possible without the historical experience of the PCI, guided by an original analysis of reality in both Italy and the whole world. On the other hand, we must also give credit to the contribution of Pope John XXIII and Vatican II. In particular, the distinction made by Pope John in his papal encyclical, *"Pacem in terris,"* between "ideologies" and "historical movements" had a very significant consequence.[6] It gave the Church, the Catholics, and the Christian movements a methodological principle to overcome the old Manichean visions of history and to look for a new approach with the different components of the contemporary world through dialogue and encounter.

So a dialogue on the diplomatic level has been started between the Holy See and the socialist countries, between the Holy See and the non-Catholic countries, between the Roman Catholic Church and the Christian movements on one side and Marxist movements on the other.

The 1960's marked the transition from ideological opposition and the cold war to the dialogue. In spite of the persistence of some contradictions, new prospects of agreement and cooperation at different levels have been initiated to solve the urgent problems of the moment. Today, we can affirm that the old theoretical picture of the traditional Christian doctrine is in crisis. And, because

---

[5]The PCI and PCF common declaration was published by *L'Unità* on November 18, 1975.

[6]There is a distinction between "doctrines which remain unchanged" and "historical movements." By acting on historical situations unceasingly in evolution, the historical movements might suffer changes that are often quite significant.

of the new orientations derived from the Council, the organizations and movements of Christians have not only renounced old loyalties to the Christian Democrats and the principle of "the unity of all Catholic members" in a single party, but also they no longer requested that their answers to the problems of the time be considered absolutely valid. On the contrary, a constantly increasing number of Catholics now see the necessity of an encounter—even at a political level—with other currents of thought and other movements of a different orientation. The last world synods of bishops that took place in the Vatican in 1971 and 1974, and on September 30, 1977, have also confirmed these points of view. The problem of "human advance" has been the central issue in the synods. In their documents, it is stated that today evangelization cannot be separated from promoting human interests, i.e., the process of emancipation of human beings.

The problem of the relationship between Christians and Marxists has been widely considered, though not from the same perspective. The Latin-American, African, French, and Spanish bishops were more tolerant. The Belgian, Dutch, and Italian bishops were more restrictive. The West German bishops oppose it. Bishops from Hungary and Yugoslavia were very pragmatic. The Italian bishops at their November, 1976, meeting on evangelization and human progress considered a new and open approach toward the Marxist ideology and the possibility for Catholics to be members of the PCI. All of the bishops had to realize that the number of socialist countries is increasing and the need for a socialist society is deeply felt in all continents, particularly by the young generations.

On the other hand, because of the total change which has taken place in this century (the Russian revolution is an unavoidable point of reference), particularly since the end of World War II, Pope John XXIII decided to call a Council not to excommunicate or to bless, but rather to face the development of history. In fact, the last chapter of the conciliar constitution *"Gaudium et Spes,"* which deals with the role of the Church in the contemporary world, is dedicated to "the dialogue among all men" without making any distinction between Catholics and non-Catholics or between believers and non-believers, because "we must work together to construct a new world with true peace." The Council, therefore, heartily welcomed the invitation that John XXIII extended to all people, without considering their ideological dissensions, to work together for the general welfare.

Pope John made the distinction between "ideologies" and "historical movements." In this way, he put an end to the religious wars and to theorizing of head-on controversies, and initiated collaboration "in clarity." "Clarifications and alliances," he said in *"Pacem in Terris,"* among the different sectors of the secular order, among believers and non-believers, or among those who do not believe in the proper way because they adhere to errors, might cause them to discover the truth and, consequently, to adhere to it." Today, the PCI fully agrees with such an approach. Exactly twenty days before the publication of *"Pacem in Terris"* (April 11, 1963), in his famous speech "The Destiny of Man" delivered at Bergamo, March 20, 1963, Togliatti said:

We always rejected the possibility of negotiating with Catholics on the basis of any compromise between the two doctrines. It is necessary, instead, to consider both the Catholic and the Communist worlds as complexes of real forces—states, governments, organizations, individuals, movements of different nature—and see if, in some way, in view of the revolutions of the present time and the perspectives of the future, we can work out a reciprocal understanding, a mutual recognition of values, and, from there, an agreement to reach goals which are common to everybody, because they are necessary and indispensable to all humankind.

The real political problem, therefore, was not, and is not, in the search for a compromise between the two doctrines. Even if, sometimes, from different starting points, it is possible to reach conclusions which are not totally contradictory, we want now to ascertain how to find an understanding and start a collaboration which are necessary for the peace and general emancipation of all countries. This means that the dialogue and encounter among different forces are the only valid approaches to construct something new and useful. But we must conduct them systematically, giving everyone the opportunity to have his or her rights respected, and ultimately having in mind the liberation of every man and woman from any kind of exploitation and limitation of his or her dignity and freedom.

On February 22, 1972, in his speech about the changes which had occurred in the Catholic world, the present secretary general of the PCI, Enrico Berlinguer, said: "The Council forced the Church to pay attention to 'the signs of the times,' as Pope John called them. People's earthly emancipation, and not solely their eternal salvation together with the certainty that their solution is in a thorough revalorization of the collective present situation, are the main outcomes of the Council."[7]

III

It is certainly true that the values related to social justice, reform of the family, human dignity, and peace obtained through a democratic order, on a national and international level, can be realized today only if we put the issue of individual emancipation at all levels at the center of political action, and only if we consider it a public value. These are typical values of a socialist movement, but we find them also in the texts that contain the Christian message. Since the Council, many theologians and Catholics have brought the message up to date and have eliminated all mythological and metaphysical references from a certain occidental philosophy.

In the last fifteen years, the dialogue between Communists and Catholics has been conducted on these new bases. It has given a valid contribution to the change of mentality and behavior, while it has caused new political, social, and

---

[7]Enrico Berlinguer, *The Communist Issue* (Rome: Riuniti Publishers), p. 401.

cultural processes, as has been widely noticed. Objectively speaking, today it is anti-historical to propose again religious wars or ideological confrontations. During the last months of 1975, some Italian prelates and the Cardinal Vicar Ugo Poletti tried to do so. In June, 1976, before the administrative elections, Poletti spoke about "a confrontation between the city of God," that is the Church, and "the city of the people without God," which is supposed to be the city of Communists. The idea of "the two cities" is no longer valid even in the minds of many Catholics and in particular in the minds of the younger generation. Today, everybody wants to live in a city that belongs to everybody. And besides that, the new leftist administration of Mayor Giulio Carlo Argon which took power in Rome in August, 1976, has demonstrated that nothing apocalyptical happened to the Church. At a meeting in the Vatican, on January 3, 1977, Pope Paul VI and the mayor of Rome, Mr. Giulio Carlo Argan, treated each other with the greatest cordiality and mutual consideration, and in the spirit of collaboration. Thereby, they intended to prepare for "the Eternal City"—so rich in monuments and in pagan and Christian remains—a different future in respect to the aggravations inflicted upon it by past Christian Democratic administrations. There is no doubt that the political elections of June 20, 1976, have given a decisive impulse to the PCI on both local and national levels. Rome, Naples, Bologna, Florence, Genoa, and others, often with complete regions, have no leftist administrations.

It is a fact that the PCI now plays a main role in Italy, in Europe, and in the world. Therefore, all the other political forces had to review their positions. This is the cause of the intense "travail" in which the Catholic world, not only in Italy, is experiencing. Of course, some sectors in the political and social movements of Christians, as well as within the Church, still refuse to acknowledge all that is new in history, and obstinately look back at the past. Yet at the same time, "the other Church," "the Church of the Council," is expanding and has taken for a guideline what is written in the conciliar Constitution *"Gaudium et Spes"*: "The Church does not stand on the privileges received by the civil authority, but it will act for the welfare of everybody, according to different times and situations." Also, "Political community and the Church are independent and autonomous entities in their own fields. Nevertheless, both of them, and for different aims, are at the service of the personal and social vocation of each fellow human."

Because these ideas are widespread among Italian Catholics, the Christian Democrats, as a party of Catholics, finds itself in a really serious crisis. It is, in fact, relevant that in polls taken in 1975 and 1976 the most conservative and "integralist" faction, led by Amintore Fanfani, was defeated in its own Christian Democratic Party and in the Catholic Church. The dismissal of both Fanfani from the Christian Democratic secretary's office and Giovanni Benelli (later elected Cardinal and archbishop of Florence) from the secretary's office of the Vatican are clear proofs of the above-mentioned defeat. Nevertheless, "Integralism," as a typical characteristic of Italian Catholicism for too long afflicted by "temporalism" and "compromising" of the Church with the political and economic power, still exists. After the elections of June 20, 1976, and because of the crisis of the Christian Democratic behavior over the last thirty years (made more severe by the European economical situation), the cultural and political forces of Italy (including, of course, the Christian Democrats) must face the "Historical Compromise" proposed by the PCI and the ideological and political implications derived from it, in both the near and the distant future.

This is why, today, the problem of the general emancipation of human beings with the consequent renewal of society is not considered in terms of antagonism among different theologies, but rather, and first of all, as a conflict between those who want to rule the commune, the region, the state by giving preference to collective prosperity over individual interests, and those who consider only the advantage of their group and their allies to the detriment of common welfare.

Only by considering austerity and justice as the bases of our government will it be possible to keep the "crisis" from becoming a burden such that the people are forced to suffer the consequences of all the contradictions of the capitalist system and all of the distortions of the previous governments of the last thirty years. Let it be, instead, the historical occasion to initiate a moral, political, and economical process which will lead naturally to a more human, fair, and free society.

With "moral clarity" and, always, starting from real problems, we intend to face Catholics and other political forces of the nation, on the issue of the features of a new democratic society, under the conditions of socialism. We consider that today the method of confrontation is the only workable way for our country to overcome a crisis which is not only economic, but also cultural and political. In fact, it totally involves a style of life which the capitalistic forces and the political and cultural movements of Catholics have praised so much up till now. After the Council, which spread a genuine Christian message, an increasing number of Catholics are willing to give priority to the common welfare. We do believe that with these people it is possible both to discuss and to construct a society without profiteers or abused members. In it, the popular participation will have the support of the entire representative system (Parliament, communal, provincial, and regional councils), and, at the same time, it will favor other direct participatory ways of political government, those which are representative of a "Superior Society," the socialist society.

It is relevant that these our ideas are beginning to make their way into the Catholic world and the circles of the "Church intelligentsia," represented by the Society of Jesus. In an essay published in *Civiltà Cattolica* [*Catholic Civilization*] by its director, Father Bartolomeo Sorge, it is stated that "Marxism has contributed to the development in the world of a hope of liberation, that is, in itself, true and good, and this hope must not be betrayed."[8] Then, after criticizing how this "Marxist hope" has been realized in the eastern socialist countries, the reliable Jesuit urges Catholics to make a "serious and fair encounter" with

---

[8]*Civiltà Cattolica* (Rome), No. 3054 (September, 1977), pp. 462–465.

the Communists, because, he says, the time of the crusades and conflicts is over, and, henceforth, "Christian hope" must be "in a complementary relationship with other human hopes" including the Marxist one, in order to construct a better new society. This recognition of "complementarity" opens new horizons for the cooperation between Communists and Christians, while it closes—forever—the time of dogmatic approaches in history.

Our theoretical search and our political action are guided by a methodology which follows the great Marxist revolutionary lesson. Against any mechanical or dogmatic interpretation of what Marx and Lenin have said or thought, the above-mentioned lesson permits the Communists to live it and to realize it today in the historical context in which they live and act.

Translated by Dr. Leda M. Jaworski,
Rosemont College, Rosemont, PA

MILESTONES OF CHRISTIAN-MARXIST DIALOGUE IN FRANCE

Francis J. Murphy

In April, 1936, Maurice Thorez, then Secretary-General of the French Communist Party, addressed the citizens of France on national radio. In fulfillment of the mandate of the Central Committee of the French Communist Party (P.C.F.), Thorez delivered what he himself considered ''a great appeal for the unification of the French people.''[1] At the climax of his speech, Thorez proclaimed:

> We stretch out our hand to you, Catholic worker, employee, tradesman, peasant; we who are laic stretch out our hand to you, because you are our brother and you, like us, are burdened with the same cares.[2]

This brief, dramatic appeal continues to reverberate in France to this day. These words have given rise not only to the name of the Communist policy of the ''outstretched hand'' to Christians, but also to an unbroken tradition of forty years of French Communist efforts toward unity with French Christians.

Dale Vree has recently described the Christian-Marxist dialogue in France as ''largely an affair limited to intellectuals—Catholic clergy and maverick Communist theoreticians.''[3] Such an evaluation overlooks the fact that in France alone have the official leaders of a major Communist party publicly and directly appealed to believers. In carefully prepared, theoretically sophisticated addresses which have become quasi-canonical texts of Communist policy, Maurice Thorez in 1937 and Georges Marchais in 1976 have made official appeals to the Christians of France. Neither Thorez nor Marchais could be considered ''maverick''; each spoke officially as Secretary-General of the French Communist Party. Therefore, a thorough analysis of their policy statements is crucial to a serious study of Christian-Communist relationships in France.

I

The first of the two crucial statements under investigation is the celebrated address of Maurice Thorez on October 26, 1937, entitled: ''Communists and

---

[1] Maurice Thorez, *Son of the People* (London, 1938), p. 106.
[2] M. Thorez, *Oeuvres,* XI, p. 215.
[3] D. Vree, ''Coalition Politics on the Left in France and Italy,'' *The Review of Politics* 37 (1975): 343.

Francis J. Murphy (Roman Catholic) is assistant professor of history at Boston College and a priest of the Boston Archdiocese. He received his education at Holy Cross College, St. John's Seminary, and Catholic University, where he received the Ph.D. degree. He wrote articles for the *Catholic Historical Review* and *Worldview* on the Christian-Marxist dialogue in France, and is the historical planning editor for the *New Catholic Encyclopedia*.

Catholics: The 'Outstretched Hand.' '' The context of its presentation was inextricably intertwined with its content. France was at that time torn domestically by the demise of the Popular Front and divided diplomatically over the Spanish Civil War. Nonetheless, the P.C.F. continued to pursue its initiatives toward both support of the Popular Front and defense of the Spanish Republic. While the vast majority of French Catholics remained unsympathetic to both these causes, a small but articulate minority, especially among Catholic intellectuals, espoused these positions, of which the Communists were the most ardent champions. It was principally from their number that response—serious, if not usually favorable—had come to the original appeal by Thorez to the Catholics of France.[4]

It was to the questions posed and the challenges raised by the Communist initiative of the "outstretched hand" that Thorez addressed his attention on October 26, 1937. Formally, his presentation was a report, commissioned by the Central Committee of the P.C.F., on the subject: "Communists and Catholics." Substantively, his address was an exposition of Party policy toward the Catholics of France. Prominently present in the audience of five thousand which crowded the Palais de la Mutualité for the address were the thirty Catholics, principally journalists, who had accepted the Party's invitation.[5] After brief introductory remarks, Thorez immediately embarked upon his eight-part address.[6]

Thorez first dealt with the original appeal which he himself had made to French Catholics on national radio eighteen months earlier. "Whether for or against," the leader of the P.C.F. noted, "a vast controversy, testifying to the importance of the problem, has started."[7]

In the second part of the address, Thorez set out to explain the Communist position, its motives, and its aims. He first repeated verbatim the appeal he had originally made on national radio on April 17, 1936. From this proposal, Thorez drew two affirmations:

1. The Communists are secularists, materialists.
2. There exists a factual solidarity—material economic and social—between Catholic and Communist workers.[8]

---

[4]For the divisions among French Catholics on these questions, see R. Remond, *Les Catholiques le Communisme et les Crises 1929–1939* (Paris, 1960). For the fuller development of the background to this policy, see F. Murphy, "*La Main Tendue:* Prelude to Christian-Marxist Dialogue in France, 1936–1939," *The Catholic Historical Review* 60 (1974): 255–270.

[5]For a detailed description of the setting and the audience, see *Humanité,* October 28, 1937.

[6]There are many sources in which this speech is reproduced. The text used in the subsequent analysis is the English version: M. Thorez, *Catholics and Communists* (New York, 1938). The division of the speech into eight parts follows the French edition: M. Thorez, *Oeuvres,* XIV, pp. 159–181.

[7]Thorez, *Catholics and Communists,* p. 6.

[8]Ibid., p. 9. As Henri Chambre astutely points out, Thorez not only: "... did not minimize the doctrinal differences that separate Communists and Catholics, but ... he forgot to mention two points which are doubtless self-evident to a Communist listener, but which it would have been advisable for a Catholic listener to bear in mind: (1) that the Communist's view of *praxis,* i.e., the relationship of thought to action, makes him or her consider it inevitable and necessary that action should determine human thoughts and ideas; action inspired by Marxism is therefore bound to lead to the adoption of

While acknowledging the fundamental doctrinal opposition between Communism and Catholicism, Thorez still saw in both "the same burning desire to answer the profound aspirations of men towards a better life."[9] Just as Engels, in a passage drawn from the *History of Christianity*, saw remarkable parallels between primitive Christianity and the modern working-class movement, so Thorez saw a comparison between the builders of the great medieval cathedrals and the "constructors of a new socialist city."[10]

The third section of the speech treated the idealism of the Communists which was described as "an inexhaustible source of generous impulses which exalts in its adherents devotion and the spirit of sacrifice."[11] Thorez then quoted at length from the French Dominican, Vincent Ducattillon, praising the "very keen sense of the ideal" which sometimes accompanied the materialism of the Communists.[12] What Communism ultimately sought, said Thorez, was to put life "on true, on real foundations . . . to create the conditions necessary for the full flowering of all human faculties." It was for this reason that Thorez could say emphatically: "Communism is indeed humanism."[13]

The forth section on the liberating humanism of Communism concluded with a strong appeal by Thorez for the union of the Catholic trade union, the C.F.T.C., with the C.G.T., which, since the reunification of September 27, 1935, had combined both the Socialist and the Communist labor unions. The independence of the C.F.T.C., Thorez declared, "can no longer be justified in any way, the more since the C.G.T. accepts in its fold all workers, whatever their political opinions, their religious philosophic ideas."[14]

The proposal of the merger of the two labor movements served as a bridge to the fifth section of the address, which dealt with mutual charity. That charity, which Thorez envisioned as "the essential aim of our policy of the outstretched hand," was not "hypocritical philanthropy," but rather "the spirit of solidarity, the devotion to the common good . . . on the model of the good samaritan."[15]

That same spirit of solidarity should likewise mark the defense of democratic liberties and the defeat of fascism. These were the themes of the sixth and seventh

---

the Marxist view of reality; and (2) that propaganda will continue its efforts in every direction. See H. Chambre, S. J., *Christianity and Communism* (New York, 1960), pp. 35–36.

[9]Ibid., p. 10.

[10]Ibid., pp. 11–12.

[11]Ibid., p. 12.

[12]Ibid., p. 13. For the actual words of Ducattillion cited here, see F. Mauriac et al., *Communism and Christianity* (Westminster, MD, 1946), p. 41.

[13]Thorez, *Catholics and Communists*, p. 13.

[14]Ibid., p. 17. Despite sympathetic words and extensive coverage of the C.F.T.C.'s activities by *Humanité* (see *Hum.*, October 7, 1937), Catholic labor leaders were suspicious of the C.G.T.'s overtures and carefully promoted their independent position. In two articles in *Dossiers de l'Action populaire*, G. Robinot-Marcy explained the position, as well as the C.F.T.C.'s fears vis-à-vis the C.G.T. See "Allons-nous vers le Syndicat unique? L'offensive de la C.G.T. contre le Syndicalisme chrétien," *Dossiers de l'Action populaire*, No. 380 (February 25, 1937), pp. 377–410; and "Vers une dicature de la C.G.T.?" *Dossiers de l'Action populaire*, No. 383 (April 10, 1937), pp. 801–834.

[15]Thorez, *Catholics and Communists*, pp. 17–18.

sections of the speech. First among those democratic liberties, in Thorez' judgement, was liberty of conscience, which included two rights precious to Catholics—free exercise of worship and free choice of education. "The Communists," Thorez affirmed, "are against all exceptional legislation aimed at one class of the community because of their opinions and beliefs, when the latter are professed with respect for Republican laws."[16]

Thorez then quoted Articles 124 and 136 of the Constitution of the U.S.S.R. to prove that "the coexistence of Communists and Catholics, collaboration between them, is possible in a democratic regime and quite obviously in that higher form of democracy, the Soviet regime."[17] In marked contrast, anti-Catholicism in Fascist countries flowed as inescapably from "the totalitarian ideology of fascism"[18] as premeditated aggression.

The conclusion to which Thorez was drawing in the final section of his speech was clear: "It is time to unite all nations, all men of goodwill."[19] Specifically with reference to France, that meant:

> The alliance between Catholics and Communists is necessary; it is possible; it is on the way to becoming a reality. It simply demands mutual good faith; a mutual spirit of tolerance. For our part, whatever happens, whatever people do, we are firmly resolved to persevere in our policy of the outstretched hand. We are certain that success will crown our efforts.
>
> As in the case of the United Front, as in the case of the Popular Front, we are not talking about a clever maneuver, a campaign promise, or an occasional tactic. The texts of the founders of our doctrine, which I have just recalled, prove clearly that our attitude toward religion and toward Catholics has not been determined on the basis of a changing situation.
>
> As in the case of the United Front, as in the case of the Popular Front, we shall not let ourselves be stopped by any difficulty, any refusal, any ban. Our patience and our persuasion will once more vanquish resistance.[20]

---

[16]Ibid., p. 19.

[17]Ibid., pp. 19–20. The full text of the New Soviet Constitution, to which Thorez referred, can be found in English in M. Oakeshott, "The Constitution of the U.S.S.R., 1936," *The Social and Political Doctrines of Contemporary Europe* (Cambridge: Cambridge University Press, 1939), pp. 154–159. Freedom of conscience in Russia, which the P.C.F. consistently considered as fact because it was stated in the Soviet Constitution, was denied with equal consistency, but even more vehemence, in Catholic circles. The actual treatment of the religious question in Russia, with reference not only to Catholics but also to the much larger Orthodox community, was regularly advanced as an argument against collaboration. The best, brief treatment of the question available at that time by an informed Catholic author was that of Alexandre Marc, "The Outstretched (?) Hand . . . in the U.S.S.R.," in Mauriac et al., *Communism and Christianity,* pp. 172–199.

[18]Thorez, *Catholics and Communists,* p. 20.

[19]Ibid., p. 23.

[20]Ibid. The correct text of this last section is difficult to determine. The second paragraph given here (which is my own translation) is found only in the text published in *Humanité* on October 28, 1937. It is in neither Thorez' *Oeuvres,* nor the English translation, both of which were reproduced from a brochure edition of the speech published by the P.C.F. In my opinion the text from *Humanité* is the most reliable.

In retrospect, it would be extremely difficult to give a resume of the speech which Thorez gave on that night at the Palais de la Mutualité. The text itself had obviously been prepared with great care. The allusions made in the course of the speech were many in number and rich in variety. Yet, four fundamental propositions can be discerned which composed the skeleton on which the flesh of the speech clung: (1) The policy of the outstretched hand was effective, as proved not only by Catholic response, but by Socialist and Radical responses as well. (2) This policy corresponded not merely to the doctrines of Marx, Engels, and Lenin, but also to the current practice of the Soviet Union. (3) The noblest human aspirations of both Catholicism and Marxism were being opposed by "economic liberalism" and totalitarian fascism. (4) Nothing could deter the P.C.F. from carrying out its policy of collaboration with Catholics.

Obviously, the prior condemnations of Communism by Pius XI and the French bishops were implicit in the fourth of these propositions. More important, however, than these objections were the profound questions asked by critically thinking French Catholics, both clerical and lay. The initiative of the "outstretched hand" stimulated probing responses from all angles of Catholic perception.[21] However, in 1937, as Gaston Fessard astutely observed, Catholics and Communists never seemed to be speaking the same language. Yet, by 1976, his prediction that the way to dialogue had nonetheless been opened by the appeal of the French Communist Party in 1936 and 1937 had proved accurate.[22]

II

Several authors have explored the development of Christian-Marxist dialogue in the period following World War II.[23] In France, the question of Christian-Marxist relations has become not only a publishing phenomenon but also a pressing political prospect.[24] In was against this background that Georges Marchais, the present Secretary General of the French Communist Party, addressed the Christians of France on June 10, 1976.

Marchais delivered his "Appeal to the Christians of France" at the Gerland Sports Palace in Lyons. The arena was thronged with an audience of over ten

---

[21]See J. Hellman, "French 'Left Catholics' and Communism in the Nineteen-Thirties," *Church History* 45 (1976): 507–523. In comprehensive analysis, Prof. Hellman distinguishes five general attitudes ranging from total irreconcilability to needed compatibility on the part of French Catholics toward Christian-Communist relations.

[22]See G. Fessard, S. J., *Le Dialogue Catholique-Communiste, Est-il Possible?* (Paris, 1937), pp. 29–35.

[23]In this regard, see especially P. Hebblethwaite, *The Christian-Marxist Dialogue: Beginnings, Present Status, and Beyond* (New York, 1977), and D. Vree, *On Synthesizing Marxism and Christianity* (New York, 1976).

[24]See, for example, H. Madelin, *Chrétiens et Marxistes dans la Société Française* (Paris, 1977); G. Marchais and G. Hourdin, *Communistes et Chrétiens: Communistes ou Chrétiens* (Paris, 1976) and M. Thorez, W. Rochet, and G. Marchais, *Communistes et Chrétiens* (Paris, 1976).

thousand, including many Catholics ranging from prelates to peasants, formally invited by the French Communist Party.[25]

Marchais' address, the second crucial statement of the French Communist Party to the Christians of France, can be divided for purposes of analysis into two main divisions, each of which has five parts.[26] After brief introductory remarks calling attention to the urgency of the question of Christian-Communist relations in contemporary France, Marchais began his analysis of the political foundations of a definition of the relations between Communists and Christians.

Marchais first cited unemployment statistics, the archaic French educational system, the plight of the poor and the aged, and depressing, often dangerous working conditions as evidence of the serious crisis in French society. Yet, France with its vast human and material riches, with its tradition of democratic liberty and its prestige in the world need not so frustrate its citizens, especially the working class.

The Communist analysis of the crisis afflicting France constituted the second part of Marchais' address. "The cause of the ills that afflict France," according to Marchais, "is the system in which grand capital exercises its domination over every aspect of national life."[27] Despite differences of ideology and political persuasion, millions of French citizens demand change. That change, which will bring an end to present poverty, injustice, and disorder, is political.

The political change which Marchais and the French Communist Party propose is "modern democracy." This "modern democracy" is to be both economic and political. On the economic level, powers will be taken from the hands of the small privileged minority of grand capitalists and will be passed "into the hands of the nation, to be put solely at the service of our people." On the political level, "power should be held by those who are productive and serve the country."[28] The road to this modern democracy will be based at every step "on the democratic expression of the popular will." This will, regardless of its verdict, will be respected by the Communists. The result will be "a socialism in the colors of France."[29]

This "modern democracy" which Marchais described in the third part of his presentation would produce a new union of the French people, which he then analyzed at length. France, according to Marchais, is divided not between Right and Left, but between a small caste of grand capitalists and an immense mass of

---

[25] All the major French newspapers devoted extensive coverage to this address, but the most comprehensive description of the gathering can be found in *Le Progrès* (Lyon), June 11 and 12, 1976.

[26] This address has not been translated into English at this time. The French text used, with all translations by this writer is G. Marchais, "L'appel de Georges Marchais aux Chrétiens de France," in Marchais and Hourdin, *Communistes*.

[27] Ibid., p. 15.

[28] Ibid., p. 20.

[29] Ibid., p. 23. For a fuller exposition of this position, see G. Marchais, *Le Socialisme pour la France: Rapport de Georges Marchais au XXII Congrès* (Paris, 1976).

workers. The latter are deliberately set into opposing groups by the former so as to mask this true, fundamental division. But, the French Communist Party, which is preeminently the voice of the working class, will forge a new union of the French people, because the triumph of the working class, which seeks to exploit no one, will free the country of every form of exploitation.[30]

In the final part of the first section of his address, Marchais examined the great diversity of the people of France. The exploited are not "an indistinct mass," but "individuals endowed with different personalities, tastes, talents and aspirations."[31] While repudiating both "barracks Communism" and modern technocracy as destructive of the individual, Marchais held fast to the ideological orthodoxy of French Communism: "No tactical reason will ever lead us to water down what distinguishes our theory from others or to seek impossible and illusory philosophical convergences. Communist theory is based upon scientific materialism."[32] It was upon this base that Marchais then proceeded to define how the French Communist Party relates with the Christians of France.

Marchais began the second half of his address by noting that the Communists take religion seriously, since it constitutes "an essential aspect of the national community" and not "a barrier between workers." This latter misunderstanding of religion had spawned an earlier tradition of anti-clericalism in the French worker movement, based on the close ties between the bourgeoisie and the Church on one side, and "infantile" socialism on the other. He then explained the Communist position:

> We do not consider the faith of Christians as "intrinsically evil"[33] and the born enemy of the worker movement.... It is for us the complex reflection in the human consciousness of a world which oppresses men and calls them to another, happy world.[34]

For Marchais, as for Marx, "religion is not merely the expression of the distress of the lowly, it is also a protest against that distress."[35] The Communists, Marchais emphasized, struggle for all who experience that distress which is at the root of religion. In this regard, the Communists have no intention of intervening in such internal affairs of the Church as "liturgy, the content of faith or the forms of temporal involvement of believers."[36] But it is precisely this temporal involvement, as opposed to resignation or escape, to which the Bishops

---

[30]This identification of the Communist Party with the working class and its liberation as the end of all exploitation is classically Marxist. See K. Marx, *The Communist Manifesto*, especially Part II.

[31]Marchais, *Le Socialisme*, pp. 26–27.

[32]Ibid., p. 27.

[33]The expression "intrinsically evil" is a reversal of the condemnation of Communism as "intrinsically evil," by Pope Pius XI in his encyclical, *"Divini Redemptoris,"* March 19, 1937, Section 58.

[34]Marchais, *Le Socialisme*, p. 30.

[35]Ibid., p. 31. The specific reference to Marx can be found in K. Marx, "Contribution to the Critique of Hegel's Philosophy of Right," *On Religion* (Moscow, 1957), pp. 41–42.

[36]Ibid.

of France have urged French Catholics and to which Marchais adds the encouragement of the Communists.[37]

The heart of Marchais' message and the most fruitful passages for subsequent dialogue concern religious liberty and constitute the second part of his exposition. The central question involved is the position of believers in the "modern democracy" which the Communists propose for France. The socialist state which Marchais here projects will be "neither atheistic nor Christian, but simply secular." There will be no "official" state philosophy or doctrine. For both believers and non-believers, such a state, "directed and controlled by workers on every level," will guarantee all civil liberties. Specifically, Marchais defines liberty of conscience and religion as "freedom to practice one's religion, individually or collectively, in public or in private; freedom of worship and freedom of religious formation by the Church."[38] Significantly, Marchais, in conformity with his earlier Marxist analysis, sees the distinction between believers and non-believers not in terms of a relationship with a transcendent God, but rather in terms of belief in a heavenly life after death.[39]

On the institutional level, the Catholic Church, like all other churches and communities of believers, will enjoy all the freedom "necessary for their activities." Specifically, this includes the rights "to hold and dispose of property, to publish and to form candidates for the ministry."[40] The churches will be strictly separated from the state, "as a guarantee of independence for the churches as well as for the state."[41]

At this point, Marchais insisted that the religious situation in a socialist France will be markedly different from that of the Communist countries of Eastern Europe. On this extremely sensitive issue, Marchais explained:

> In order to make an objective appraisal, it must be noted that in several of those countries, the churches were previously linked tightly to the old order. They themselves sometimes participated directly in the exploitation of the peasants. They fought to prevent first the establishment and then the consolidation of worker states. This did not favor the establishment of harmonious relations between the churches and the new state. In turn, these were negative influences on the attitude of the state toward religion and indeed believers.[42]

But, Marchais hastened to add, such would not be the case in France for two reasons. On the one hand, the contemporary French church does not play a comparable role in the economic and political life of the country as did the

---

[37]Ibid. Marchais here refers explicitly to the document adopted by the Plenary Assembly of the French Bishops. The precise statement can be found in: "Pour une Pratique Chrétienne de la Politique," *Documentation Catholique* 54 (1972): 1011.

[38]Marchais, *Le Socialisme*, pp. 33–34.

[39]Ibid., p. 32.

[40]Ibid., p. 35.

[41]Ibid.

[42]Ibid., pp. 36–37.

churches in Eastern Europe. On the other hand, the French Communist Party has long held "a clear and open position in this regard" and follows no foreign model, but rather pursues its own road "which corresponds to the conditions of our own time and our own country."[43] This is precisely why, Marchais emphasizes, "we assign such great importance to reflection, to dialogue and to common action between Christians and Communists."[44]

It is the future of France, not electoral success, which impels the Communists to reach out to Christians, according to Marchais. The goal of a "modern democracy" will be realized only by a "broad union of the French people" of which "the Christians are an essential component."[45] The continuity of the policy of the "outstretched hand" from the time of the first appeal to Christians by Thorez in 1936 should dispel any claim of a tactical ruse by the French Communist Party. Marchais continues in this third part of his exposition to make the insightful observation: "I am not sure that our civilization is simply western and Christian, as it is termed."[46] Materialism and atheism are also an integral part of the western tradition. Therefore, "the future will be what we together today make it."[47]

That future will be the product of the shared aspirations of Communists and Christians who are "while different, profoundly attached to their respective traditions."[48] In support of this "community of aspirations," which constitutes the fourth part of his statement, Marchais cited official statements of remarkable similarity. First, the French Bishops are quoted: "No Christian man or woman can be indifferent so long as one of his brothers is, in any measure, the victim of injustice, oppression or degradation."[49] Then, Marchais quoted his own words: "Everywhere there is poverty to be relieved, injustice to be fought, or right to be defended, there is where the Communists should be."[50]

How will this "community of aspirations" be realized? Marchais concluded with this consideration. Simple coexistence, "without hostility, but without friendship," will not be enough. What is both possible and necessary is that Communists and Christians come to know each other and work side by side, with full respect for one another's uniqueness, in the task of preparing and building a more human society."[51] If Christians wish to join the Communist Party, they are most welcome and will enjoy "the same rights and the same responsibilities as all Party members."[52] However, Marchais realistically acknowledges that the

---

[43]Ibid., p. 37.
[44]Ibid.
[45]Ibid., p. 39.
[46]Ibid.
[47]Ibid., p. 37.
[48]Ibid., p. 41.
[49]Ibid., p. 42. The reference is to the same page and document of the French Bishops cited in note 54 below.
[50]Ibid., p. 42.
[51]Ibid., p. 45.
[52]Ibid., p. 48.

majority of Christians will not make this personal choice. This latter group will work, not among, but alongside the Communists. Together they can transform both France and the world. ''Peace on earth! Liberty for all peoples! Justice and social progress! Yes, all this, from today on, compels the mutual understanding and the common action of Communists and Christians.'' The Communists are prepared to meet with Christians on every level to strive for union. Union is the keynote on which Marchais concludes:

> In sum, the appeal which we are making to Christians, both Catholic and Protestant, is contained in one word: Union! Union in action for a more human society; Union for the victory of the Common Program; Union for socialism![53]

Marchais' appeal had been carefully constructed and powerfully presented. The immediate reaction of the audience was excitedly enthusiastic.[54] The later reaction of the French press was reservedly reflective.[55] The continuing reaction of both Christian and Communist spokespersons constitutes a new chapter in the Christian-Marxist dialogue.

III

Taken together and comparatively, these two crucial statements of leaders of the French Communist Party to their Christian compatriots have unique significance for dialogue. First, these statements underline the specifically national context in which Christian-Marxist relations develop. Second, within France, the Communist Party is most concerned about relations with Christians at times in which the P.C.F. is seeking to unify the political forces of the Left.[56] In 1937, the goal was the Popular Front. In 1976, it is the Common Program. Third, by 1976 the P.C.F. had openly assumed an identity independent of the model of the Soviet Union, which was the admitted ideal in 1937. Fourth, in both addresses references to Marx, Engels, and Lenin were largely eclectic, with little effort at systematic argumentation based on the authoritative Communist texts. Finally, a comparison of the central themes of both addresses, while signalling a more fulsome embrace of the traditions of French democracy and civil liberties on the part of the P.C.F. over the past forty years, indicates even more dramatic change in the

---

[53]Ibid., p. 49. The ''Common Program'' herein cited is the joint platform of the major parties of the French Left, the Communist Party, the Socialist Party, and the Movement of the Left Radicals. See *Programme Commun de Gouvernement* (Paris, 1973).

[54]See *LeProgrès* (Lyon), June 11 and 12, 1976.

[55]See especially *Le Monde* (Paris), June 12, 13, and 18, 1976; *Le Figaro* (Paris), June 12 and 13, 1976; *France Soir* (Paris), June 12, 1976, in which the harsh atack on Marchais in the first edition was replaced by a different article in the second edition; *Le Croix* (Paris), June 12, 1976; the *Quest France* (Rennes), June 11, 1976.

[56]In this capacity, the P.C.F. assumes the ''role of political tribune,'' to use the terms of R. Tiersky, *French Communism 1920–1972* (New York, 1974). In this scholarly analysis, Tiersky distinguishes four distinct roles assumed by the P.C.F. at different periods of its history.

Christian tradition, especially in terms of social involvement and political pluralism.

So far as the future of Christian-Marxist dialogue is concerned, valuable lessons can be drawn from the French experience. First, dialogue, despite the proclivities of intellectuals, both Christian and Marxist, must be sensitive to the unique historical and political situation of each country. Second, the special fruitfulness of specific moments in the history of Christian-Communist relations should be acknowledged and put to maximum avail. Third, the emergence of self-confident, independent Communist movements, especially the incipient Eurocommunism, demands a new openness and responsiveness among Christian intellectuals. Fourth, for the present at least, the French experience validates Paul Mojzes' generalization that "the Marxists are currently less eager to dialogue about theoretical matters."[57] Finally, Christians must be appreciative that the pluralism and renewal which have been characteristic of their tradition are now appearing in different forms within the Marxist tradition. The French experience, therefore, offers a uniquely fertile field for the future of Christian-Marxist dialogue.

Striking confirmation of the fertility of contemporary Christian-Marxist dialogue in France can be found in two recent statements of the French hierarchy. Together these documents demonstrate the problem and the potential of dialogue. Separately, their examination reveals markedly different approaches and significantly different conclusions.

The first statement, entitled "Marxism, Man and the Christian Faith," was issued by the Permanent Council of the French Bishops on June 30, 1977.[58] This document, although commissioned in 1975, constitutes the first comprehensive, collective statement of the French hierarchy on Catholic-Communist relations since the appeal of the P.C.F. to the Christians of France in June, 1976.[59] Therein, the French Bishops adopt what is now an almost classic Catholic approach that the central problem in Christian-Marxist dialogue is not "the opposition of atheism and faith," but rather "the divergence between two conceptions of nature, man, society and history."[60] While acknowledging the positive protest against injustice which is at the root of Marx's theory, and while distinguishing between Marxism as a philosophy and as a tool of analysis, the French Bishops conclude:

---

[57]P. Mojzes, "New Impulses for Christian-Marxist Dialogue," *Worldview* 20 (June, 1977): 44.

[58]For the full text of this document, see "Le Marxisme, L'Homme et la foi Chrétienne: Déclaration ou Conseil Permanent de l'Episcopat Français," *La Documentation Catholique,* No. 1724 (July 17, 1977), pp. 684–690 (hereafter cited as "Déclaration").

[59]Very brief, general remarks of the French Bishop concerning Catholic-Communist relations can be found in the "Compte rendu de la réunion du Conseil Permanent de l'Episcopat français," Paris, June 14–16, 1976; *La Documentation Catholique* (hereafter cited as *D.C.*), No. 1701 (July 4, 1976), pp. 635–636. For statements by individual bishops, see "A près l'appel de Georges Marchais aux Chrétiens," ibid., pp. 636–637, and "L'impossible alliance entre la vision Marxiste et la vision Chrétienne de l'homme," *D.C.*, No. 1711 (January 2, 1977), pp. 37–38.

[60]"Déclaration," p. 687.

If we, like the Communists themselves, affirm the theoretical and practical incompatabilities of Christian faith and Marxism, we nonetheless accept the risk of dialogue and confrontation; but it is necessary to set down precise guidelines...[61]

The Bishops spelled out their guidelines in four propositions.

1. It is indispensable to work with mutual respect for one another. Loss of identity benefits no one.
2. When a decision is made to work together, collaboration can be only on specific projects. It is important to define the projects clearly, to draw up a plan of action, and to evaluate the completed work.
3. This demands that different social commitments and options be debated among brothers in the faith, within the Church, in the light of the fullness of man in Jesus Christ.
4. Finally, in full awareness that no one has total knowledge of the future of man or the title of his happiness, Christians should apply themselves intellectually to the renewal of their faith and their knowledge of the Word of God in the living tradition of the Church.[62]

These guidelines acknowledge and seek to forestall the experience of loss of faith which frequently accompanies Christian contact with Communists. However, they continue to overlook a crucial distinction which Paul Droulers noted in his research in nineteenth-century social history and which is no less valid today: "The masses of workers, for their part, and undoubtedly a number of their militants, adopted socialism not because of its ideology, but as the sole means which was offered to them to improve effectively their lot, which they felt unjust."[63] The second of the previously mentioned statements of the French Bishops reflects a sensitive awareness of this distinction and will undoubtedly prove a catalyst for future dialogue.

That statement, entitled: "Faith and Marxism in the Worker World," was issued on July 4, 1977, by the Commission of the French Bishops on the Worker World.[64] The starting point of that document is not Marxist theory or Catholic theology, but rather the shared experience of Christian and Communist militants in the French labor movement. That shared life experience has resulted in bonds of mutual respect and even friendship between Catholic and Communist workers. For the former, it has engendered the conviction that "... no genuine transformation of existing society is possible without the support of the Communists."[65] For the latter, it seems to have produced "... a more positive awareness of the

---

[61]Ibid., p. 689.

[62]Ibid., p. 690.

[63]P. Droulers, "Catholicisme et mouvement ouvrier eu France au XIXe siècle: L'attitude de L'Episcopat," in F. Bédarida and J. Maitron, *Christianisme et Monde Ouvrier* (Paris: Les editions ouvrières), 1975, p. 64.

[64]For the full text of this document, see "Foi et Marxisme en monde ouvrier: Note de la Commission Episcopale française du monde ouvrier," *D.C.*, No. 1724 (July 17, 1977), pp. 690–696.

[65]Ibid., p. 691.

bond between the life of faith of militant Christian workers and their participation in the labor movement; the link between the Gospel and a more just, fraternal society."[66]

This "habitual dialogue" between Christian and Marxist workers takes place in a world of experience almost completely unfamiliar to scholars and theologians. Yet it is precisely in that world that the Commission sees "a seed which is just beginning to grow and which gives hope for future fruitfulness."[67] The proposals which the Commission then makes constitute a genuine challenge to the French church as well as an exciting incentive to Christian-Marxist dialogue. The Commission proposes: that the church be more receptive to the dynamic forces of liberation; that Christians who are in close contact with Marxism be urged to deepen their understanding of the faith; that the faith be presented in a less intellectual language, more understandable to workers; and that the Church promote the growth of "a genuine, ecclesial experience firmly rooted in the life and activity of the workers."[68] The Commission concludes that such an apostolic attitude is the indispensable prerequisite for "a truly evangelical dimension" in the relationships between Christian and Communist workers as well as the guarantee of the "authenticity and vigor" of the faith of the Christian worker.[69]

These two French documents illustrate the continuing urgency of the question of Christian-Marxist dialogue. The first highlights the impasse to which a preoccupation with theory invariably leads. The second opens up a whole new approach to dialogue. To be sure, the unique historical development of both the Church and the labor movement in France have created what René Rémond, the foremost historian of the modern French church, has described as: "a working class and a Catholicism, which for a century, have belonged to two worlds, if not always hostile, at least radically foreign to one another."[70]

At last, the French Bishops are taking cognizance of this reality, assuming responsibility for much of its development and proposing positive principles to explore its apostolic potential. It is not surprising, therefore, that Roger Garaudy, the foremost Marxist champion of dialogue in France, hailed the document, "Faith and Marxism in the Worker World," as an historic initiative which " . . . opens up a future perspective and points out new lines of research."[71]

The long experience of Christian-Marxist relations in France is of compelling interest, therefore, for all future dialogue. It challenges the Church and the Party, the scholar and the worker, the theologian and the philosopher. Above all, it proves that Christian-Marxist dialogue can enrich both its participants when each realizes the special contribution of the other's tradition.

[66]Ibid., p. 692.
[67]Ibid., p. 694.
[68]Ibid., pp. 694–695.
[69]Ibid., p. 696.
[70]R. Rémond, "Eglise et monde ouvrier," in Bédarida and Maitron, Christianisme, p. 293.
[71]R. Garaudy, "L'Eglise et le Marxisme," Le Monde, July 27, 1977. It must also be noted that while this document brought "hope" to Garaudy, the first document brought "great sorrow" (ibid.). For a sample of various Protestant and Orthodox as well as Catholic opinions on the state of Christian-Marxist relations in France, see "Chrétiens et Marxistes: Quel Dialogue?" LaVie, No. 1665 (July 27, 1977), pp. 16–24.

CHRISTIAN AND MARXIST RESPONSES TO THE CHALLENGE OF SECULARIZATION AND SECULARISM

Ans J. van der Bent

I

The so-called process of secularization has been a primary focus of theological attention for several decades. Secularization is defined as the historical process by which the world is de-divinized or as a social and cultural process by which non-religious beliefs, practices, and institutions increasingly replace religious ones in all spheres of life. More negative definitions view secularization as a gradual conformation to this world, the world which rebels against God, its Creator and the Lord of all history. Most Christian theologians agree that secularization should be distinguished from secularism, which signifies the systematic denial of religious principles in the interpretation of the world and existence, and which consequently is to be equated with an anti-religious ideology promising total human liberation.

As theism has been linked with Christianity, Marxism has been identified with atheism. As long as Christianity defended theism—the word denotes a philosophical system which accepts a transcendent and personal God who not only created but also preserves and governs the world—it faced tremendous difficulties recognizing and evaluating the modern process of secularization. Marxism, on the contrary, as an outspoken form of secularism, from its inception took the process of secularization for granted. Other secular and atheist schools not sharing the Marxist platform, along with a good deal of liberal democracy which is neither Christian nor religious, have also promoted secularization. But it is Marxism as secularism that has still further and more vigorously accelerated the process.

On the following pages I wish to develop the thesis that hardly any Christian theologians to date have sufficiently analyzed the secular order. In spite of their attempts to break away from theism and to view the secular world in its own development and right, theological scholars continue to concentrate on the new outlook and tasks of the individual believer and the Christian community and not on the world at large. Still worse, they have not dealt yet with the even more complicated problem of secularism. Hence all "theologies of secularization" have until today an a-political character. The institutional Christian church has

Ans J. van der Bent (United Church of Christ) has been the director of the Library of the World Council of Churches in Geneva since 1964. At the University of Amsterdam he studied economics and theology and received a Master of Theology degree. Simmons College granted him the M.S.L.S. degree. He compiled a multi-lingual bibliography of the early stages of the Christian-Marxist dialogue and wrote a number of articles for English, Dutch, and German theological journals. He has published *The Utopia of World Community* (1973) and *God So Loved the World: The Immaturity of World Christianity* (1977).

been so obsessed with the destructive influence of Marxist atheism and so preoccupied with crusades against godless communism that it has not only also totally underestimated the question of secularism but also has benefited little from the positive impact of the twentieth-century secularization process. The worldwide church has been rather poorly served by the modern "secular theologians" who treated the doctrine of dialectical and historical materialism as a side issue. A few conclusions will be drawn from these arguments for the future dialogue between Christians and Marxists.

Since World War II a great deal of Protestant and Roman Catholic literature has concentrated on the phenomenon of secularization. As a process it is seen to have a certain historical inevitability. For centuries the explanation of the world was strongly linked with mythologies, and social life was firmly based on forms worked out under the influence of religion. Atheism and secularism remained rare and transient phenomena until the beginning of the modern era. Yet, despite that, it is widely taken for granted that the Christian faith itself should favor, and has favored, secularization. Among several official documents of the World Council of Churches the Report of the Assembly in Uppsala (1968) states: "In secularization, understood positively, man refuses to absolutize any authority or structure of the created order and insists on maintaining an open view of the future. In this way man becomes responsible for the shape of his own future and the future of the world. This process need not imply the denial of God, although it may often involve a rejection of religious language and customs."[1] The Old Testament contains, biblical scholars point out, a clear orientation to secularization. Faith in creation meant for the Israelites that the world and all that it contains is for humankind, that any image of God, in order to localize God's presence in the world, turns out to be an idol and that the promise of salvation is extended to all "secular" nations. The New Testament abolishes still further the distinction between the sacred and the secular. According to Jesus Christ the Creator is not to be worshipped in a holy place but in spirit and in truth. The Sabbath is made for human beings. Sacred customs such as fasting, rules for pure and impure, and circumcision have become superfluous. Saint Paul stresses that "nothing is unclean in itself" and that "the world or life or death or the present or the future, all are yours."

Institutional Christianity, though unconsciously and against its will, also contributed to the process of secularization. The very success of the church's civilizing activities in the Middle Ages spelled the inevitable ending of its paternalistic authority. With the advent of the Renaissance, the Reformation, nation-states, and concern for empirical natural and social sciences, a plurality of conceptions developed concerning Christian society. Religious unity was shattered as several disciplines claimed competence in many areas of life. Ever since the sixteenth century, Christendom has been hard pressed to justify its theocen-

---

[1]Norman Goodall, ed., *The Uppsala Report, 1968* (Geneva: World Council of Churches, 1968), p. 79.

tric universe and to explain the sustaining power of an almighty God miraculously intervening in history and nature. The Enlightenment contributed further to the disintegration of the medieval worldview and the gradual secularization of European thought and institutions. Widescale confiscation of church property by the state took place after the French Revolution. The term "secularization" itself, until well into the twentieth century meant precisely the expropriation of ecclesiastical lands, buildings, and institutions for worldly ends. In Roman Catholic canon law, "secularization" also signified the granting of permission to members of religious orders to live outside their monasteries for the rest of their lives. Only in this century was the term "secularization" coined to describe parts or the whole of individual and social life ceasing to be determined by religion. In the French language the term "sécularisation" still primarily denotes the taking over of the church's and the clergy's belongings by the state and the secularization of public education. It is difficult to explain why in French terminology no appropriate words exist to refer to the process of secularization and to secularism as a set of anti-religious dynamics expressing the interests of social groups with the purpose of radically changing social structures and human behavior.

Contemporary Christianity has just started to examine seriously the causes and the consequences of secularization and secularism. The Protestant side has felt the influence of dialectical theology. According to Karl Barth, humanity has always been aware of the possibility that life may be sacred or at least sanctified. Human beings have always projected pictures of gods or a God who would perform this function. Religion so understood is a human activity, a contradictory enterprise which gives a person ultimate security and yet expresses his or her anxiety. The revelation of God, however, is the abolition of religion. "In the outpouring of the Holy Spirit," it "is the judging but also reconciling presence of God in the world of human religion, that is, in the realm of man's attempt to justify and to sanctify himself before a capricious and arbitrary picture of God."[2]

Dietrich Bonhoeffer launched the notion of a "religionless Christianity." Discarding God as the *deus ex machina,* the stop-gap where human knowledge and effort fail, he urged Christians to live in this world as if God does not exist. Friedrich Gogarten took up the theme of the powerlessness of God, contending that, because of the cross, we can now know that the world is left to human responsibility. It is God who justifies men and women on the cross. They no longer need to justify themselves. Following partly in the footsteps of Rudolf Bultmann, Paul van Buren pleaded for a radical reinterpretation of the Gospel by asking how a Christian who is a secular person could understand the Gospel in a secular way. In his book *Secular Christianity,* R. Gregor Smith maintained that only in relation to historical action can faith and reflection about faith take on their true nature. Thomas Altizer, one of the representatives of the "death of God" school, asserted that when God died in Christ on the cross God performed an act of self-annihilation. Since Christ was not resurrected and glorified, accord-

---

[2]Karl Barth, *Church Dogmatics,* Vol. I, 2 (Edinburgh: T. and T. Clark, 1956), p. 280.

ing to Altizer, we can know Christ now as a secular presence in a world which is freed from the traditional concept of God as the almighty Creator, reigning in distant transcendental glory, and judging humankind in a far-off future. In his book *The Gospel of Christian Atheism,* Altizer challenged Christians with the claim that the God they worship existed only in the past. The "good news" is that God willed to die in order to enter more completely into the world of creation.

Among Roman Catholic theologians a positive verdict on secularization has also gained ground and influence, which showed itself at Vatican II in, for instance, the Pastoral Constitution on the Church in the Modern World. Karl Rahner has expounded that the church must take a stand between "integrism" and "esotericism." The former views the world as mere material for the action and self-manifestation of the church desiring to integrate the world into its own community. The latter suffers from a latent dualism regarding the secular world as a matter of indifference for Christianity. Rahner has repeatedly emphasized that the world is not only an ongoing history but has become a history which can be planned and guided by people in its empirical space-time reality without any knowledge of Christian notions of salvation and perdition. This was hardly possible in earlier times. In several works, *Theology of the World* in particular, Johann B. Metz has emphasized that the Incarnation marks the beginning of the effective secularization of the world. He sees God's free acceptance of the world in the Christ event—enabling the world to begin to be itself. The secularization process is to Metz the driving force of history and it must be reappropriated by Christians if they mean to understand what their faith truly is. "To Christianize the world means to secularize it."

II

This very brief survey of the use of secularization as a concept and a process reveals some limitations and shortcomings. Curiously enough, in spite of all modern efforts to understand and to explain correctly the long historical "coming of age" process undergone by the autonomous world, Christian theologians concentrate almost exclusively on what has happened within the church and not in the world. All are far more interested in reinterpreting the meaning of the Gospel and in updating the mission of the true people of God in the world than in analyzing the structures, the motivation, and the behavior of that mature secular world. Scholars agree that Christians must change their "churchy" and pietistic attitudes and participate in the common life of society if the church is not to be relegated to the narrow area of ecclesiastical activity and personal devotion. But none of the theologians mentioned spells out concretely the implications of such conduct, and they are even less aware of the very problem of cooperating with "secular" people and ideological forces, struggling for a more just, participatory, and sustainable society. Their preoccupation with erroneous beliefs and with the misfortune and the many failures of the Christian community hinders them from taking seriously into account the reasoning, ingenuity, and achievements of the secular world.

Modern theologians are so keenly aware of the weakness and falsehood of inveterate Christian theism and trying so zealously to replace traditional belief in an omnipotent, omnipresent, and omniscient God by a genuine and mature Christian faith that they fail to observe that institutional Christianity itself is still unable to catch up with its dubious past. Here are three quotations that illustrate how the process of secularization has not yet invaded Christian churches around the world, notwithstanding all the claims that the non-secular Constantinian period has finally come to an end during the twentieth century. All three statements presuppose the validity of theism and passionately condemn atheism and secularization. It is rather incredible that for more than sixty years in this "modern" era, the universal church until today has made hardly any progress in understanding the necessity of atheism's attack on theism and the inherent fallibility, impotence, and inhumanity of both theism and atheism.

Representatives of churches and missionary societies meeting at Edinburgh in 1910—the start of the twentieth-century ecumenical movement has been dated from this year—expressed their concern about "materialistic and socialist ideas" as follows:

> Literature of indecent or, more commonly, of agnostic and atheistic character is an obstacle which is of growing seriousness. These books are from Japan and Europe mainly, and in some cases attack Christianity with the utmost boldness. Many of them are the more insidious because of their advocacy of materialistic views and extreme evolutionary positions. The increasing use of foreign liquors and new forms of gambling are other items of a similar kind. The importation of prostitutes and the immoral life of members of foreign communities, which is supposed to represent modern civilisation, has harmed the cause in Manchuria, as well as proved a bane to young Chinese. Western education at home and as obtained by students in America and Europe, has weakened the old moral teaching in some cases without adding Christian correctives. These examples suffice to show how important it is for Christianity to multiply its agencies for overcoming hostile influences... Only the religion commended by the most convincing examples in dominating individual and social life and commercial and international relations will be earnestly sought after and permanently accepted.[3]

In his 1937 Encyclical Letter, *Divini Redemptoris,* Pope Pius XI condemned Communism more strongly than had any other church authority. Quoting Pope Leo XIII, who defined communism as "the fatal plague which insinuates itself into the very marrow of human society only to bring about its ruin," he warned all the faithful that "communism is intrinsically wrong, and [that] no one who

---

[3]World Missionary Conference, 1910, *Report of Commission I: Carrying the Gospel to all the Non-Christian World* (Edinburgh: Oliphant, Anderson & Ferrier, 1911), pp. 97 and 25.

would save Christian civilization may collaborate with it in any undertaking whatsoever."[4]

At the recent inauguration of the Institute for the Study of Atheism of the Roman Catholic Pontifical Urban University in Rome, Father Battista Mondin, its Director, made the following statement:

> A considerable number of non-Christians today are no longer followers of Mohammed, Buddha, Confucius or of primitive religions; they are atheists. Thus while missionaries in the past preached to pagans, today they must often preach to atheists. . . . Our purpose is not merely to defend the interests of the Church, but rather to defend the interests of mankind. Dostoyevsky said that if God does not exist, then anything is allowed. Atheism, in fact, legitimizes egoism, oppression, violence. It is thus not a form of humanism but of barbarism, not freedom but oppression, not truth but obscurantism.[5]

As just indicated, these three almost identical positions during nearly seven decades—numerous other examples could be given—confirm that the church at large, confronted with atheistic movements and communist powers, has been quite unable to change its outlook and teachings on the secular, non-religious world. Still, today, the vast majority of Christians abhor atheism as an impossible possibility of interpreting the world and dealing with human problems. Atheism is a terrifying vacuum which must immediately and by all means be filled with some kind of theism. Whether theoretical or practical, the systematic rejection of God starts from an "immoral" or "sub-human" understanding of human beings. There must be, therefore, something basically wrong in the minds of atheist humanists and communists; their theories and suggestions for radical reform of society cannot aim at anything positive. Until they are converted to Christianity or another religion, their behavior has to be questioned seriously and their actions must be checked carefully.

The story of primitive anti-communism and anti-communist crusades in the churches is long, sad, and still unfinished. The parallel story of theism and religious idealism also continues; only a small minority of Christians stress theism and neo-platonic idealism as invalid theoretical options for interpreting the world or invalid practical approaches to changing society. I do not think that the pronouncements of the Second Vatican Council on the modern world, atheism, and ideology have made any real impact. *Gaudium et spes,* to be sure, rightly distinguishes between different types of atheism, holds Christianity responsible for the birth of modern atheism, and urges the Catholic Church to work with unbelievers together for "the rightful betterment of this world in which all alike live." This is a significant step forward. But a single naive and unreflected sentence on "ideological propaganda" in the same Pastoral

---

[4]Pius XI, *Divini Redemptoris* (New York: Paulist Press, 1937), pp. 4 and 26.
[5]International Fides Service, February 19, 1977, no. 2781, NE 95.

Constitution on the Church in the Modern World waters down the evaluation of the secular world and gravely underestimates the necessity of hammering out a concrete, coherent, and practicable social ideology in given national situations. The isolated reference to "ideologies" reads as follows: "If an economic order is to be created which is genuine and universal, there must be an abolition of excessive desire for profit, nationalistic pretensions, the lust for political domination, militaristic thinking, and intrigues designed to spread and impose ideologies."[6] These few trifling, simplistic, and unrealistic words reveal the Catholic Church's incapacity to view secular and ideological societies in their own right and integrity. These words in fact piously and benevolently gloss over the fierce and inevitable ideological struggles in which each ideology (in particular an ideology of an aggressively anti-religious nature) aims precisely at the creation of a genuine socio-economic order which will abolish all individual and collective greed, exploitation, and selfishness.

III

It is not only the church's hierarchy that bypasses the secular world. Christian thinkers, interpreting the process of secularization, as we have seen, also seem to be unaware of the fact that modern history can now be ideologically planned, radically changed, and actively guided without any perception of the transcendent meaning of salvation and perdition. That Marxism has really been the first to work out a genuine theory of the world to be constructed by humans alone in order to master their own "self-alienation" escapes most theological attention. This negligence is the logical consequence of the failure to observe that institutional churches in many countries are at their wit's end when they have to face the claims of the right explanation of this world and the successful change of social structures by atheist communist regimes and parties. Urging church members to become critical of theistic Christianity in order to act as true Christians in society is of no use when avowedly secular political groups and movements are taking the lead in worldly affairs, while ignoring all Christian disclaimers about divine governance, divine judgment, and divine eternal victory.

Even much Christian reflection on the spectacular advance of modern science and technology, bringing a degree of enlightenment and of this-worldliness with them that cannot be withstood, does not penetrate sufficiently into the very problem of secularization. Certainly technology is more than the sum total of machinery; it is the product of attitude which thinks in purely historical rather than religious terms. Having radically changed their contemplative attitude toward nature to a pragmatic one, the natural sciences are now more or less exclusively the servant of technology. Both science and technology are less concerned with the world's origin than with its future. Instead of delving into the past they are planning for the well-being of tomorrow's society. All human

---

[6]Walter M. Abbott, ed., *The Documents of Vatican II* (New York: Guild Press, 1966), p. 299.

insight and ingenuity is made to serve production and consumption. Human beings have become the product of planning. A specific type of human being has become subject to scientific and technological manipulation. Christian theology is even more right to prick up its ears when ecologists warn against a rapid depletion of world resources; when physicists predict some form of "death" of the universe, or at best perpetual, meaningless recurrence; and when science is unable to give any guarantee of greater success in the future. On the contrary, it may be hastening doomsday. All these enormous problems indeed have to be dealt with by both liberal-democratic and socialist-communist societies in East and West.

Yet the heart of the problem of secularization is not the unpredictable success or failure of science and technology but the problem of how to evaluate the modern phenomenon of secularism. Secularism in Christian circles is almost unanimously interpreted in a pejorative way as an anti-religious ideology promising total liberation from antiquated inhuman conditions. It is in this respect that the theologians concentrating on the process of secularization have little or nothing to contribute. I would make bold to say that the Chinese experiment since 1949 is a greater event in human history and a more "logical" factor in the secularization process than the exploration of the moon, the creation of atomic energy, and even the discovery of post-religious, post-ecclesiastical Christianity. Within a few decades Maoism has achieved the miracle of wiping out hunger, unemployment, and utter poverty of 800 million people who were dominated, exploited, and humiliated for centuries. In the three sections of its national economy—agricultural production, industrial output, and creation of energy sources—China has swiftly surpassed India where initial internal conditions for socio-economic development were very similar, following independence in 1947. The Peoples' Republic of China had the great courage to tackle radically the problem of land reform. It mobilized the peasant masses and concentrated on ecological planning. Today every citizen can lead a minimally secure and relatively prosperous life. Adequate basic medical care for all ages is provided, and all Chinese children have an opportunity to learn to read and write. The Maoist way of self-reliance functions. China has hope and a future. This development is even more unprecedented if one keeps in mind that today fifteen percent of the world's population consume eighty-five percent of the world's resources and production.

The progress of Maoism is due to the fact that it is an advanced form of secularism. It continues to change all traditional structures and aims at the creation of a new communitarian ethos with as few loopholes as possible. Can the church continue to reject and condemn this coherent secular ideology as easily as sheer totalitarianism, preposterous manipulation of the masses, and brutal elimination of all individual freedom? Can communists so sweepingly be accused of arrogance, dishonesty, injustice, stupidity, and tyranny, all resulting from their adherence to the doctrines of dialectical and historical materialism? Are Christians free from arrogance, dishonesty, injustice, stupidity, and tyranny as long as they defend the superiority of religious idealism over materialism? Does not Christianity still trail behind in finding its place in the secularized world, in spite of its new search for an authentic "non-religious" Christian community and its increasingly critical approach to the blessing of modern scientific and technological progress? Can it ever catch up with its past?

In his recent book, *Post-Theistic Thinking,*[7] Thomas Dean also reflects on the future of Christianity in a secular world. After having argued that an ontology of radical secularity provides a theoretical alternative to theistic and antitheistic metaphysics and that the new Marxist humanism can express this ontology in a more radical form, he examines the Marxist thesis that religion will wither away in a communist and classless society. The place of religion in human life, according to Dean, can no longer be considered an ultimate one; its status has been reduced to a penultimate one, because it is the task of religion in the secular future "to eliminate the need for itself as religion by overcoming secular, not religious or ecclesiastical, alienation." Believing to be in line with "the hidden secret of the biblical tradition" itself, Dean asserts that "the answers of religion can become real only if they move beyond the realm of religious and ecclesiastical life as well: education, law, society, work, economics, politics, culture." Thus "religious answers will not become real answers until they are no longer religious answers at all."[8]

Marxists on their side will also have to draw a similar conclusion from their thesis that the state will wither away in an advanced communist society. As long as Marxism is an ideology of alienation and not entirely free of the contradictions that characterize the alienated world it reflects, neither Christianity as a penultimate religion nor Marxism as an incomplete future philosophy of perfect freedom will disappear. Marx's comment in his *Capital* that "the religious reflex of the real world can, in any case, only then vanish when the practical relations of everyday life offer to man none but perfectly intelligible and reasonable relations with regard to his fellowmen and to nature" equally pertains to the decline of Marxist ideology and the withering away of the communist state apparatus, no longer governed by the law of material necessity and the conditions of alienation. But as it is utopian to expect that alienation can ever be completely overcome, Christianity is right to assert that religion is a "permanent penultimate" necessity of human life, neither withering away because of successful anti-religious propaganda campaigns nor because of effective eradication of the different social classes, but only totally disappearing in the Kingdom of God. This does not imply that the one (religion, Christianity) will ultimately triumph over the other (Marxist ideology, communism). It does, however, imply that both Christianity and Marxism are constantly challenged to assess the validity of the secular answers they give to humankind's questions and the possibilities of overcoming the real sources of human alienation.

---

[7]Thomas Dean, *Post-Theistic Thinking: The Marxist-Christian Dialogue in Radical Perspective* (Philadelphia: Temple University Press, 1975).
[8]Ibid., pp. 232–233.

Thomas Dean is not overly optimistic about the promising future of the secularization process when he raises the questions whether "the self-proclaimed universalism of Christianity and Marxism are not in fact vehicles for white, European cultural imperialism" and whether "the universal humanity is not a code name for the world-historical supremacy of a particular religious or national tradition." Speaking of "the revolt of Black, Brown, Red and Yellow peoples against the myth of universal humanity which turns out to be the White Christian's tribalism imperialistically imposed on the universe," he wonders whether we should note hope for "a universalism which will rest on a vision of man far richer, more varied, and more comprehensive of the global aspirations of men, East and West, secular and religious."[9]

Though I find it difficult to share this long-range hope and vision, I believe that Dean has far more adequately dealt with the problem of secularization than many Christian thinkers mentioned earlier. His important observation that the penultimate function of Christianity is to give secular answers to political and socio-economic questions fills in the gap of the curiously individualistic and existentialistic ethics of "secular theologians," unrelated to the hard and complicated problem of secularism. But strangely enough, despite the pertinent conclusions which Dean draws from his study on post-theistic thinking, he also stays too much in an academic realm of non-political and non-ideological reflection. The course of the secularization process and the validity of secularism can be more adequately interpreted, I believe, by a new exegesis of an important biblical text, namely Mt. 25:31–46. In the framework of this text not only the deficiency of Christian theism and Marxist atheism but also the central place of Jesus Christ—not as victorious Lord over history but as the suffering servant—in the secular order are clearly emphasized.

IV

In the prophecy and warning of the Last Judgment of the "Son of Man," several common assumptions are turned upside down. It is not Christian churches and their believers assembled on the one side and all other religious and secular communities on the other side of the throne of the Supreme Judge, but all *nations* are gathered before God. There are many who have given food to the hungry and drink to the thirsty, clothed the naked, and cared for the sick without knowing that they were serving the Lord. They are invited to enter the Reign of God. Many, however, who were convinced they belonged to and served the Lord by serving their neighbor do not inherit eternal life. Being aware of the needs of one's neighbor and alleviating his or her lot is of course not only a matter of individual and collective charity today, but of deep concern for changing politico-economic structures which cause hunger, thirst, sickness, and nakedness. In the Mt. 25 passage it is not churches and Christians who have drawn the

---

[9]Ibid., pp. 242–243.

ideological consequences from their faith that are singled out. The only criterion of judgment is the ministering of *all* (individually and jointly) to the needs of others with or without an explicit knowledge of serving the Lord. This criterion, however, is far more radical than many Christian social ethics and "secular" theologies can fathom and express. It is indeed implied that the decisive factor is not the "religious" approach to one's neighbor (and the whole of society), but the very factual serving of fellow men and women. This does not mean that the parable can be interpreted as a description of those who will enjoy the Reign or as a universal command to action. If this were the case only very few heroes and saints would have a chance to enter it, and most would be turned away as having been utterly self-righteous and insensitive to what is fully involved in loving one's neighbor. As "all have sinned, and all fall short of the glory of God" (Rom. 3:23), the acceptance of every creature is wholly gratuitous and remains the sole prerogative of the suffering Lord who has gained the victory, and who supremely judges the religious answers given to secular questions, which cease to be religious answers at all.

The prophecy of the Last Judgment, it seems to me, confirms the historical fact that in the secularization process religions constantly turn into ideologies, and ideologies constantly into religions. All those who are trapped in this sinful confusion run grave risk of being rejected as vain and deceitful when stock of their life is taken. It is so extremely difficult to give truly secular (religiously valid) answers to truly secular questions. Who will the Lord turn away? Those who concentrate on Christianizing the world in order to secularize it (but still secretly long for the continuation of the "liberal" and "free" western world protecting above all precious individual human rights)? Or those who prophetically warn of the limits of scientific discovery and technological growth (but in fact are quite contented with the affluence of ingenious consumer society)? One cannot be sure. Will those among the eighty-five percent who consume only fifteen percent of the world's total resources, who are preoccupied with wiping out hunger, poverty, and disease, raising the average age of the people to forty years instead of twenty-five years, and guaranteeing a minimally dignified human life—will they not pass more easily through the last Judgment? There is no doubt that in Mt. 25:31–46 the ideological engagement in raising dismally low human living standards takes precedence over all other religious (missionary) and secular (subduing the earth) activities. But on the other hand, what about those who are raising agricultural production so successfully that they are well protected against the calamitous food shortages that increasingly afflict the underdeveloped world? Might they not fall prey to an unworldly dream of collective happiness and well-being and thereby fail to be prepared to meet the one and only Judge?

As humankind is by nature inclined not to receive the world from God as the one *to* whom it is responsible and thinks that it alone is responsible *to* the world, it fails to be responsible *for* it. The suffering Christ, continuously present in the hungry to be fed, the naked to be clothed, and the sick to be healed makes this perfectly clear. Christ's suffering in the world keeps the secular process of being responsible *for* the world truly open and leads its course unexpectedly and uncontrollably to the ultimate goal. Christ resists all "more comprehensive and global aspirations of people, East and West, secular and religious," even the timely Maoist model of secularism, although not for "Christian" reasons. From Christ secular humankind learns that it should be prepared for the total surprise of the separation of the sheep from the goats. In spite of the persistent inhumanity of one human being to another, the joy of hearing the words "well done, good and faithful servant" can be anticipated.

V

In terms of the dialogue between Christians and Marxists, we can now ask how Christianity should face the secularized world and Marxism as an institutionalized secular ideology. The theologies of secularization, particularly in view of the development of various forms of Marxism, are partial and in need of elaboration and application. The "secular Christian" notion that Christ was emptied and annihilated himself on the cross remains valid. So, too, do Bonhoeffer's words that "God lets himself be pushed out of the world on the cross" that "only the suffering God can help and that this is a reversal of what religious man expects from God" and that "man is summoned to share in God's suffering at the hands of a godless world."[10] But all this wisdom does not help the problems of opting for a consistent, coherent, and practicable social ideology, of facing together massive suffering and of struggling jointly against nations' injustice to nations. Much Christian talk of being involved in the secularization process rings hollow, and the decisive story of Mt. 25 of human sharing with Christ in overcoming our inhumanity to one another is ignored at our peril, so long as Christians fail to give evidence of having more effectively participated in changing western structures of exploitation, greed, and injustice, and so long as the churches remain embedded in these structures, helping to prolong them and guilty of their own religiously-veiled inhumanity. Those who urge Christians to live in this world as if God does not exist, but do not spell out what an ideological commitment to the world entails in all its irreversible consequences, especially with regard to the minimal raising of the very precarious standards of living of millions of human beings, end up in defending a pseudo-religion of a modern, just, and sustainable society.

Facing Soviet and Chinese Marxism, the most developed and overt models of secularism, the church and its believers should far better understand that the communist parties and others in these countries are retaliating against violent attacks on Marxist atheism. They do so by means of uncompromising critiques of religion. Christians should also understand that the atheism of Karl Marx himself

---

[10]Dietrich Bonhoeffer, *Letter and Papers from Prison* (London: SCM Press, 1971), p. 360.

was primarily a war cry in the name of the downtrodden proletariat, against belief in a God who provides for creatures and on behalf of a new order in which people would finally provide for themselves. The essence of Marx's atheism was not the theoretical denial of God. Instead, it resulted from the necessity of fighting against the church and political clericalism. Marx, Engels, and their followers became convinced that the road to self-liberation of the working class could be travelled only apart from Christianity and its institutions.

Still more important, the church and its theologians should realize that Soviet, Chinese, and other present forms of Marxism-Leninism cannot be primarily attacked on the ground that they are merely desperate and blasphemous coercive systems, unworthy of humanity, suppressing all individual privacy, initiative, and full development. Especially in the case of the new China, the blessings of advanced western liberal democracy for each member of society cannot be played off against the radical conditioning of the happiness and behavior of the entire nation. The Roman Catholic Church and the World Council of Churches are behind the times by still refusing to state officially that strong one-party socialist regimes in many under-developed countries are the only way of coping with seemingly unsolvable problems of over-population, massive unemployment and underemployment, vast urban slums, desperate agricultural backwardness, and the slow upbuilding of an industrial infrastructure. Such regimes do make some progress on these huge problems, regardless of their present internal political conflicts and their inability to achieve more humanizing socio-economic goals.

Christianity cannot continue to be preoccupied with challenging the Soviet Union on its violation of human rights, its suppression of religious liberty, and its harsh treatment of enemies of the state and political dissidents. A far more important question is whether Soviet Marxism has not exchanged the spirit of the October Revolution for a primitive and aggressive pseudo-religious messianism and a naive belief in ever-progressive industrial and scientific achievements for the benefit of humankind, all of which distorts Marx's humanist philosophy as it reflects on the harmony between human beings and between humans and nature. Socialism is not merely the production of ever more material goods, nor even a more equal distribution of these goods. It is a new society, a classless society of real and not merely formal equality from which the differences between city and country, mental and manual labor, and industry and agriculture have been eliminated. To approximate such a society, a great deal more is required than quantitative technological and industrial progress, and the imposition of the belief in ever greater economic advance on the rest of the world. The crucial question is whether Marx's protest against the dehumanization and automatization of people, inherent in western industrialism, has not been covered up by the Soviets with a system of conservative state capitalism in which people are still alienated, an appendix to machines, and still transformed into a thing.

Furthermore, it is no use asking whether the Peoples' Republic of China could have travelled the same road to national independence and dignity without the acceptance of the Marxist-Leninist ideology and a thorough indigenization of communist principles in a Chinese context, generally decried in the West as messianic nationalism, cultural aggressiveness, and xenophobia. "Secular Christianity" is, for the time being, only entitled to raise such questions as these. In their efforts to transform every person into a new human being by consistently conditioning and controlling his or her behavior, can the Chinese communists be so sure that they are not basing their efforts on megalomania and self-deception, desperately but in vain seeking their own preservation and salvation? Even if Mao stated that the cultural revolution has to continue for ten thousand years and more, is there a real possibility of overcoming the last sources of human alienation? The other question is related to the problem of death, death not understood in a metaphysical sence of the separation of the immortal soul from the mortal body, but in the "secular" sense of being, totally severed from the richness, joy, and satisfaction of this human society?

Precisely these questions can be raised by the Christian community, because it knows that Christ's suffering in every person's neighbor and the process of secularization are identical. The secular history of humankind will climax in a total victory over human alienation and abasement. This will be achieved through Christ's immeasurable capacity to revaluate men's and women's wavering commitment and feeble love. Karl Marx had only a dream when he predicted that "the practical relations of everyday life will offer to man none but perfectly intelligible and reasonable relations with regard to his fellowmen and to nature." It is the "secular humanity of Christ, stripped of its religious embellishments and ecclesiastical disguises, which renders one individually, collectively, and fully responsible to the world and make Marx's dream become true. That humanity, reconciling the inhuman world with its Creator, changes the self-righteousness and frailty of both who are for and against secularism into righteousness and wholeness. This will become tangible and visible in the Reign of God when all people will know God as God has always known them, and God will be all in all.

How does Marxism interpret the process of secularization, and to what extent is its defense of the necessity of secularism valid? These questions cannot be answered by Christians. Marxists themselves should state at length their own position and their critique of Christianity vis-à-vis secularism. I wish to add, however, one last point to this article.

Forty years ago I was taught in high school in the Netherlands that during the second half of the nineteenth century and the first three decades of the twentieth century tens of millions of Chinese were wiped out by famines. That history lesson did not shake my conscience, as I firmly believed together with fellow Christians that many people—in particular ignorant, idle, and indolent non-white people—in God's providence are destined to suffer and to die an untimely death. Today I firmly believe that so long as the Christian church and its faithful dare to argue that the China of Mao, so far from being a revolutionary paradise of egalitarianism, is a monstrous tyranny ruled over by a new privileged class of bureaucrats and generals, stopping short of all the more ultimate goals of Christian hope, the Chinese cannot but be suspicious of any kind of dialogue. They have every right to ask how Christians who denounce violent and totalitarian methods actually propose to achieve the ends which both admit to be good. How deeply is Christianity concerned with these goals? In comparison with the past the new China has made great progress. Its socialist construction represents a step forward toward human dignity, responsibility, and creativity. It is now also up to the Chinese communists (and socialists and communists of other nations) to move beyond the old question of whether the individual exists for the sake of the social institution, or the social institution for the sake of the individual. They have to continue to struggle for a more genuine community with less hypocrisy, boredom, submissiveness, and restraint, showing that their society is preferable to a community in which only a smaller part of the people live not by bread alone, but enjoy the freedom for the full flowering of the human spirit, the gaiety and perspective of humor, and the complete exercise of personal responsibility. Can communists prove that the sentence from the mouth of Christians, "the sabbath is made for (individual) man," is only a half-truth because "the sabbath is made for all men, all women, and all children?"

HISTORICAL DIALECTICAL MATERIALISM: A SECULAR METHOD FOR CHRISTIAN THOUGHT AND ACTION

Gerhard Melzer

Young people are always asking questions; but in the Christian churches today old people are asking the same questions. Science is in demand. For the individual, hand-to-mouth formulas no longer are satisfying. Answers must be to the point. In setting down principles for living, our answers must bring about a better, growing command of our natural and social environments. Science has come to mean that system or totality of knowledge which satisfies the demands of praxis. Praxis, therefore, concurrently ties science down to an ongoing process of testing.

In a letter from students in a church trade school, I was asked:

> In what respect can we work out a reconciliation between Christianity and the socialist movement? How can Christians and Marxists share a common cause? Can we be Christians and members of Marxist student groups and workers parties? This is a serious question for us because our school administration always tries to fend off both the student body's unity and the cooperation of students and other trade school personnel in this matter. In our FSH [trade school] anti-communism is still having a wild heyday.

Another letter says: "Many people, even when they must work as future social workers, no longer are happy with our capitalist society and are looking for an alternative. Many students, however, undergo considerable difficulties in trying to harmonize their Christian self-understanding with a socialist society."

I. Occupational Discrimination [Berufsverbote] in the Economy, State, and Church

On February 25, 1975, Karl Immer, the president of the Evangelical Church in the Rhineland, wrote to the evangelical clergy, regional synods, various concerned committees, and divinity students reporting the church leadership's policy on the question of pastors' membership in the German Communist Party. The letter spoke of mounting inquiries from congregations, ministers, and divinity students regarding pastors' support of strikers at Mannesmann-Duisburg in the Summer of 1973, and asked the church's publicity committee to work out some guidelines in this case.

Gerhard Melzer (Lutheran) is a pastor in Duisburg, West Germany. He studied at the Kirchliche Hochschule in Wuppertal and the University of Göttingen. Contributor of articles on theological, social, and peace issues, he is active in the Christian Peace Conference and in the movement for atomic disarmament and democracy in the Federal Republic of Germany. Three attempts on Pastor Melzer's life have been made by neo-fascists for these activities.

Just mentioning this occasion for a church declaration on the incompatibility of ministry and Communist Party membership points to the socio-economic background of occupational discrimination in private and public employment in West Germany as well as in the Evangelical Church. Usually this sort of job discrimination begins with a person's being born into a working-class family. Under the most favorable circumstances, the worker's child usually becomes a skilled worker. The school system looks after that. But even if they have studied hard, working-class children do not look forward to the same chance at getting ahead as do middle-class children. Prof. Karl Heinz Sohn, managing director of the German Developmental Aid Corporation in Cologne and Chairperson of the Social Ethics Committee of the Evangelical Church in the Rhineland, states: "Social disadvantage experienced after their college education is the big disappointment for these students . . . because in getting a job, so much depends on having just those right connections which these students do not have."[1]

If the workers defend themselves, the usual job discrimination is aggravated. Active trade unionists and youth representatives will be fired and blacklisted. It also happens, and can be readily admitted, that special investigative police units are used against strikers. Fifty years ago, students and academics, including theologians, formed an almost united front with the propertied class against the working class. In the 1920's, student volunteer corps shot down demonstrating strikers; today, however, teachers and ministers are deeply involved in the struggles of the workers' party. Students no longer draw their sword against the workers but join them in common demonstrations. Today academics are discovering that they too are subject to the very arbitrary squeeze of the labor market which workers have experienced all along. Moreover, since academics are beginning to defend themselves, they are being disciplined as are the workers. *Unsere Zeit* reports:

> *Manager-Magazin,* which is published in Hamburg and supplies information
> and opinions for the leading powers of the domestic economy, disclosed in
> its November issue just a little of the extent to which large industry practices
> job discrimination. . . . Perhaps the most dismaying news in the article was
> the disclosure that, since at least 1971, these large industries maintained their
> own informants on the faculties of German universities. Following the in-
> structions of their industrial bosses, these professors report their evaluations
> of the latest crop of graduates. *Manager-Magazin* writes that three giants of
> the chemical industry, Hoechst, Bayer, and BASF, may have even recruited
> as an informant a renowned professor on the examination committee of
> Regensburg University.[2]

Anti-communism is the theory behind the practice of job discrimination in both the private and the public economy. Job discrimination, however, is used

---

[1]*Rheinische Post,* January 21, 1976.
[2]*Unsere Zeit,* November 27, 1975.

not only against communism; more often, it is used against any innovation leading to, or suspected of leading to, a democratic change oriented more toward the objective needs of working people and less toward the profit motive.

It is characteristic of anti-communism to demonize every such democratic alternative which is already being realized. This demonization—an irrational roll call in which one sees the controlling anxieties of capitalist society—helps itself to a simple trick. It is, of course, a trick if anti-communism tears real socialism's development and the present state of its development out of every historical context. (The adjective "real" serves to note the distinction between socialism and unrealized theories and models. Realities exist whether we like them or not. At least the reality of the socialist states pleases anti-communists.) Two aspects of real, existing socialism have been intentionally overlooked in anti-communist doctrine. These particular aspects, without which real, existing socialism is inexplicable, will not be repeated in Western Europe and the U. S., so no one need be afraid of their consequences. First, in the USSR and East Germany the industrial base, without which socialism is unrealizable, had to be worked on. That was hard. Secondly, building this structure had to be accomplished under the constant, massive threat and vigorous opposition of imperialism. Given an inherited underdevelopment, this was even harder. Both these crucial historical conditions will cease when the West changes over to socialism. Here the socialist structure might be launched immediately as a result of economic conditions. A socialist structure could be introduced into the West only if the imperialist powers were weakened. An objective point of departure for an immediate development of socialist democracy—something unknown in socialist history up till now—might, therefore, be given. For that reason it can be said with certainty that the sacrificial path of the USSR, as well as East Germany and Cuba, can not be repeated in Western Europe and the U.S. It could not happen even if there existed a closer agreement on the principles of a socialist structure—perhaps especially not then.

The theological problem of the incompatibility of secular science and Christian belief, of atheism and ministry in the socio-economic connection, is to be seen not only in those who are characterized by the practice of job discrimination and anti-communism; it is also established by President Immer's circular letter. This theological problem also proves what Prof. Hanfried Müller surmises in an expert opinion on the practice of job discrimination in the Hessian Evangelical Church:

> As with all churches in West Germany, the Hessian church, for whatever reasons, tolerates the notorious God-is-dead theology, the theology of "Whence comes my disorientation" [*"Woher meines Umgetriebenseins"*] —not only pure and simple atheistic worldviews, but even atheistic theologians! What is worse, they even tolerate the abuse of the Name of Jesus Christ as has happened everywhere when ministers are members of an imperialist party and employ the name of Jesus Christ in making political propa-

ganda. If with so much "tolerance" (which this evaluator does not approve of) they suddenly have become scrupulous, when a minister (widely removed not only from atheistic theology, but also after his own public declaration against atheism generally) works only politically in a party which is intrinsically oriented in a scientific-atheistic direction, then such a church evidently stands under the judgment of Mt. 23:24. Such a church is politically suspect, that it is not condemning the German Communist Party's attitude toward the existence of God, but rather the Communist Party's position toward private ownership of the means of production (Phil. 3:19).[3]

A theological answer needs to be given not to those people who evasively maintain the incompatibility of ministry and cooperation with the Communist Party, but rather to those who in justifying their Christian faith do not come to terms with the actual conditions of capitalism. Since the atheism of socialist theory assails their faith, it is these people who are trying to find an alternative who have considerable difficulties in relating their Christian self-understanding to a socialist order.

II. Faith and Worldview

1. Divine Revelation and Human Thought

The Christian faith lives only in terms of God's self-revelation. The believer does not invent this revelation for himself or herself, but hears and obeys it as God's self-revelation. As Luther wrote, "Christ Jesus it is he, Lord Sabaoth his name, from age to age the same." For a "natural being," God's self-revelation is simply out of the question (1 Cor. 2:14). The believing congregation witnesses God's self-denial only when the congregation denies itself. The self-revelation of God as God's self-denial, the hearing congregation's faith, and the self-denying witness of the congregation of God's own self-denial do not happen one after the other. Thus they cannot be separated from one another. They must be differentiated, for it is only the Subject, only the revealing God, who is believed and witnessed.

Human thinking is Christian thinking to the extent that it reflects God's self-revelation rather than its own self-revelation. Human behavior is Christian behavior insofar as it does not seek out its own justification, but declares to both the individual and the whole human race God's promised justification of the unrighteous. Historical dialectical materialism is not in keeping with Christian human thinking and action, but it is in keeping with human thinking and acting. Historical dialectical materialism, therefore, can be a method for Christian think-

---

[3]*Internationale Dialog-Zeitschrift*, 3, 1973. Evaluation of the question, "Whether the political work in an atheist party fundamentally excludes work in the church," by the director of the theological section of Humboldt University, Berlin, G.D.R., for the Christian Peace Conference, published in *Internationale*.

ing and acting, a secular method for historical exegesis and research, a method for systematic reflection. It can be a method for the conscious and methodological realization of that human well-being which love demands and faith achieves. The Christian who is less ready to help himself or herself to scientific ways of thinking and acting can also fully realize that love which faith intends, for truly God is the author of the believer's acts who leads us where we would not go. One who knows the help one needs from God and does not ask for that help is a poor steward of God's gifts.   .

2. The Mature Christian's Worldview

"As long as a designated heir is not of age his condition is no different from that of a slave" (Gal. 4:1). No longer a minor, the child of God, like the son in the business of Meyer and Son, has authority, has a voice. "One asks, what comes afterwards? Another asks, is it right? That is the distinction between the free and the servant."[4] "Is it right?" asks the servant who searches in law and dogma. The free person is responsible for his or her own deeds. "Men become real . . . without God through questions about death, sorrow, guilt, and it is simply not true that only Christianity has answers for these questions."[5] "God himself forces us to come to this realization. Our becoming free leads us to a true knowledge of our position before God. God has us know that we must live a complete life even without God."[6] May the Christian, or must the Christian, live "without the help or working hypothesis of God?"[7] May the Christian, or must the Christian, have a godless world picture insofar as atheism is right that there is no God? "May the Christian, or must the Christian, think and act in an atheistic fashion, in the sense that all being is accessible to human knowledge, clear to human eyes, and necessarily to be controlled by man as an ethical postulate for the self-domination of human society?"[8] In the cited passages, Bonhoeffer does not make the differentiation between nature as a lawfully subjugated sphere and human society as a sphere for freedom and grace. He understands human autonomy in terms of "discovering those scientific, socio-political, artistic, ethical, and religious laws according to which the world lives and becomes complete."[9] Of course, these laws, as they were intended by Freud and carried out by Konrad Lorenz, do not infer a levelling out of nature and society.

For Bonhoeffer, a worldview is a systematic view of everything that is evident. Ideology is to be differentiated from this concept of worldview; ideology, then, denotes the system which is produced out of a systematic worldview as a conclusion for human action. Worldview and ideology, therefore, are in-

---

[4]Theodor Sterm. In German this passage rhymes (translator's note).
[5]Dietrich Bonhoeffer, *Widerstand und Ergebung* (München, 1953), p. 211.
[6]Ibid., p. 241.
[7]Ibid., p. 215.
[8]Hanfried Müller, *Von der Kirche zur Welt* (Leipzig, 1961), p. 1152.
[9]Bonhoeffer, *Widerstand*, p. 215.

struments of thought, systems for dominating nature and human self-rule. Whether he or she knows it or not, every believer has and needs both a worldview and an ideology, even if the believer disputes this and through the ideology of "ideological freedom" allows himself or herself to gloss over the domination of the powers that be. Perceiving the perceivable and thinking the thinkable may not and can not file God away among the perceivable and thinkable. It is just this sort of idolatry which is emphasized not only in the Decalogue but also in the church's Trinitarian doctrine. Even the Christian's worldview and ideology are, therefore, the natural human being's theory and praxis and hence atheistic, even if this Christian worldview and ideology are mistakenly considered as grounded in, or the specific consequence of, Christian faith. For this reason, "Christian" worldviews and irrationally grounded religious ideologies neither ease nor strengthen the Christian faith, but oppose it. This is especially true if these "Christian" worldviews and irrational ideologies are seen or promoted as proving, facilitating, or strengthening Christian faith.

Knowledge, gained with or without faith, is not atheistic but religious if this knowledge turns out to be worshipped on its own account and not something in human service. If eating and drinking become the dominant aim in life, then one's belly will end up being one's God (Phil. 3:19). This does not mean that one cannot fill the belly without making the belly into God. It is absurd, therefore, to call scientific knowledge a substitute for religion. Physical science replaces the superstition that thunder is God's voice. Is scientific knowledge then a substitute for superstition? Does the lightning rod replace the superstitious prayer for protection because we still have not mastered nature? Is the domination of nature with the help of the lightning rod a substitute for religion? It is just nonsensical to call physical science a substitute for religion.[10] Scientific knowledge will replace religious faith as the stopgap measure of our knowledge and action. However, the natural human being's scientific knowledge simply is not religion. If it is religion, then it is not scientific knowledge of natural human beings.

3. The Marxist Critique of Religion

Religion is used as the "opium for the people" in the interest of those who rule, not those who govern. It is people such as Wilhelm II, Stocker, Franz Hitze, Budelschwingh, and Wichern, with their attempts at staving off the workers' coming of age, who both own the means of production and whose interests are championed in state, church, and school. Religion is for the powerless and confused; Christianity is "the opium of the people" (Marx) which gives comfort to the weak and courage to the self-fearing. And to the given age it gives the courage to break the domination of those who, holding the masses in contempt, deny them the equal voice of nature people. Biblical religion, the Old Testament's prophetic preaching, the New Testament's anti-pharisaic and anti-

---

[10]Müller, *Von der Kirche zur Welt*, p. 1051.

spiritualist preaching, the religious critiques of the Reformers, dialectical theology, and the Marxists rise against the emergent, stopgap function of religion.

> Religion, of course, is man's act of self-consciousness and self-feeling which he either has not yet gained or has already forfeited.... Religion is the universal theory of this topsy-turvy world, its encyclopedic compendium, its logic in popular form, its spiritual *point d'honneur,* its enthusiasm, its moral sanction, festive completion, general comfort, and reason for justification.... Religion is both an expression of and a protest against this world's real misery; religion is the afflicted creature's groan, the feeling of a heartless world, the spirit of an unintellectual state of affairs. It is the opium of the people.... The critique of religion challenges people to give up their illusions about the human condition. This is a challenge to abandon the very need for illusions.... Inasmuch as this critique disabuses man of his illusion, man thinks and treats his disappointingly shaped reality in terms of understanding his own future.... The critique of heaven, therefore, turns into a critique of earth. The critique of religion turns into a critique of privilege, the critique of theology into a critique of politics.[11]

In the same sense, Engels condemned Duhring's pretended revolutionary idea of forbidding religion in socialist society. Similarly, Marx and Engels disapproved of bringing into the workers' party program a direct avowal of that kind of atheism which is a combative program against religion. According to Engels, to declare such a war against religion was "to out-Bismarck Bismarck," viz., to repeat Bismarck's folly of warring against the clergy. Bismarck, thereby, pushed religious divisions, not political ones, into the foreground and forced the attention of certain ranks in the working class and the democratic movement onto an entirely superficial, bourgeois, and deceitful anticlericalism.[12]

III. The Philosophical Contradictions and the Praxis of Faith

1. Materialism and Idealism

The dialectic as science not only formulates and practices the most general dynamic and evolutionary laws of nature, society, and thought; at the same time, it also recognizes and articulates the lawful correlation and mutual dependence of connected parts as coherent material and historical phenomena within a whole. Dialectic is not simply the passive mirror of matter, but it also creates and reacts on the material life of nature and society.

According to historical dialectical materialism, since there is an interaction of being and thought, matter and ideal superstructure, philosophical idealism is not just nonsense, but "a one-sided, overstated, high-flown development."[13]

---

[11]Karl Marx, *The Critique of Hegel's Philosophy of Right, Selected Works of Marx and Engels* (Frankfurt/Main, 1970), vol. 1, pp. 9–10.

[12]Lenin, *Marx-Engels-Marxism* (Berlin, 1958), pp. 258–259.

[13]Ibid., p. 317.

Idealism is one facet or frontier of human knowledge which gets blown up into a deified absolute cut off from nature. As metaphysics' mistake is cutting off a particular phenomenon from its material and historical context, so too idealism's mistake is detaching ideas from matter. In this sense, Christian faith agrees with historical dialectical materialism; both matter and idea are created things which are different from the Creator. "God is a God, not of confusion, but of peace" (1 Cor. 14:33). Since the God of the Christian faith can be known as an "Other" over and against all that can be seen or thought, Christian faith can only be thought of as idealistic. Believing what it does not see—what it does not see even with Stefan Heym's "eyes of reason"—this Christian idealism may not soften a materialistic knowledge of what is rationally knowable. What the "natural man" of 1 Cor. 2:14 can understand the Christian as a materialist also can understand. As a materialist whose faith owns up to its idealism, the Christian can act as a person driven by God's Spirit (Rom. 8:14). Otherwise, the Christian materialist will end up with a worldview coming out of his or her faith, but given to an understanding of God as being accessible, as part of the world of human imagination, as subordinated to human thought.

Christian faith, therefore, does not find itself in an ideological coexistence with the worldviews of either believers or nonbelievers. Rather, faith is in conflict with what the believer both sees and affirms; that with this reason, with "the eyes of reason," natural being truly sees what is visible. The believer does not call into question the fundamental visibility of God's whole creation; at the same time, however, the believer hopes against every merely rational, calculative hope (Rom. 8:24) for what he or she cannot exactly picture (Heb. 1:11). Though it is foolishness to the natural being's reason (1 Cor. 2:14), the believer's hope is, in the strict sense of Mt. 19:26, impossible, inconceivable for the natural being's reason. In the words of the Psalmist, the believer's hope is a wonder God brings about (Ps. 139:6). "God's Spirit witnesses with our Spirit" (Rom. 8:16). "Faith comes by hearing and hearing by the word of God" (Rom. 10:17), but this is a hearing heard only by the person whose ears have been opened by God (Is. 50:4). In terms of the natural being's knowing, the Christian's knowing of God is "objective idealism." The Christian, however, acknowledges and wonders at his or her faith (Ps. 139:6). Also a natural being, the Christian does not justify his or her faith by putting it before the specific knowledge of the natural being; nor does he or she defame the natural being's knowledge as foolishness, as if our natural eyes and "the eyes of reason" were unreliable tools which, although God-given, were not put to any thankful use since God's creation is at bottom shoddy work (Gen. 1:31; 1 Tim. 4:4).

2. Capitalism and Socialism

Just as with Christian faith, historical dialectical materialism is realized as a method of secular thought and action only in a unity of thought and praxis. The promise, "I am the Lord your God" (Ex. 20:2), first is concretized in the renunciation of other gods: "no other gods besides me" and not instead of mine. This renunciation is translated exactly in the explanation of the Decalogue found in the Sermon on the Mount: "You cannot serve both God and mammon" (Mt. 6:24). Mammon is deified money, just like capital in the progressive phases of capitalism: money, or the increase of money, as an end in itself, or "Money makes the world go round." This popular rendering of the dogma of Mammon signifies that humans do not rule the world as they were created to do (Gen. 1; Ps. 8), that humans do not rule the world for human ends as they were commissioned to do.

The total subjection of human beings follows upon this close-fisted increase of money, this growing concentration of capital in fewer and fewer hands, required by capitalism's inherent dynamics. By no means extreme for it, capitalism blindly or knowingly produces human sacrifices. Entering into the jungle's law of the war of all against all, capitalism characteristically requires colonialism and neocolonialism as well as wars. Insofar as they either intend, support, or lead to colonial and neocolonial exploitation, imperialist wars sacrifice people to the empire of profits. To illustrate the explanation, at a Governors' Conference on August 4, 1953, President Eisenhower proved why the U. S. had almost completely financed the last phase of the French colonial war against the Vietnamese people: "If Indochina is lost, then something connected with the loss will happen. Tin and tungsten . . . will be in short supply. If instead of letting that happen, the U.S. spends $400 million supporting this war, then we won't have thrown our money out the window. So that we can get certain things we need from the riches of Indonesia and Southeast Asia, we've decided on the cheapest way we have of halting what would be terrible for the U.S."[14]

This description of the reality of capitalism's cult does not exhaust the demonic character of the capitalists. Capitalism has a religious character which its critique does not have. Capitalism's apologists irrationally base it on the assertion of the human inability to be the image of God, or by asserting that absolute forces have given people the destiny of an industrial society.

The renunciation in which the assent is concretized would remain an interpretation which changes nothing if it does not intend the alternative. If it is not realized in concrete political action to bring about socialism, then the critique of capitalism remains without obliging force. "Critical distance" and "independence" also practically mean denial of concrete political action. Concrete political action, partisanship, however, is not a fresh cult, no confession of faith, and also not an adjustment to the inevitable. It is, rather, plain solidarity with all of capitalism's human sacrifices. It is, therefore, an optimistic praxis for humankind which suits the epistemological optimism of dialectical historical materialism, or finds its reflection in this epistemological optimism. This partisanship is also found by participating in struggles for an alternative to the dominance of

---

[14]*War and Atrocity in Vietnam*, p. 27. Cited in *Informationen zur Abrüstung*, April 4, 1965.

deified money, as well as in cooperating in the building of socialism which has really already begun. Political action does not mean giving up all claim to freedom, but the realization of freedom, the liberation of human nature, even for the capitalists when they no longer lift a finger for Mammon.

3. The Impossibility of Belief and the Possibility of Unbelief

The alternative's realization, the struggle for an alternative to deified money's domination, for socialism's upbuilding, can be worked out only consciously—and that means methodically—by being organized. The atheism of allied or leading responsible organizers does not limit cooperation, does not allow Christians to be led astray from political action, or not to be obliged to participate in political action.

An unbeliever speaks: "Can a minister join or belong to an organization or alliance which denies God's existence?"[15] Such an explanation of incompatibility denies God's incarnation, strikes at God's coming down from solitude to the knowledge of faith, forbids the Christian to think. Christ and human being are so incompatible with one another as God's word moves away from believing to secular thinking. So God and human person are incompatible with one another.

What we believe in, however, is truly reconcilable with our human nature, with our human thinking, but only in the hope of the Holy Spirit, the Creator, who works miracles: "He emptied himself and took the form of a slave, being born in the likeness of men" (Phil. 2:7). The church leaders' opinion on the incompatibility of Christianity and socialism is not the expression of the apostles at the impossibility of being a Christian (Mt. 19:25). What is speaking in that opinion is the unbelief of the leaders of the People of God who, even though under the call of the God who works miracles, still deny, doubt, and laugh at God's wonders (Jn. 3:9, 8:54–59; Mk. 15:32). In divine truth, according to the biblical witness, it is incompatible with the Christian faith to declare the incompatibility of the believer's Christian faith and his or her secular existence, his or her conscious, methodical action which is shared with the nonbeliever. Even the atheism of dialectical historical materialism marks the profane character of this means for helping the human thought and action of both the Christian and the non-Christian. In thought and action, the Christian helps himself or herself to such profane methods; hence, insofar as these are proper thought and action of humans, the atheism of these methods is appropriate to prevent the Christian from confusing faith with viewpoint. Once more, the compatibility of faith with different viewpoints does not mean "ideological coexistence." Materialism and idealism are and remain rationally irreconcilable. The reconciliation of faith and viewpoints is and remains a wonder of the Holy Spirit, who makes both hearing and faith and which permits the hearing faith to hope the impossible against all

---

[15]*Stimme der Gemeinde*, June 15, 1973.

hope without that "idealistic" hope in faith, being a hindrance to responsible thought and action, *etsi Deus non daretur*.[16]

Finally, however, rarely is the Christian faith or a worldview the condition in partaking in the alliance which joins humans together in the struggle for the humanity of all.

Translated from German by
Lance P. Nadeau, Temple University, Philadelphia

---

[16]Bonhoeffer, *Widerstand*, p. 241.

TEACHING A COURSE ON THE MARXIST-CHRISTIAN DIALOGUE

Robert G. Thobaben and Nicholas Piediscalzi

"The Marxist-Christian Dialogue" has been team-taught by the authors at Wright State University in Dayton, Ohio, since 1970.[1] The purpose of the course is to introduce students to the history of the dialogue and its different branches and characteristics; the major issues, themes, problems, and points of convergence and divergence which emerge from the encounter; and the most recent developments in the dialogue. This paper summarizes how the authors attempt to fulfill this three-fold purpose.

I. History, Branches, and Characteristics

After the course is introduced, the students are asked to write short responses to the following three questions: How do you define a Christian? How do you define a Marxist? Can a person be both a Christian and a Marxist? The purpose of this exercise is to help the instructors and the students discover the preconceptions and attitudes each brings to the course and how these factors assist or impede the learning process. It also is used as a measuring device. At the close of the course the students are asked once again to write responses to the same questions. Then they compare their first and second sets of replies and discuss whether they differ. If they do, the instructors and students seek to ascertain what caused the differences, and they are able to measure and evaluate the course's effectiveness. This exercise usually results in the group discovering that most of the students believe that Marxists and Christians are by their different natures opposed to each other and that it is impossible for a person to be both a Marxist and a Christian. Also, very few of them see any basis for dialogue between the two groups. These discoveries prepare the way for a presentation of how it is that Marxists and Christians came to treat each other as natural opponents.

---

[1] As far as the authors are able to ascertain, this is the only team-taught course in the U.S.A. on the Marxist-Christian Dialogue which is offered on a regular basis over an extended period of time, and it is one of very few full-length courses devoted to the dialogue.

Robert G. Thobaben (United Methodist) is associate professor of political science at Wright State University, Dayton, OH. He received his education at Ohio University and Miami University and the Ph.D. from the University of Cincinnati. With N. Piediscalzi he was the co-editor and contributor to *From Hope to Liberation: Toward a New Marxist-Christian Dialogue,* as well as other articles.

Nicholas Piediscalzi (Unitarian) is professor of religion and co-director of The Public Education Religion Studies Center at Wright State University. He received his education at Grinnell College and Yale University, and the Ph.D. from Boston University. With R. Thobaben he attended the Salzburg Congress of the Paulus-Gesellschaft in 1977. He is the co-editor and a contributor to *Teaching about Religion in Public Schools.*

First, the students are introduced to the Christian community's contributions to this conflict. The church's insensitivity to the grave social injustices and deep human suffering which occurred during the rise of industrialized capitalism and the Christian community's alignment with reactionary forces in efforts to block individuals and groups who worked for socio-economic reform and redress of the wrongs inflicted upon the working classes are discussed. Next, we lecture briefly on the Roman Pontiffs who have pronounced anathema upon Communism on at least twelve different occasions during the past hundred years. Moreover, Pius XI declared that "there is no sphere whatever in which it is permissible to cooperate with it or countenance it."[2] This review is followed by summaries of the hostile statements and activities of many Protestants and their leaders, e.g., Billy James Hargis, the editor of *Christianity Today,* and the "Better Dead than Red" group. In addition, detailed attention is given to the meaning, significance, and religio-socio-political function of the United States' long-standing crusade against Communism.

After examining these Christian contributions to this period of anathema we consider those of the Communists. First, Marx's and Engel's criticism of religion, their avowed atheism, and their call for the violent overthrow of capitalist systems whose leaders called themselves Christians are presented as contributing factors to the polarization of Marxists and Christians. Second, Lenin's and Stalin's polemics against religion, e.g., Lenin's description of religion as "spiritual booze," and their systematic programs designed to exterminate the church and eliminate all forms of dissent are presented.

Finally, careful attention is given to the division of the world into two hostile blocs with the Soviet Union as the leader of one and the United States as the leader of the other, and to the detrimental effects this division has upon Marxist and Christian relations.

Following this review, we consider the forces and factors leading to the period which Roger Garaudy calls "From Anathema to Dialogue." First, we consider José Miranda's assertion that almost simultaneously some Christians began to claim that Christian faith is "completely falsified when it becomes . . . a world view . . . ," while some Marxists stated that dialectics is denied totally when it is "petrified into a 'conception of the world'. . . ."[3] These criticisms stem, according to Miranda, from each group's understanding "faith and dialectics in much greater depth than that achieved by their official respective representatives."[4] Moreover, each group discovered that the universal justice for which its community aspired was denied by their official representatives. This revelation slowly and imperceptibly began to draw these Christians and Marxists toward dialogue with each other. Both had a common enemy—officials who de-

---

[2]As quoted by Robert Adolfs, "Church and Communism," in Paul Oestreicher, ed., *The Christian Marxist Dialogue* (London: The Macmillan Co., 1969), p. 30.

[3]John Eagleson, tr., *Marx and the Bible: A Critique of the "Philosophy of Oppression"* (Maryknoll, NY: Orbis Books, 1974), p. 201.

[4]Ibid.

nied the heart of their community's eschatological vision. Second, we consider the encyclicals and efforts of Pope John XXIII, Pope Paul VI, and the actions of Vatican II, along with Khrushchev's rejection of Stalin's abuses of power in his dramatic speech to the Twentieth Party Congress and his liberalizing of Russian society. In addition, the positive overtures and statements of Togliatti and the new sets of relationships which developed between Communists and Christians living and working side by side in Italy, Hungary, and Yugoslavia are summarized. Third, the recent recognition by Marxists and Christians that the survival of the planet and the human race is threatened by worldwide pollution and the possibility of thermonuclear war is presented as a factor leading to dialogue. Fourth, the inescapable facts that over one billion people now live in regimes that claim to follow the theories of Marx and that religion in these areas and everywhere else in the world has not faded away but continues to flourish move some Marxists and Christians to conclude that it is more productive for them to dialogue with each other rather than remain in antagonistic tension.

Next, we provide a brief history of the dialogue, in three periods: the origin, ascendency, and descendency of the encounter in the First and Second Worlds; the rise and recent decline of the dialogue in Latin America; and new attempts at dialogue in the First and Second Worlds.

We trace the origin of the dialogue in the First and Second Worlds, along with the subsequent eclipses and revivals (1956–1968), to the early private encounters which took place between Marxists and Christians in seminars of the Comenius Faculty in Prague and the pioneering public dialogues conducted by the Paulus-Gesellschaft in Salzburg, Herrenchiemsee, and Marianske Lazny. In our presentation of this period, we include a description of those who participated in the encounters and how they defined dialogue and carefully established its limits, what topics were discussed, and what appeared to be some of the philosophical, social, and psychological preconditions for the encounters. This is followed by a consideration of the first period of eclipse which resulted from the Russian invasion of Czechoslovakia and the United States intervention in Vietnam. This encounter with very few exceptions involved only intellectuals who dwelt upon theoretical issues.

The second period of encounter, which we label "Revolutionary Praxis," occurred in Latin America. This is presented as a new and different Marxist-Christian Christian encounter. Here Marxists and Christians joined in revolutionary activities to correct social, political, and economic injustices. We include in this presentation the rise of Liberation Theology and its criticism and rejection of the theology of Hope. It is pointed out that the Marxist and Christian participants involved in this encounter are not only intellectuals and clergy but also activists and revolutionary leaders who refuse to devote their time to theoretical and ideological discussions. Since they all are dedicated to creating a more just society, they hold that it is more important for them to involve themselves jointly in revolutionary activity which will achieve their common goals rather than in abstract discussions. The Marxists realize that they have not been able to motivate and raise the consciousness of the masses. They feel the Christian church has the means and power to do so. The Christians believe that the churches and Christian Democratic parties have not been able to solve the socio-economic problems confronting their nations. In fact, they contend that all attempts on their part to do so have been blocked by imperialistic forces within and without their countries. Hence, they see Marxism as the only adequate "scientific" tool available to solve their countries' problems. Thus, they distinguish between Communism as an absolute ideology and Marxism as an analytic tool which may be used by Christians to solve societal problems. This allows them to cooperate with Marxists without having to resolve ideological differences. The struggle for justice takes precedence over theoretical debate. These vigorous efforts were brought to a virtual halt by the overthrow of Allende in Chile and the adoption of repressive measures to stem the tide of revolution in other Latin American countries.

The rise of Eurocommunism provided conditions for a new type of dialogue in Europe and the United States. This third period of development is traced in origin to the Paulus-Gesellschaft's 1975 meeting in Florence, Italy. For the first time, high ranking officials from a Communist Party (Italy's) participated in a dialogue. They also agreed to co-sponsor a 1977 Europa-Kongress to discuss "Towards a Socialist, Democratic, Christian, Humanist Europe." In the interim another dialogue took place at Rosemont College (Pennsylvania) in January, 1977. This encounter, the first major and official one to take place on American soil, was a joint venture of the Institute for International Understanding at Rosemont College, the Institute for Peace Research of the Roman Catholic Theological Faculty at the University of Vienna, the International Institute for Peace (headquartered in Vienna), Christians Associated for Relationships with Eastern Europe (American), and the *Journal of Ecumenical Studies*. The USSR, the GDR, and Hungary sent delegates to discuss with North Americans and West Europeans "Peaceful Co-existence and the Education of Youth." The emphasis shifted from purely ideological and theoretical issues to a combination of these and practical issues. Seven months later the Paulus-Gesellschaft's Kongress convened in Salzburg. Unfortunately, the Italian Communists withdrew their co-sponsorship and support of the dialogue. No official Communist Party officials attended. Only a small number of individuals came from Hungary, Spain and Italy. These most recent encounters will be followed by one in Kishnyev, Moldavia, U.S.S.R., in the Spring of 1978. Both point to an emerging new form of dialogue among First, Second, and Third World nations which bears careful observation concerning both what it augurs for the future and the motivations and expectations of those in authority who sanction and finance these encounters. The participants come from the ranks of political leaders, activist groups, and intellectuals.

These lectures on the history of the dialogue provide students with the historical perspective necessary for understanding the next section of the course—a study of the major issues, themes, problems, and points of convergence and divergence which emerge from the dialogue.

II. Issues, Themes, and Problems

Before turning to specific topics, we lecture extensively on a set of theses that we present as the keystone for the remainder of the course. We summarize the views of Adam Smith, Karl Marx, and Jesus of Nazareth on human nature, alienation, and the resolution of this predicament. We contend that only a comparative inquiry into the anthropology of Capitalism, Communism, and Christianity provides an adequate understanding of the critical points of convergence and divergence in these three ideologies. We want our students to come face to face with these categories early in the course because they mediate all the work that follows. They function, in a very real sense, as intellectual prisms through which all else may be understood. We try to get students to test and appraise the validity of their conceptions and misconceptions of what Smith, Marx, and Jesus said, primarily because these men have been misrepresented so often. We argue that these concepts are very important themes in all three belief systems and that there is much that each can learn from the other. Therefore, we present a formal lecture entitled, "Three Images of Man/Woman—Smith, Marx, Jesus: A Critique of the Sweetest Yoke of All."[5] The direct juxtaposition of the ideas of these three men makes possible quick comparisons which provoke some of the most exciting classes we have experienced in teaching the Marxist-Christian Dialogue.

The ideas of Adam Smith are dealt with first, because his thought impregnates the conscious and unconscious values, beliefs, and attitudes of every student. Initially, we argue that the old image of Adam Smith as the ideologue of absolute human egoism is simply not correct or complete and that any thorough review of his intellectual contributions demands that we construct a new and accurate model. We maintain that Smith's model of human nature is dualistic: sympathy (what Smith calls "fellow-feeling"), as well as self-interest. We prove our argument by drawing extensively from Smith's first major work, *The Theory of Moral Sentiments,* which outlines in great detail the nature of sympathy, and from *The Wealth of Nations,* which presents his views on self-interest. To Smith, both sympathy and self-interest must be kept in a polar relationship in order to have an accurate understanding of human conduct. We go on to show that Smith, like Marx, was concerned with human estrangement, but that Smith viewed this estrangement as *natural.* Isolation of owners and the powerlessness of workers characterize Smith's discussion, but there is little if anything that one can do to overcome the unbridgeable gulf between man/woman, rich/poor, worker/boss, or elite/follower. Civil society is *naturally* class society. Finally, we point out that Smith's naturalist philosophy presupposes an inherent, natural order in the world and in social life and that any efforts to achieve public good inexorably tend toward disaster, while the "invisible hand" is ultimately the only effective mechanism available to resolve the problems of humanity. Nevertheless, Smith

---

[5]Nicholas Piediscalzi and Robert G. Thobaben, "Three Images of Man/Woman: Smith, Marx, Jesus—A Critique of the Sweetest Yoke of All," *Proceedings,* pp. 146–171, of the Conference on Adam Smith and the Wealth of Nations, 1776–1976, Eastern Kentucky University, Richmond, KY, 1976.

believes that even the "invisible hand" occasionally needs some assistance from citizens to monitor and keep in check the propensity of business leaders' conspiracies against the public.[6]

We develop Marx's ideas on these three concepts under the rubric of New Marxism versus Old Communism. Marx's theory seems to differ fundamentally from the traditional communist construction, in that Marx stresses the concrete individual in his or her social praxis, while the traditional communist focus has been on the mode of production and technology. This emphasis of authentic Marxism is demonstrated theoretically in two basic concepts—alienation and *praxis*. One of the greatest misconceptions about Marx is that he was interested only in the group (the proletariat) and not in the individual. This misinterpretation is handled by quoting from Marx and by presenting Adam Schaff's claim that "the acting and acted upon individual" is the central category around which Marx organizes all his non-human variables.[7]

The human predicament for Marx is alienation (human estrangement) and we maintain in our presentation that it is the organizing principle of all of Marx's writing. Without a thorough understanding of this concept no really fundamental question raised by Marx on political economy makes sense. "Alienation" is the term Marx employed to refer to the unfulfilled human condition, our lack of correspondence with our authentic mode of being. To develop these ideas, we draw on Marx's writing in the *Paris Manuscripts* of 1844, through the *German Ideology* (1846) and the *Grundrisse* (1857), to *Capital* (1867). We lecture on the major forms of economic alienation and also on the social, religious, and political expressions of this human problem, pointing out that Marx begins with human categories (human beings and alienation), while Stalin and his followers begin with non-human constructs (technology and mode of production). We also introduce the notion of transcendence in discussing Marx's prescription for the resolution of the human predicament of alienation. Marx's dialectical interpretation of social change involving reciprocal relations between the economic base and superstructure is juxtaposed to the conventional communist interpretation of economic determination. This demonstrates the gap between the two views as well as its significance, that Marx believed that humans can transcend the present "pre-history" and achieve the epoch of Communism, the New Society.

Following our discussion of Marx we turn to Jesus, whose relationship to the prophetic tradition is shown. The popular presentations of Jesus as one who preached only long-suffering and inactivity in the face of grave injustices are rejected by referring to Lk. 4:18–19, wherein Jesus' ministry is presented as one of active liberation. Also considered are Jesus' use of force to drive the money changers from the Temple and his severe criticism of those who kill prophets and

---

[6]See Adam Smith, *An Inquiry into the Nature and Causes of the Wealth of Nations* (New York: The Modern Library, 1937), p. 128: "People of the same trade seldom meet together for merriment and diversion, but the conversation ends in a conspiracy against the public or in some contrivance to raise prices."

[7]Adam Schaff, *Marxism and the Human Individual* (New York: McGraw-Hill Book Company, 1970).

refuse to help people in need. Jesus did not write a systematic treatise on human nature; however, it is possible to infer at least four themes in his teachings: (a) all human beings are children of God who wills that they live in just and merciful relationships (Mt. 22:37–40); (b) individuals and groups establish either just or unjust relationships and societal structures (Lk. 6:45); (c) human beings possess the power through faith to deliver themselves from enslavements (Mt. 10:22); and (d) human fulfillment and the arrival of the Kingdom of God require leaders who are devoted to serving the welfare of others to the same degree they serve their own (Lk. 22:25–26). Thus, Jesus affirms human responsibility for events and human capacity to change unjust conditions. Human beings are "co-creators" of history with God and are called to join God in working for a just order.

Jesus' view on the human predicament is best summed up by the word "sin," the breaking of the Mosaic covenant as interpreted by the Hebrew prophets, namely, a failure "to do justice, and to love kindness and to walk humbly with . . . God" (Mic. 6:8b). Failure to fulfill the Covenant results in estrangement of individuals from each other and from God, the destruction of supportive communal structures, and gross injustices and hypocrisy. In condemning sinners, Jesus always was more harsh on the religio-political rulers than on the common people. The former create the structures which make it impossible for people to fulfill the Covenant. Jesus' basic resolution for sin is twofold. First, God's Reign is breaking into history and cannot be stopped from establishing a new order. Second, individuals and groups may become renewed by joining the Reign through an act of repentance (*metanoia*—a radical change or reorientation of one's ultimate loyalties and lifestyle). Jesus calls for two types of repentance— those who are responsible for perpetuating an unjust society are called to accept responsibility for their corrupt ways and to make restitution, and the victims of the unjust society are called to a *praxis* which overcomes their estrangement and denigration and produces a new sense of personal meaning and a new set of supportive relationships. Finally, Jesus' resolution is dialectical: the Reign of God is breaking in but is only partially present. Eventually it will come completely. In the interim, human beings are called to live out the life of the Reign by doing justice, loving kindness, and walking humbly with God.

Our work in this area concludes with a discussion of the common fate of Smith, Marx, and Jesus, i.e., the transformation of their radical ideas into oppressive and reactionary dogmas by the leaders of all three groups—leaders who are separate from the people they rule, and are "atheist" in the sense that they themselves do not believe in the magnificent eschatological visions they espouse. When students begin to recognize this, they discover that there is a basis for dialogue among Marxists and Christians and Socialists and Capitalists.

Having completed our comparative analysis in anthropology and prior to our examination of the sociological issues and themes of the dialogue, two lectures that focus on a critique of religion are presented. The central thesis is twofold. First, the traditional image of Marx's critique of religion is distorted and misrepresented seriously, and needs correction. Second, the prophetic criticism of established, self-seeking religious institutions found in the Hebrew and Christian Scriptures has been equally distorted and misrepresented, and it, too, must be presented in its original form.

We argue that Marx's critique of religion is dialectical and not positivistic in its nature, then show how Marx's rejection of established religion corresponds to the prophetic condemnation of self-absolutizing religious institutions. Two essays are used to accomplish these goals—Reinhold Niebuhr's "Introduction" and Marx's "Contribution to the Critique of Hegel's Philosophy of Right."[8] We employ eleven theses in our critique of Niebuhr's "Introduction" to demonstrate Marx's deep commitment to Hegelian dialectics rather than positivism, how he differed from his disciples (Engels, Lenin, and Stalin), and the unity of his thought. Niebuhr argues that Marx was "vague" on the problem of knowledge, that he was anti-Hegelian, that his materialism can be equated with Locke's, and that he (Marx) lapsed into positivism. We criticize these assertions and try to show just the reverse. In so doing, we transmit the basic principles of dialectics (inter-relatedness, reciprocal action, motion, and transformation) and compare these doctrines with the principles of Aristotelian logic and positivism. We then show that Niebuhr is incorrect in equating Marx and Engels (as he does) and that, in a number of areas, the work of the two men should be viewed separately. Here we particularly note Engels' tendency to lapse into philosophical positivism and economic determinism. Finally, we demonstrate that Niebuhr's claim that Marx's humanism is only a "subordinate part" of his writing is erroneous, by citing the work of outstanding scholars such as David McLellan, Shlomo Avineri, Adam Schaff, Leszek Kołakowski, Gajo Petrović, Roger Garaudy, etc. All of Marx's writing is a continuous meditation on the humanist theme of alienation.

To put Marx's critique of religion in its correct perspective we focus our analysis and comments on two ideas he expresses in "Contribution to the Critique of Hegel's Philosophy of Right." First, on religion as an opiate:

> Religious distress is at the same time the expression of real distress and the protest against real distress. Religion is the sigh of the oppressed creature, the heart of a heartless world, just as it is the spirit of the spiritless situation. It is the opium of the people.[9]

In this famous quotation, Marx makes five positive statements and one negative one on religion. This paragraph is an excellent example of Marx's dialectical method. We maintain that Marx views the world as a totality, that in his perception of reality politics, economics, religion, education, etc., are all different expressions of the same thing, that religion arises continually in history, and that people need religion for sustenance in this inhuman world. One gets a distorted image of Marx's position when only the opium phrase is heard. Marx talks of religion as a genuine expression (manifestation or evidence) of distress, as a

---

[8]Karl Marx and Friedrich Engels, *On Religion* (New York: Schocken Books, 1964).
[9]Ibid., p. 42.

protest (a challenge, an expression of indignation) against that distress, as a sigh (a hoping or yearning) by oppressed people, as the heart (a metaphor that recognizes the very root of life itself) of a heartless world, and as the spirit (the passion, the vehemence, the guardian) of a spiritless world. Religion is a relation through which people have historically expressed their agony. Religion, according to Marx, fulfills a human need, and it would be counter-productive to destroy or attempt to destroy such a relation. Then, *after* these positive statements, Marx characterizes religion as a sedative—a painkiller. Religion is both positive and negative—these are clearly two sides of the same coin. In the same essay Marx argues that the Peasant War in Germany, 1524–1525, was "the most radical fact of German history."[10] Thomas Müntzer, a pastor, was a major leader in this war. The first and last demands of "The Twelve Articles" made by the peasants to the nobles were religious (autonomy in choosing pastors, and use of the Scriptures as the basis for justice). Marx knew who led the revolt and what they demanded. This was clearly a socio-religious war, yet he characterized it as "the most radical fact of German history." Religious activity in the radical, prophetic tradition clearly had a positive, transcending, and revolutionary dimension for Marx.

The next task is to present how and why many Marxists and Christians agree that the major thrust of the Jewish and Christian contributions to western culture are contained in the prophetic dimensions of the Bible. Moreover, they agree that there is a link between this tradition and Marx's vision. Therefore, Marxists and Christians, according to them, share a common point of origin. Some Marxists and Christians now agree that both the Prophets and Jesus exemplified what Marx meant by praxis. Here is another meeting ground for Marxists and Christians.

Another important issue is introduced during this part of the course to demonstrate another area where some Marxists and Christians find a point of convergence. According to many Christians, the Bible's major concern is with idolatry, not atheism. The battle to be fought is not with atheists but with idolators who perpetuate gross injustices in the names of their idols. Often the most serious idolators, according to biblical writers, are people devoted to what we call today "institutionalized religion." Many Marxists today—e.g., Gardavsky—contend that Marx's atheism must be understood methodologically and historically. Methodologically, Marx's atheism was a rejection of the alienation of reason implicit in positivism and its internal relation to and expression through the institutionalized church. Historically, Marx was reacting against and rejecting idolatrous religious communities which were sanctioning gross injustices in the name of their gods. Some Marxists and Christians also agree that Marx's concept of the fetishism of money is a penetrating analysis of idolatry in western Capitalism. The concept of fetishism as Marx used it is rather difficult to transmit to students. Presenting it as a "double abstraction" seems to work best.

---

[10]Ibid., p. 51.

For example, Marx describes people as alienated in that they work not for use but for exchange. This is the first abstraction. The second abstraction (fetishism) occurs, according to Marx, when one works not for exchange but for the medium of exchange—money. Hence, both Marxists who now view the atheism of Marx methodologically and historically and some Christians who hold that one of the Bible's major themes is combating idolatry rather than atheism discover that they have another point of convergence in their desire to bring about a more just social order.

Teaching a course on the Marxist-Christian Dialogue is comparable to teaching mathematics. The theory is cumulative and one must build one's intellectual base slowly and thoughtfully. The time spent on historical development of the dialogue along with efforts to correct misconceptions and myths about human nature and religion have created the proper conditions for analysis of the next topic which is sociological in nature. Our primary concern here is to demonstrate the validity of the hypothesis that, paradoxically, there is a unity of opposites in Marxist and Christian thought. Although there may be a number of differences between the two groups, they reflect a common methodological perspective (prophetic and dialectical) and may share a number of substantive viewpoints about what constitutes a just society. This thesis is demonstrated by employing two sub-theses: "The Developmental Mentality of Marx and de Chardin," and "The Dominance of Bourgeois Ideology."

To transmit the first sub-thesis, we have constructed a simple matrix which is presented in lecture-dialogue format:

Common Criteria	Marx	de Chardin
Perspective	Evolutionary: Developmental	Evolutionary: Developmental
Basic Unit of Analysis	Man is *Praxis*	The Human Phylum
The Context	Alienated Society	Social Ramification
Origin of Change	Class Struggle	Divergence & Convergence
Forms of Change	Revolution	Change of State
Functions of Change	Communism	Megasynthesis
Object of Concern	Man as Species-Being	Hyper-Persona Man

There is a broad range of similarity between Karl Marx and Teilhard de Chardin as thinkers of the modern era. The basic thought of both men fits easily into a common set of formal criteria which follow a developmental pattern of change, and it is relatively easy to find concepts and phrases that match these criteria. Both thinkers have thoroughly anthropological points of departure in seeing human beings as active and social individuals. Both envision a forward movement in time whereby forms of matter, life, ideas, and social structure constantly transform themselves in ascending order of complexity. Both thinkers seek to provide a precise explanation for the processes whereby these changes take place. Finally, both are supremely aware of human existence in the conditions of the present as the best source for discovering a plan of action in the future course of development.[11]

The second sub-thesis is the dominance of bourgeois ideology as manifested in the control and manipulation of human beings by the major social structures of family, state, church, economy, and education. These socio-economic and political structures are related to various expressions of the cult of individualism in all its philosophical and social dimensions. We usually start our analysis with the state, which seems to be the easiest idea to transmit. We discuss the state as a set of relationships characterized by the estrangement of citizens from the center of political power so clearly present in both the U.S.A. (Vietnam) and the U.S.S.R. (*The Gulag Archipelago*). People of both countries have lost control of their political systems. The particular problems of social justice (U.S.A.) and freedom (U.S.S.R.) are discussed in an effort to demythologize the relations of political economy and the extreme nationalism of both nations. Then we try to show the radical character of both Marxism and Christianity in their universal outlooks and universalistic utopian visions. Both systems of thought cut across national barriers in their converging notions of loving one's neighbor and the solidarity of all workers. In discussing economic relationships, capitalist and socialist doctrines are compared and contrasted with Christian values. Cooperation, rational planning at the social as well as the individual level, production for the general welfare, concern with the quality of human relations, and collective ownership and control of major productive forces correspond with a Christian ethic of love, sharing, and concern for the corporate welfare. Finally, we criticize the sexism and hierarchical structures inherent in the nuclear family, and we close with a commentary on the role of the Christian community in sanctioning the unjust socio-economic structures of the bourgeoise state.

The next set of issues and recurring themes in the dialogue is introduced by presenting the socio-political criticism of some leading dialogists, so that students can understand the nature, meaning, and significance of the ideological fatigue that exists in both the East and West. This provides an effective introduction and transition to our presentation of the categories of hope, faith, and utopian vision. Marxists Leszek Kołakowski, Milan Machoveč, Roger Garaudy, and Vitezslav Gardavsky, and Christians Jan Lochman, Jürgen Moltmann, José Bonino, and Johannes Metz agree that the operative surrogate belief systems in East and West are nationalism at the social level, materialism-consumerism at the individual level, cynicism at the psychological level, and crass pragmatism at the public policy level.

We next demonstrate that Marxism and Christianity are rooted in escatological "hopes" which are capable of revitalizing and reforming their respective institutionalized forms of theology, theory, and praxis because they hold out the promise of a new future. *The Communist Manifesto* and the Bible demonstrate

---

[11]Robert G. Thobaben and Herbert T. Neve, "The Developmental Mentality of Marx and de Chardin," formal lecture presented in May, 1976, at Wright State University, Dayton, OH.

that the category of "hope" is central to both faith systems. Each holds out a hope of salvation (Communism and the Reign of God), each depends upon hope as a source of renewal, and each speaks of how hope sustains one in the face of adversity, pain, and setbacks. The analysis and rhetoric of the Bible and *The Communist Manifesto* must be read and understood within the framework of the radical perspective of achieving-renewing hope. Without this view, neither one makes much sense. Next, we discuss Ernst Bloch's and Jürgen Moltmann's views on hope. Their convergence and divergence are pointed out. The Bloch/Moltmann dialogue is instructive because it reveals the mutual enrichment of Marxist and Christian thought which results from honest dialogue. The session on hope ends with reading and discussing the essays of Herbert Aptheker and Thomas Ogletree on the topic, "What May Man Really Hope For?" and by studying their answers to questions put to them before a live audience.[12]

As we study hope, we also address ourselves to two other concepts of great importance—faith and eschatological vision. We employ Milan Machoveč's commentary on Jesus' command, "Let the children come unto me." According to Machoveč, Jesus teaches that children do not alienate themselves by objectifying their faith, as adults do. Machoveč argues that adults who retain from childhood a capacity for openness, directness, innocence—even naiveness—are true followers and reflect genuine faith.[13] Christian and Marxist faith respectively, in love and solidarity, and in the coming of the Reign of God and Communism is genuine faith according to Machoveč, while church and party doctrines are mere ideological fetishism.

The nature and role of eschatological vision is examined thoroughly (it is a recurrent theme throughout the course). Eschatology is defined, and its central role in biblical thought is developed. We ask what it means to live eschatologically. This question stimulates dialogue on the issues of eschatological promise, the relationship of present and future, the common characteristic of Marx and Jesus as eschatological thinkers, and the tendency of people with an eschatological attitude to be more concerned with altering the world rather than merely explaining it. We draw on the work of two other authors to develop the relationship of the future to the present. Thomas Thorson in *Biopolitics* provides a convincing argument for the necessity to go beyond our tendency to envision history in linear terms with the past at one end and the future at the other. This is done by viewing history not as a "clothesline" of connected events but an organic unity in which the present and the future are related. Moreover, this vision of the inter-relatedness of present and future provides a basis for meaningful and responsible activity in the present.[14]

---

[12]Nicholas Piediscalzi and Robert G. Thobaben, eds., *From Hope to Liberation: Towards a New Marxist-Christian Dialogue* (Philadelphia: Fortress Press, 1974), pp. 28–51. We organized and conducted this dialogue at Wright State University in the Spring of 1972.

[13]Milan Machoveč, *A Marxist Looks at Jesus* (Philadelphia: Fortress Press, 1976), pp. 99–101.

[14]Thomas Thorson, *Biopolitics* (New York: Rinehart and Winston, Inc., 1970), pp. 6–11, 74–89.

We draw on Garaudy's "confession" in *The Alternative Future* to develop these ideas. His presentation of Christian transcendence as the only sufficient condition for authentic revolutionary action[15] parallels and complements Thorson's organic view of history and his understanding of living responsibly in the present. Students are fascinated with these theses. These theses minimize many positivistic obstacles to our resumes and discussions of the Marxist vision of Communism and the Christian vision of the Reign of God. We point out the convergence of Marxist and Christian thought in both method (existence of vision) and substance (common content). To demonstrate substance we use contemporary interpretations of Marx and Jesus. For Marx, Communism is the solution to alienation. It is the new civilization and new community. It is a qualitatively different social milieu that is the end of human pre-history and the beginning of the real human history in an authentic ontological relation with nature and human activity. Communism is the fulfillment of Marx's revolutionary idea. For Jesus, the breaking in of the Reign of God and the immediate claim the new reality places upon men and women is presented as the core of his transforming vision. This wholly eschatological description of the future is the foundation of the message. Here we also comment on the fact that many now view the message of Marx and Jesus as particularly significant because both acted out their ideas and values. Students often know something of Jesus' love-acted-out, but nothing of Marx' lifelong revolutionary activities.

Following this presentation we turn to a consideration of Moltmann's definition of "God as man's future" and Gardavsky's interpretation of love as an "eternal category," and show how these two seemingly disparate views are complementary.

This session concludes with a summary of suggestions for alternative futures, so as to keep the encounter linked to actual proposals and to make certain that students are exposed to several different viewpoints and opinions.[16] We begin with a discussion of how and why the First and Second World have centered on hope, while the Third World encounters zero in on liberation and justice. Without dynamic hope, strivings for political liberation and socio-economic justice end in cynicism. However, with hope, one is psychologically prepared to work to achieve these two goals over a longer period of time in the face of adversity and defeats. Pedagogically, consideration of the categories of liberation and justice follow the actual evolutionary pattern of the dialogue between Marxists and Christians—especially in the Third World.

Although the words certainly are not mutually exclusive, liberation is usually emphasized as it affects political relations, and justice as it pertains to social and economic realities. These ideas are introduced with a lecture on their status and

---

[15]Roger Garaudy, *The Alternative Future* (New York: Simon and Shuster, 1974), pp. 80–86.

[16]Kenneth A. Megill, *The New Democratic Theory* (New York: The Free Press, 1970), pp. 65–79, 149–164; Garaudy, *The Alternative Future*, pp. 127–166; Michael Harrington, *Socialism* (New York: Bantam, 1973), pp. 421–456.

prospects in the world today. We have found the word "control" extremely helpful in bridging the gap between liberation and justice, and we comment on the world crisis, first by characterizing the First World crisis as primarily a reflection of loss of control of economic relations as manifested in the multi-national corporations and in authoritarian economic structures that tend increasingly toward more centralization in decision-making; second by arguing that the primary crisis in the Second World is a loss of control of political relations as witnessed by bureaucratic collectivism, Charter 77, and the "Gulag mentality" of the power holders; and finally we maintain that the Third World crisis involves both the loss of control of politics by the people to indigenous autocratic rulers and the loss of control of economic relations to foreign exploiters—both capitalist and "socialist."

Following this presentation, we move directly into a discussion of Marxism and Christianity on the concepts of liberation and justice. Since liberation clearly is central to Marxism, we begin with Marx and his views on class. This is difficult because American students tend not to think in group terms, but are much happier "explaining" politics at all levels of decision-making in terms of individuals (Napoleon, Churchill, Stalin, Roosevelt, Nixon, etc.). We try, frankly with limited success, to get them to think about politics in terms of group (class) struggle. From class, we can move to class struggle. In Marx's theory, the origin and dynamic of social change is class struggle: "The history of all hitherto existing society is the history of class struggles."[17] We put great emphasis on the idea (as Marx did) that the engine of change is class struggle—social praxis. Marx's liberation involves the "withering away" of political relations and his justice implies the end of egoism and the distribution of necessities on the basis of need. Needless to say, we have some heated debate in class on these points. We draw on *The Communist Manifesto,* "Theses on Feuerbach," and *The German Ideology* particularly in developing these themes. Marx's ideas on liberation and justice are supplemented with the contributions of Mao Tse-tung (theory of guerrilla warfare) and Che Guevara (efforts to build a new person and society by uninterrupted revolutionary activity).

Next we focus on how some Christians interpret the Exodus as the central meaning-giving event of the Hebrew Bible. They maintain that the liberation of the enslaved Hebrews and the establishment of a Covenant society governed by God's justice is a major and constant theme of the Bible. We summarize some Christian views on liberation and justice, beginning by considering contemporary interpretations of "The Last Judgment" story found in Mt. 25:31–41. Some Christian leaders make this story the foundation of their liberation theology and their belief that socio-economic justice can be achieved only through socialism. Next, we present Shepherd Bliss' views on liberation. He addresses himself to a host of questions on the encounter in Latin America where, as Bliss says, "The

---

[17]Karl Marx, *The Communist Manifesto* (Baltimore: Penguin Books, 1968), p. 79.

dialogue becomes praxis.'' Bliss argues that Latin American theology centers on liberation and justice rather than on hope because, whereas liberation theology speaks directly to the concrete circumstances and needs of the masses of people of Latin America, the theology of hope ignores this reality by remaining in the realm of theory.[18]

It is important for students to learn that the First and Second World dialogues are almost exclusively a series of intellectual encounters, while the Third World dialogue is one of co-operative efforts to reform society. Thus the focus and emphasis of the dialogue varies with the objective circumstances that confront those who are involved in the encounter. Hope is critical if we are to live life fully. Liberation is crucial if we are to live at all. Such seems to be the major assertion of the theology of liberation.

The necessity of theoretical convergence as a basis for practical cooperation is not difficult to demonstrate. However the problem in the encounter to date has been to find such clear complementary and unambiguous constructions. We present ''love'' and ''social solidarity'' as two important categories now emerging from the Marxist-Christian Dialogue that meet this need. They are found in the works of such leading thinkers as Machoveč, Gardavsky, Bonino, Petulla, Lochman, and Moltmann. We try to show how these theorists and theologians view love as the category capable of linking Marxists and Christians in praxis by enabling them to work together to transform alienated society into human community. They derive these views from the heart of Marx's thought as expressed in the ''umbrella'' concepts of alienation and community which he spread out over all he wrote, and from the center of Jesus' message and ministry.

According to the Marxists mentioned above and others, e.g., Ché Guevara, one becomes a communist out of love for others. Knowledge of the class struggle is not enough—passionate love for humankind is also necessary. This love is the relation that makes work creative and life adventurous, and it transforms the quality of relations from I-It to I-Thou. Love is the ''eternal category'' that demands a radical decision to step across historical times. The Christians involved in the dialogue emphasize that God is manifested in just and loving relationships. The question we raise is how Christians seek to make this love efficacious. The most difficult task that confronts us in presenting the views of Christian thinkers on this topic is overcoming ''positivistic'' views of God. It is difficult—almost impossible—for most people to think of God except as objectified existence. They find it very difficult to comprehend relational definitions of God. God as the source of a love which seeks to overcome estrangement— especially in the socio-economic realm—is most difficult to transmit to those who view God as a moralistic police officer. The same is true for presenting God as man's and woman's future. Yet it must be done because theologians involved in the dialogue conceive of God relationally.

---

[18] ''Latin America—Where the Dialogue Becomes Praxis,'' in Nicholas Piediscalzi and Robert G. Thobaben, eds., *From Hope to Liberation* (Philadelphia: Fortress Press, 1974), pp . 77–114.

Next, we conduct a comparative study of the major doctrines of Capitalism and Socialism. Then, in class discussion, we attempt to measure the degree of correspondence between these two ideologies and Christian love. Almost without exception, Christian theologians involved in the dialogue view classical Capitalism with its emphasis on unrestricted individualism as anti-Christian, and Socialism, with its central concern for social solidarity and justice, as the only political economy that fulfills the demands of Christian love. This concept is then related to the notion of celebration. Marx calls for the celebration of life in his critique of an ascetic Christian ethic that suggests that the more one saves and foregoes life, the more one lives—that a person who somehow denies life lives life. Marx ridicules this idea and calls for a life lived fully and spontaneously. To demonstrate the Christian perspective we draw on the work of Harvey Cox and his interpretation of the Christian concept of celebration as conscious excess (overdoing it), affirmation (saying yes to life), and juxtaposition (contrasting life as it is and might be). This topic generates a good deal of surprise and interest in our students—surprise, because by this point most view Marxism and Christianity as such serious faith systems that such conduct seems out of place, and interest because this view of life corresponds to their own conception of life as exciting, promising, and experiential.

Finally, we show how those who seek to live a life of love confront a major ethical question, "How do I remain human and responsible in the face of death?" This question paves the way for a full discussion of the various answers offered by Marxists and Christians. Herbert Aptheker begins to outline the boundary of the Marxist position in chapter nine of his book, *The Urgency of the Marxist-Christian Dialogue*. Here he reviews and criticizes four theoretical perspectives on death: as absurdity, as a source of hope, as a source of despair, and as a matter of indifference. He rejects all in favor of a Marxist conception that views as an implicit, postponable, biological, and challenging finality to live life fully.[19] He also deals with death existentially when he describes how he felt when he faced death during a surprise assault by a number of men.

> I resisted . . . I felt mad . . . I felt I didn't waste my time here. I did as well as I could. I could have done better in this or that, but I've been lucky in being able to join the struggle for justice and equal economic opportunity for all human beings. The main issue for me is this struggle. It's right. There's no alternative. That's the way to live.[20]

Vitezslav Gardavsky also does pioneering work on the concept of death when he discusses the atheistic theory of subjective identity which bears the imprint of the fact of death but not hopelessness. Gardavsky argues that to embrace the "honorary" title of human being implies that one accepts the possibility of transcend-

---

[19]Herbert Aptheker, *The Urgency of the Marxist-Christian Dialogue* (New York: Harper Colophon Books, 1970), pp. 121–125.

[20]See Herbert Aptheker's response in Piediscalzi and Thobaben, eds., *From Hope to Liberation* pp. 65–66.

ing all limits in our lifetime. Love alone, he maintains, provides the driving force which moves humans inwardly to accept the tragedy of their own death (defeat) with ethical responsibility. This in turn is an expression of love and communal hope for all humankind. Only love permits me to transcend oneself and say, ''I am a gift to you and you to me.'' This is the source of transcendence. Gardavsky concludes, ''I do not believe although it is absurd.''[21]

The question at this point is, ''Can humanism energize the necessary eschatological vision necessary for human beings to make life meaningful and death acceptable?'' Before reviewing several different Christian views on humanism and death, we deal with the charges made against Christians by many Marxists, namely, that Christians deny responsibility for transforming the here and now by promising and over-emphasizing preparation for life after death. Following this presentation we seek to understand why some Marxists state that they have much to learn from some Christians in resolving the problem of death. We draw on Jürgen Moltmann's book, *Man,* as an example of a contemporary theology of humanism. Moltmann is particularly instructive in his warning to modern people of the dangers to humanity implicit in our technology. In addition, his development of Buber's concept of the human as relationship (I-Thou) and his relation of hope to humanism with its implied promise that life can be different is very helpful in class work. Some of the alternative interpretations of the resurrection of Jesus are introduced, including Garaudy's, which suggests that we should view the resurrection as neither a fact nor an event that took place ''literally'' on a specific day at a specific time. Rather, it should be interpreted as a creative act that opens up the future to us all. The ultimate meaning of the resurrection is in the promise, vision, and hope it holds for human praxis and transcendence. Dealing with the problem of death reveals that the gap between Marxist and contemporary Christian thought on this problem is imaginary. Both Marxists and contemporary Christians have unresolved problems. Neither contemporary Marxism nor contemporary Christianity offers adequate solutions for most of their followers. Both ideologies as practiced are lacking in their capacity to nerve people to live life fully and accept death creatively.

III. Recent Developments

The course moves toward conclusion with a discussion of the most recent developments in the dialogue. The reactionary and oppressive actions of Latin American dictatorships are presented as the major factor in the eclipse of the praxis-oriented encounter in that part of the world. The ramifications of this development for other dialogues also are discussed. Next are considered the attempts to develop new types of dialogues between First and Second World Marxists and Christians—Florence, Rosemont, Salzburg (1977), planned dia-

---

[21]Vitezslav Gardavsky, *God Is Not Yet Dead* (Harmondsworth, Middlesex: Penguin Books, 1973), p. 7.

logue sessions for the upcoming international convention of philosophers in
Düsseldorf, the announced dialogue to be held in Moldavia as a follow-up
to Rosemont, Rosemont-1978, and the continuation of the seminar on "The
Future of Religion" in Dubrovnik. These developments are viewed within the
context of the rise of Eurocommunism and as reactions to it. Since all but the
Düsseldorf sessions and the Dubrovnik seminar seek to include a mixture of
intellectuals, political leaders, and activists, the students are invited to watch for
the possible emergence of a more praxis-oriented First and Second Worlds encounter. However, the students are asked to watch closely political developments
in Europe, the emerging interaction of political parties with the Vatican and
major Protestant bodies in Europe, and the reactions of the United States and the
Soviet Union to determine how genuine and long-lasting the move toward practical and cooperative encounters will be.

The course concludes with the students defining for a second time the terms
"Christian" and "Marxist," discussing whether it is possible to be a Marxist
and a Christian at the same time, comparing these responses to their first ones,
and sharing their assessments of, and reactions to, the course. They tend to agree
that their eyes are opened to the destructiveness of stereotyping. They express
appreciation for being introduced to the difference between Marxist theory and
the way it is practiced in various countries. They come to see that there is a
serious discrepancy between Marxist ideals and Leninist, Stalinist, and Maoist
practices, and they learn how to search out the causes of these discrepancies.
Likewise, they deal more critically and responsibly with the discrepancies they
find between Christian faith and practice. Here too they acquire a modicum of
sophistication in discovering the causes of this paradox. The students agree that
they have not been converted to Marxism. On the other hand they admit that they
no longer view Marxists according to their formerly held stereotypes, viz., as
godless, unprincipled revolutionaries. Rather, they see Marxists as complex
individuals who seek to solve some of the serious socio-economic problems
confronting our globe. This new understanding does not include an uncritical
acceptance of Marxist theories and programs—especially as they are acted out by
nations in the arena of world politics. But it does include a new apprecition for
the need of dialogue between Marxists and Christians for the purpose of discovering ways of resolving conflicts without resorting to armed conflict. Moreover,
like the participants in the dialogue, the students come to see that both Marxists
and Christians face the same ecological problems threatening the survival of their
planet, which makes it necessary for them to transcend their differences and
conflicts in order to address these critical problems. Likewise, the students come
to see that this problem is not unique to Marxists and Christians but confronts all
people and their many diverse religious commitments. Therefore, the students
begin to discover the need to extend the dialogue to include Muslims, Hindus,
Buddhists, and other religious communities.

The students also agree that the course forced them to examine and take more
seriously their own religious commitments and affiliations. They also report that

they no longer can mouth platitudes about the unreconcilable differences between Marxism and their religious faith. They discover that there are areas of convergence, e.g., the Jewish and Christian commitment to human solidarity and equal justice for all, which can no longer be denied or ignored. The discovery of this convergence makes them more dedicated to "reforming" their own religious communities rather than becoming Marxists.

The instructors find their team-teaching to be a constant source of intellectual growth. Their own presuppositions and conclusions constantly are called into question by their team-research, -planning, and -teaching, and by their students. As a result, their theories and practices are widened and begin to approach the holistic goal set for interdisciplinary studies at Wright State University.

EDUCATION FOR PEACE AND IDEOLOGICAL DEBATE

Maurice Boutin

A four-day symposium on "Peaceful Coexistence and the Education of Youth" took place in January, 1977, at Rosemont College, Rosemont, PA. The symposium was sponsored by the Institute for International Understanding (Rosemont), the Institut für Friedensforschung (Vienna), and the International Institute for Peace (Vienna), with the co-sponsorship of Christians Associated for Relationships with Eastern Europe and the *Journal of Ecumenical Studies*. The symposium was a sequel to four previous symposia which included only European participants and which were held beginning in 1971 in Vienna, Moscow, Wallersee (Austria), and Tutsing (West Germany). About sixty-five prominent Marxist and Christian scholars participated in the symposium. The eastern European contingent included seven from the Soviet Union (including a Russian Orthodox Archbishop), three from East Germany, and one from Hungary. From western Europe, there were five from West Germany, two from Austria, one from the Vatican, and one from Sweden. In the North American group of about forty there were one Canadian and one from the Dominican Republic; the others were from the United States.

Two major papers were presented, one by Professor Yuri Zamoshkin, a sociologist from the Institute on the U.S.A. and Canada in Moscow, and the other by Professor Charles West of Princeton Theological Seminary. The two respondents were Professor Rudolf Weiler, head of the Institut für Friedensforschung, and Professor Christoph Wulf of West Germany. Professor Weiler and Dr. Vladimir Bruskov, director of the International Institute for Peace, who was also present, had initiated the series of peace symposia, while Professor Paul Mojzes of Rosemont College had initiated American participation in the symposia and organized the Rosemont symposium.

The account which follows is not an attempt to summarize the proceedings of the symposium in chronological order, but a series of analytical remarks concerning some key issues discussed in the symposium. An important decision was made at the end of the symposium, namely to continue with this tri-partite constituency at a symposium to be held in 1978, in Kishnyev, Moldavia, U.S.S.R. A short conference on "Aspects of Detènte" was held at the end of the symposium to which no specific reference is made for lack of space.

Out of the many questions raised at the Rosemont Symposium on "Peaceful

Maurice Boutin (Roman Catholic) received his education at Collège de Saint-Laurent and the Université de Montréal and his doctorate in theology from the University of Munich. He is assistant professor of theology at the Faculté de théologie, Université de Montréal. Participant in a number of the symposia of the Paulus-Gesellschaft in Europe, he is a member of the Council of the Internationale Paulus-Gesellschaft. Since 1975 he has been a member of the Colloques Internationaux sur l'Hermeneutique in Rome. He has published articles in German and Canadian journals, a number of which dealt with Christian-Marxist questions, and the book *Relationalität als Verstehensprinzip bei Rudolf Bultmann* (1974).

Coexistence and the Education of the Youth for Peace"[1] the following, I feel, forces attention: what does the call for *intensifying* ideological debate require? This urgency was suggested by Yuri A. Zamoshkin, during the discussion following his report. Other participants at the Rosemont Symposium also stressed the importance of ideological debate, calling for establishment of "genuine faith in our respective Christian and Marxist ideologies rather than fanaticism or cynicism," in order to "act as an instrument of ideological development."

The quest for a new understanding and practice of ideological dialogue should bring about a radical change in the way ideological conflict between capitalism and socialism, as social and economic systems, was initiated and is still all too often carried out today. This is an important element in peace education.

It is not possible here to consider more than a few aspects of the problematic implied in education for peace and ideological debate. Neither is it possible to analyze the process of education or to focus on certain facts pertaining to it, as it was done at Rosemont, especially in Christoph Wulf's paper on "Perspectives for Peace Education." It is also obvious that what is here called "ideological debate" is different from the commonly assumed negative meaning of ideology since the time of Karl Marx, though Marx insisted on some very important aspects of ideology that cannot easily be set aside.[2]

Actually ideological debate is not the most urgent issue. From a "realistic" point of view, one may consider disarmament as the imperative today, but at the same time confront the practical need for disarmament with the concrete pursuit of a diametrically opposite strategy. Charles West stated in his paper that the present world situation seems to conform to the imperative once expressed by the Romans: *Si vis pacem, bellum para.* The more we talk about peace, the more concerned we are about weapons, thus setting threat and fear as the basis for a peace subservient to the arms race and neglectful of the North-South conflict, the ecological crisis, and social tensions of all kinds.

Though not as urgent as this concrete problem, the ideological debate is, nevertheless, important. To expatiate on this seems even more difficult than to examine "concrete steps in the process of disarmament and to substantiate these measures theoretically." This was the opinion of Robert Steigerwald, a member of the Central Committee of the Communist Party of West Germany, at Rosemont when he stressed the difficulty in dealing with education for peace. But this opinion also concerns the question of intensifying the ideological debate, thus drawing attention to its relationship to education for peace, though from a formal, and hence still quite unsatisfactory, perspective.

In western European countries, as indicated by Christoph Wulf, there has

---

[1]The proceedings of this scholarly symposium were published in March, 1977, by one of its sponsors, the International Institute for Peace, Vienna ["Peace and the Sciences" series], 87 pp.
[2]On this question, cf. M. Boutin, "Idéologies et foi," in *Review Laval théologique et philosophique* (October, 1977), pp. 253–271, published by the Laval University, Québec.

always been more interest in ideological debate than in peace education. The latter is a rather recent phenomenon, which explains—but by no means excuses—the lack of emphasis on it so far according to Siegrid Pöllinger, a Catholic scholar from Vienna. The question now is whether a more explicit concern for peace education will change the way in which the ideological debate is carried out between persons belonging to different cultural traditions and living in different social and economic systems, e.g., capitalism and socialism. Can education for peace be achieved through a kind of cooperation that would eliminate ideological debate? Can ideological debate be considered only a remnant of the cold war mentality or "psychological warfare"?

The relationship between education for peace and ideological debate was constantly present at the Rosemont Symposium and was often referred to during the discussions. The participants in the symposium clearly indicated that the question should not be minimized and that they were willing to consider the crucial issues at stake in ideological debate within the issue of peace education.

The problem can be stated as follows: First, the irrational impact that prevents intensification of ideological debate is not the fact that there are differences between persons, groups, and social systems, but rather because of the concrete experiencing and interpreting of these differences *in terms of limitations*. Second, education for peace requires considering the *dynamic* dimension of peace. In fact, peace cannot be had once and for all, because it implies the discovery of the *creative* aspect in differences. Third, intensifying the ideological debate belongs to the dynamic character of peace, though it cannot be identified with the latter because the problem of peace is not primarily theoretical, but indeed disturbing and inexorable. It is disturbing on account of the precarious nature of peace. It is inexorable because peace is the only viable human alternative today.

Awareness for peace today means concern for peace *education* that brings about an action, by which peace would no longer be instrumentalized as a means of reaching some other goal (order, e.g.), based on the assumption that the arguments of the strongest are always the best. This attitude can only bring forth a "lousy world," in the words of the American Marxist Barrows Dunham. The question then arises whether it is possible to live decently in such a lousy world. According to Dunham this question characterizes American youth since the end of the 1960's, whereas young people at the beginning of the 1950's, shortly before the spread of McCarthysm, were eager to find social solutions to social problems.

Peace education is not at all necessary for the instrumentalization of peace. It rather demythologizes peace, which encompasses a respect for, and sharing in, differences, without destroying them or letting them be destructive of one another. This is the realm of a new rationality emerging from the process of peace education.

If each society could provide the people living in it with the best of everything, it would be foolish to pay attention to the differences between social and economic systems, except for the sake of comparing achievements of one's own society with the failures of others. This is the way closed systems relate and present themselves as the fittest, counting on their own survival and supremacy. What is at stake is integration within one's own system and a united front against those outside. Ideological debate gives the opportunity to justify, legitimate, and defend one's own position against others, as if each stand were a *given entity* already established prior to the debate itself. One can hardly speak here of intensifying ideological debate, since the latter consists then in *"substantiviz-ing"* one's own historical experience against that of others, which means iden-tifying what one stands under and what one stands for. Such identification results in duplicating theoretically the confrontations in economic and military affairs.

In order to make sure that the ideological debate does not become sterile, some feel the need for a common denominator. Particularly since the eighteenth century, human nature is considered a common denominator according to a twofold purpose: the building up of a constitutive resemblance among people, and, consequently, the relativizing of the differences between them. The attempt to subordinate historical data to a metaphysical *"référent"* corresponds indeed very well with the process of ideal-making.[3] But the kinship of all people dictated by human nature, and hence pre-institutional, is a grandiose and nevertheless disappointing ideal because of the abstract character of its universality.[4]

Ideological debate does not have to look for a common basis aside or above differences. The common basis is already there in the present situation, though it is ruled more by fear and mistrust, sometimes leading to consider the mere existence of others a threat to oneself. This destructive way of relating to dif-ferences among people is a luxury that can hardly be afforded today.

In his paper, Charles West asked where education for peace begins. Most likely, the answer cannot be theoretical, for it depends on specific conditions and on achieving a certain number of requirements, the identification of which was proposed by participants at Rosemont. Intensifying ideological debate implies that such a debate takes place not only despite differences, but within them. At the same time we know that differences do not fade out along with the destructive approach to them, but differences are there in order to help overcome one's own limitations without bringing about nostalgia for uniformity.

Peace can no longer be understood as *tranquillitas ordinis,* whatever it is. Otherwise education for peace is but a caricature of both education and peace, and it renders impossible a positive answer to the question of Rudolph Weiler as to "whether our ideologically oriented educational aims can be presented con-vincingly to the youth of today."

---

[3]Jean Pouillon's study, *Fétiches sans fétichisme* (Paris: Frs. Maspero, 1975), offers important critical considerations on this question; e.g., pp. 16, 21, and 299–321.

[4]E. Schilebeeckx, "Seigneur, à qui irions-nous? (Jean 6,68)," in J.-P. Jossua, H.-M. Legrand, and D. Guillou, eds., *Théologie: Le service théologique dans l' Eglise* [Coll. "Cogitatio Fidei," 76] (Paris: Cerf Publishers, 1974), p. 270.

THREE DIMENSIONS OF "PEACEFUL COEXISTENCE"

George L. Kline

I wish to discuss the concept of peaceful coexistence as it applies (I) between nation states and (II) between social groups, and then consider (III) the Marxist-Leninist repudiation of the "peaceful coexistence" of ideas, values, and ideologies.

I

I interpret the principle of "peaceful coexistence of states with [radically] different social systems" to be a theory or doctrine, and not just a tactic or strategem, for three reasons:

(1) Although peaceful coexistence is not a *Marxist* doctrine (there is no such idea in Marx himself), and its doctrinal toehold in certain late utterances of Engels is precarious,[1] it *is* rooted quite solidly in Lenin's thought.[2] And, although there is no reference to it in the current Soviet constitution (adopted under Stalin in 1936 and for twenty years regularly referred to as the "Stalin Constitution"), the new "Brezhnev" Draft Constitution, published on June 4, 1977, clearly includes, in Art. 28, among the aims of Soviet foreign policy, the "consistent implementation" of the "principle of peaceful coexistence of states with different social systems" (*Pravda*, June 4, 1977; *New York Times*, June 5, 1977).

(2) In the light of the sudden fall from power of Soviet President Nikolai Podgorny on May 24, 1977, it is important to note that the doctrine of peaceful coexistence has for two decades survived the fall of the leader who enunciated it in the period after World War II, namely, Nikita Khrushchev. The authoritative

---

[1]In general Engels agreed with Marx that the socialist revolution would occur at about the same time in *all* advanced capitalist countries. Hence there would be no occasion for "peaceful coexistence" between states with categoreally distinct social systems.

[2]According to the current (third) edition of the *Great Soviet Encyclopedia*, the "working out of the conception of peaceful coexistence was one of the most important achievements of Leninist political theory" (*Bol'shaya Sovetskaya Entsiklopediya* [hereafter "*BSE*[3]"], Moscow, 1974, XVI, 314). However, Lenin's legacy is not unambiguous. For a careful discussion of its ambiguities with respect to peaceful coexistence and the "exporting of revolution," see Gustav Wetter, S. J., "The Soviet Concept of Coexistence," *Soviet Survey*, No. 30, 1959, pp. 19–34.

George L. Kline (Unitarian-Universalist) is a professor of philosophy at Bryn Mawr College, Bryn Mawr, PA. His specialty is Russian and Marxist philosophy, on which he has written numerous articles and translated many works from Russian. He is the author of *Spinoza in Soviet Philosophy* and *Religious and Anti-Religious Thought in Russia*, and the editor of and contributor to *European Philosophy Today* and *Russian Philosophy*. He has received the Cutting, Fulbright, Ford, Rockefeller, and National Endowment for the Humanities Fellowships.

textbook, *Fundamentals of Marxist Philosophy,* in a section entitled "The Coexistence of Socialism and Capitalism and the Inevitability of the Victory of Socialism in All Countries" (Ch. XVI, sec. 9) correctly, if somewhat effusively, identifies this doctrine with Khrushchev: "The principle and policy of peaceful coexistence has been grounded in a comprehensive and profound way in the [public] statements of Comrade N. S. Khrushchev."[3] Only five years later the even more authoritative *Philosophical Encyclopedia,* in a four-column article on "Peaceful Coexistence," made no reference to Khrushchev at all.[4] A Soviet leader had been toppled, but the Soviet commitment to peaceful coexistence was unchanged. This gives some basis for assuming that when Brezhnev leaves the political scene the Soviet commitment to peaceful coexistence will continue.

(3) The most important reason for regarding peaceful coexistence as more than a strategem or tactic is that it has a serious conceptual foundation in the Marxist-Leninist philosophy of history. In this view not all capitalist states will reach socialism at the same time. During the interval between the appearance of the *first* socialist state and the disappearance of the *last* capitalist state—an interval which may continue for generations or even centuries—there will be a mixture of socialist and not-yet-socialist states in the world. The theory of peaceful coexistence specifies the relations between the socialist and non-socialist states throughout this transition period. This period was *preceded* by a (finite) historical period in which there were only warlike not-yet-socialist (i.e., either capitalist or feudal-monarchic) states. It will be *followed* by an (infinite) historical period in which there will be only peaceable socialist states. Peaceful coexistence is thus an intermediate condition—both conceptually and temporally—between the *past* condition of interrupted war among non-socialist states and the *future* condition of uninterrupted peace among socialist states.

This is a perfectly consistent *theory,* but it runs afoul of a massive contemporary *fact:* Sino-Soviet conflict. During the Rosemont Conference our Soviet colleagues twice dramatized this fact: (a) asking rhetorically whether the United States wouldn't allocate as large a share of its resources to defense as does the Soviet Union if it faced, on its southern border, not the Republic of Mexico but the People's Republic of China, and (b) asserting that if a Chinese submarine should fire a nuclear-tipped missile at the Soviet Union from a point near the United States coast, the Soviet leaders would have to retaliate against the United States without stopping to determine the precise source of the incoming missile.

The fact of Sino-Soviet conflict has been evident for almost twenty years. For

---

[3]*Osnovy marksistskoi filosofii,* 2nd printing (Moscow, 1959), p. 545.

[4]*Filosofskaya Entsiklopediya* (Moscow, 1964), III, 452–454. Interestingly enough, this volume was "cleared for printing" (*podpisan k pechati*) on September 22, 1964, more than three weeks before Khrushchev was deposed (on October 15). References to Khrushchev were presumably deleted in the course of proof-correction. The 5½-column article on peaceful coexistence in the *Great Soviet Encyclopedia* also fails to mention Khrushchev by name. but both encyclopedia articles refer to, and quote from, documents with which Khrushchev was closely associated, such as the Central Committee Resolution of June 21, 1963. (See *BSE*[3], XVI, 314–316.)

nearly that long the Soviet leaders have identified the People's Republic of China as a major threat to world peace. In this situation only two courses are open to Marxist-Leninist theorists of peaceful coexistence: either to deny that the People's Republic of China is a socialist state, or to admit that at least one socialist state is warlike. But the first alternative is blocked by the plain fact that the Chinese Communists have abolished private ownership of the means of production, eliminated—or at least reduced—class antagonisms, and met the other Marxist-Leninist criteria of a "socialist state." Yet Brezhnev appears to have taken this course, first in 1972, and more recently in his 1976 speech to the Twenty-Fifth Party Congress, when he offered to normalize relations with Peking "on the bsis of the principle of peaceful coexistence." This clearly implies that China is a state with a "different," i.e., non-socialist, social system. But in such a usage the term "non-socialist" loses its distinctive meaning, and becomes a mere synonym for "non-peaceful" or "warlike."

The second alternative undercuts both the Marxist-Leninist theory of history and the doctrine of peaceful coexistence, and for this reason appears even more unacceptable from the Soviet point of view than the first alternative. Since our Marxist-Leninist colleagues at the Rosemont Conference declared repeatedly that *only* non-socialist states are warlike, I would hope that on some future occasion they might address themselves to this central and disturbing question.

II

Archbishop Vladimir of Dmitrov made the interesting statement during the Rosemont Conference that Christians and Marxists in the Soviet Union have engaged, do now engage, and will in the future engage, in "peaceful coexistence." He is aware, of course, that a majority of Soviet citizens are neither Marxists nor Christians; he would presumably be willing to extend coexistence to include this third group.

However, since our theme is "education for peace," I want to point out that the peaceful coexistence of diverse groups within Soviet society cannot be isolated from the Marxist-Leninist proscription of "coexistence" of the groups', or their members', ideas, values, or "ideologies." This proscription has a particularly stultifying effect on Soviet education.

(1) As Archbishop Vladimir well knows, since he is the current Rector of the Moscow Theological Academy at Zagorsk, there is in Soviet higher education almost no coexistence of Christians and Marxists—or, more broadly, of religious believers and non-believers. Religious instruction is limited to the two Russian Orthodox divinity schools, in Zagorsk and Leningrad, which together graduate only a few score students each year. Secular higher education is in principle closed to believers, although—by way of exception—there is a scattering of graduates of Soviet dental schools among Soviet Evangelical Baptists. But the proportion of religious believers among recent graduates of Soviet institutions of higher learning is vanishingly small, representing probably no more than one or

two per cent of all religious believers in the relevant age group, say, ages twenty-one to twenty-five.[5]

(2) The proscription of lay religious instruction, which dates from 1929, is still the law of the Soviet land. Children under eighteen years of age are permitted to receive religious instruction only in groups of not more than three and only in private homes. Sunday schools, Bible schools, religious discussion groups, and, of course, parochial schools of any kind are absolutely forbidden.

For A and B to coexist peacefully they must be *equal* in certain important respects.[6] As between religious believers and non-believers such equality is explicitly denied by the current 1936 Soviet constitution as well as by the Draft Constitution of 1977, which defines "freedom of conscience" (in Art. 52) as involving, for believers, "the right to profess any religion and perform religious rites" but, for non-believers, the right "not to profess any religion and to conduct atheistic propaganda."[7] As I once had occasion to point out in the case of the 1936 Constitution:

> There is no equality here, even on paper. Believers have the right to believe and to worship but are denied the right to instruct others and to attempt to persuade others to share their belief. In contrast, non-believers have not only the right to disbelieve, but also the right, opportunity, and systematic encouragement of the party and the state to attempt to persuade others to share their atheism.[8]

III

Since to permit religious instruction (other than for divinity students) would open the way to a peaceful coexistence in Soviet society of Christian and Marxist-Leninist *ideas* and *values*—not just of Christians and Marxist-Leninists as *individuals* and *social groups*—we are brought directly to the sensitive question of ideological coexistence. What do Marxist-Leninists mean by "ideological coexistence," and why do they reject it with such violence?

The absolute and categorical nature of the Soviet rejection of "peaceful coexistence of ideologies" is not always appreciated in the West. I therefore offer a few quotations from authoritative Soviet sources, beginning with

---

[5]Yuri Zamoshkin's claim, at the Rosemont Conference, that no such statistics are available—because Soviet law forbids any mention of a student's religious preference on educational records—is unconvincing in the light of the fact that (a) a high proportion of Soviet university students are members of the Young Communist League (Komsomol) and thus, by definition, non-believers, and (b) their Komsomol membership is a matter of public record.

[6]Soviet authorities recognize "equality of rights [*ravnopraviye*] between states" as a necessary condition of peaceful coexistence (*BSE*[3], XVI, 314).

[7]Art. 124 of the 1936 Constitution grants to "all citizens" the "freedom to carry out religious cults and the freedom of anti-religious propaganda."

[8]See my *Religious and Anti-Religious Thought in Russia* (Chicago: The University of Chicago Press, 1968), pp. 147–148.

Khrushchev: "He who defends peaceful coexistence in the realm of ideology places himself, willy-nilly, on the path of betrayal of socialism, betrayal of the cause of communism" (*Pravda*, June 29, 1963). To accept such coexistence, he insists, is "to give the enemy [of socialism] an opportunity to blacken all that we hold most dear, to stir up slander, to corrupt the people's consciousness."[9] A leading party ideologist, L. F. Ilichev, adds that "there has never been, is not now, and will never be any peaceful coexistence of ideologies" (*Pravda*, June 19, 1963). An editorial in *Voprosy filosofii* refers to the "peaceful coexistence of ideologies" as a "reactionary slogan."[10] And a Soviet Marxist-Leninist calls it "a slogan of the most malicious opponents of the policy of peaceful coexistence."[11] Another Soviet philosopher equates it with "betrayal of genuine science [*izmena podlinnoi nauke*], of Marxism-Leninism."[12] Moreover, the prospect is for a *very* long haul: ". . . so long as the two social systems of socialism and capitalism . . . exist on our planet, there will be an irreconcilable struggle between their ideologies."[13]

Current Soviet statements on the peaceful coexistence of ideologies are more restrained and generally avoid the ominous terminology of "betrayal" and "treason"; but they continue to insist that the *peaceful* coexistence of *states* implies the "*struggle* [*protivoborstvo*] of *ideologies*," identifying the "unity of conflict and cooperation" as a "characteristic feature of peaceful coexistence."[14] In similar vein, our Hungarian colleague, Prof. Jozsef Lukács, declared at the Rosemont Conference that "ideological disarmament" is neither valuable nor desirable.

That the leaders of socialist states should want to do everything in their (considerable) power to prevent the *acceptance* of "hostile ideologies"—e.g., Christian, or existentialist, or pacifist,[15] ideas and values—by their own people is quite understandable. But socialist governments in fact have gone much further, interpreting the denial of all peaceful coexistence of ideologies as entailing that their citizens be denied the opportunity even to *consider* the ideas and values of the "class enemy." Thus the denial of the coexistence of ideologies amounts in

---

[9]A statement of June, 1963, as quoted in an editorial in the journal *Voprosy filosofii* [Problems of Philosophy] [hereafter "*VF*"], No. 7, 1963, p. 6. A Central Committee Resolution of the same period brands the "preaching of the peaceful coexistence of ideologies" a "betrayal [*izmena*] of Marxism-Leninism, treason [*predatel'stvo*] to the cause of the workers and peasants" (*Pravda*, June 22, 1963).

[10]*VF*, No. 7, 1963, p. 6.

[11]A. Ya. Popov, "Bor'ba ideologii—zakonomernost' nashei epokhi" ["The Struggle of Ideologies Is the Law of Our Epoch"], *VF*, No. 7, 1963, p.15.

[12]A. F. Okulov, "Gde zhe vasha ob'ektivnost', gospoda iz 'Philosophy'?" ["But Where Is Your Objectivity, Gentlemen from (the Journal) 'Philosophy'?"], *VF*, No. 7, 1963, p. 113.

[13]Popov, "Bor'ba ideologii," p. 16.

[14]*BSE*[3], XVI, 314; italics added.

[15]To struggle for peaceful coexistence, Soviet readers are informed, is to help in the "unmasking of pacifist ideology" (*Filosofskaya Entsiklopediya*, III, 453).

practice to a walling out of unwanted ideas and values.[16] The Rosemont Conference was a welcome, if only partial and temporary, breach in such walls.

Unfortunately, it appears that the Marxist-Leninist repudiation of the peaceful coexistence of ideologies will prevent any free give and take, among the educated and interested public of the socialist countries involved, of the ideas freely discussed at our Conference. I therefore conclude with a modest proposal: Let this issue of the *Journal of Ecumenical Studies* be translated into Russian, German, and Hungarian, and let it be made available to all interested readers in the Soviet Union, the GDR, and Hungary. That would be a plain and welcome indication that it is, in fact, only the *acceptance* of, not the mere *exposure* to, non- or anti-Marxist-Leninist ideas and values which is judged to be incompatible with a commitment to socialism or Marxism-Leninism.

---

[16]Soviet officials boast that the Soviet Union publishes one-fifth of all the books and pamphlets published in the world (*VF*, No. 7, 1963, p. 12). But they fail to mention that—because exposure to, not just acceptance of, "hostile" ideas and values is proscribed—among the tens of billions of books published in the Soviet Union over the past half century there has not been a single volume of the works of St. Augustine, St. Thomas Aquinas, Luther, Calvin, Pascal, Kierkegaard, or Cardinal Newman, to say nothing of twentieth-century western religious thinkers, and not a single reprinting of the works of Russia's own religious thinkers—Chaadayev, Kireyevski, Leontyev, Rozanov, Solovyov, Berdyaev, or Shestov.

Robert G. Thobaben and Nicholas Piediscalzi

The Paulus Gesellschaft Internationale's 1977 European Congress (Salzburg, September 6–10) was to mark a new era for the Marxist-Christian dialogue. Planned originally as a joint venture of the Italian Communist Party and the Paulus Gesellschaft, the Congress was to include leaders from Europe's major Communist parties and major Christian communities. The dialogue's announced topic, "Toward a Socialist, Democratic, Christian and Humanist Europe," focused on the new type of Europe toward which emerging Eurocommunism is pointing. Hopes ran high for the Congress since it was conceived at the 1975 Paulus Gesellschaft symposium in Florence, in which key members of the Italian Communist Party's Central Committee participated. They were instrumental in calling for the 1977 European Congress and pledged to attend, in addition to inviting Communist leaders from the other countries of Europe. Also, Willy Brandt reportedly assured Dr. Erich Kellner, Paulus Gesellschaft founder and chief executive officer, that West German political leaders would attend.

Unfortunately, and for reasons still not entirely known to the Paulus Gesellschaft, the Italian Communist Party withdrew its co-sponsorship of the Congress. Willy Brandt's colleagues did not attend. The only Communists to attend were unofficial participants—two from Hungary, a group from Spain, and the president of the Italian "Christians for Socialism" who identified himself as a member of the Italian Communist Party. The Vatican, as in the past, sent neither official representatives nor observers, for, as a Vatican official explained to these reporters in Rome, the Congress does not involve major political leaders, but only intellectuals. The Vatican, according to the official interviewed, does not expect any significant, concrete results from such dialogues. Only a meeting of official leaders and/or their official representatives can produce long-range advances.

Informed observers suggest that the impending elections in France and the nearness to majority power of the Italian Communists made it politically inexpedient for them to participate in the Congress. The French Communists do not want to do anything which would affect adversely their relationship with the radical elements in their constituency, and the Italian Communists, like the Vatican, now are interested in relating only to those in power.

The Spanish Communists find themselves in a position similar to that of the Italians in 1975. They are far from possessing majority power. They are in need of the maximum amount of support they can muster. Hence they came to Salzburg, according to some observers, to convince as many as possible of their dedication to a democratic and pluralistic Spain and Europe, in order to establish their credibility with those whose support they need if they are to grow and advance. On the whole, the Spanish Communists made a favorable impression on the entire Congress. They recounted how their years of persecution and

imprisonment under Franco made them acutely aware of the evils of totalitarianism and how the constant need to protect all minority groups and loyal
dissidents requires complete dedication to democracy and its survival. They also
affirmed the beneficial results of a free society in which free debate keeps alive
the dialectic of human history. At one point one of the Spanish leaders informed
the Congress that the Spanish Communist Party welcomed Christians into its
ranks and that Christians are assured equal treatment and opportunities for leadership positions. According to him, neither belief in God nor the practice of
religion is by definition an expression of escapism. On the contrary, each can be
a source of positive, revolutionary involvement in building new societies. Therefore, Christians dedicated to building a new Europe are welcomed as co-workers.

The Italian Marxist-Christian speaker stated that Marxism is not a dogma to
be accepted blindly but only a heuristic scientific tool to be used to analyze
empirical problems. This being the case, there is no natural antipathy between
Marxism and the Christian Gospel of liberation.

Many of the Christians present—most of whom were West Germans and
Austrians—questioned the sincerity of the Communists. They doubted whether
the Communists will remain loyal to their newly proclaimed commitment to
democracy and pluralism and asked for concrete assurance that they would. A
small number of West German and Dutch Christians objected to this expression
of fear and demand of assurances by reminding the group that both the Vatican
and Protestant churches in Europe have not and do not always practice democracy or respect pluralism within their own communities and in relationship to the
various political groups in their societies. Hence, according to them, the Christians voicing their fears of Communist insincerity are in need of casting the beam
from their own eyes before pointing to the splinters in the Communists'.

Many of those in attendance agreed that the new emerging Europe requires
major structural changes if it is to succeed. These changes must include economic and political equality and justice for all, as well as decentralized participatory democracy for everyone.

With the exception of the lengthy statements made by the Spanish Communists and the rather short one made by the Italian Marxist-Christian, the 1977
European Congress turned out to be a discussion among Christians of different
persuasions. It could not be a dialogue since there were not enough Marxists
present to dialogue with Christians. Hence, the expectations of those who attended were not completely fulfilled. Moreover, even the Christians failed to
dialogue. With the exception of four or five well-prepared papers, the remaining
presentations turned out to be a series of statements, frequently taking the form of
sermons on the major sub-themes of the Congress established for each day:
"Antagonistic Politics: A Threat to the Future of the Young Generation,"
"Europe between America and the Soviet Union," "Europe and the Third
World," "Christianity—Carrier of a Socially Humane Ethos," "Theology of
Liberation," "Antagonistic Structures of Ruling Social and Ecclesiastical Sys-

tems," "Dissent and Terrorism: Symptoms of a Frustrated Generation?" "A Social and Democratic Society: Principles and Structures," "Historical Alternatives: The Hypercomplex Society," "Evolution or Revolution of Social Structures?" "Structural Peace Policy," and "The Right of the Young Generation to a Future."

The most important roles at the Congress were played by Professor Udo Bermbach, a political scientist from Hamburg; Professor Jozsef Lukács, a Marxist professor of philosophy from Budapest; Professor Maurice Boutin, a theologian from Montreal; Professor A. Dall'Olio, a Jesuit theologian from Florence; Professor Louis Dupré, a philosopher from Yale University; and Dr. A. Comin Ros, a Marxist from Barcelona.

On several occasions Dr. Erich Kellner reminded the Congress that the Paulus Gesellschaft is dedicated to open dialogue in which objective and concrete analyses are made which have long-range ramifications for all participants. The Paulus Gesellschaft refuses to be used as a propaganda platform for any ideological group. Only those who are interested in and devoted to self-analysis which leads to self-reformation and growth can benefit from participation in Paulus Gesellschaft dialogues. For this reason, Kellner insists that all dialogues must include discussions of ideological issues in addition to practical cooperative programs. Hence, the Paulus Gesellschaft eschews dialogues devoted solely to the latter. This being the case, the Paulus Gesellschaft may lose, if it has not already lost, its leadership role in the Marxist-Christian dialogue, since the Vatican, established Protestants, and Communists in power or near to achieving majority power are not interested in dialogues which lead to self-criticism and institutional reform. Rather, they are eager to find means of accommodation and compromise without engaging in self-criticism. (An Italian Communist leader is reported to have said, "Ideological and theoretical dialogues are dead.")

The western European Marxist-Christian dialogue stands at a new crossroad. It is too early to tell what direction it will take. If the French and Italian Communist Parties come to power, they, in all likelihood, will seek cooperative alliances with Christian groups who will support them. These alliances will require compromises on both sides. Both established Roman Catholics and Protestants will be willing to join in such alliances so long as such relationships are beneficial to them.

One other factor bears watching. The Roman Catholic Church sponsored a meeting of West European Christian and democratic political leaders in Southern Germany shortly after the European Congress adjourned. It appears that the Vatican and West European leaders are seeking to stem the tide of Eurocommunism as long as they can in addition to blocking dialogues which lead to self-criticism and institutional reform.

Eurocommunism may be a reality. But the road to a Socialist, Democratic, Christian, and Humanist Europe and future Marxist-Christian dialogues is a long and arduous one fraught with innumerable obstacles and pitfalls. The European

Marxist-Christian dialogue probably will take place on two levels—the intellectual, ideological, and theoretical as exemplified by the European Congress, and the practical which will emerge among political parties, activist groups, and church bodies. Along this line, it will be important to note whether the upcoming dialogue at Kishnyev in Moldavia (a follow-up to the Rosemont dialogue), a special session at the international meeting of philosophers in Düsseldorf, and the seminar on "The Future of Religion" in Dubrovnik will reveal the shape, content, and direction of future First and Second World dialogues.

DATE DUE

FEB 2 1 1982		
JUN 9 1983		
JUL 9 1983		
JUL 2 5 1983		
11/6/84		
APR 2 7 1987		
NOV 2 6 1988		
DEC 1 9 1989		
GAYLORD		PRINTED IN U.S.A.